MONTREAL AT WAR

1914–1918

THE CANADIAN EXPERIENCE OF WAR

Series Editor: Mark Humphries

This series of monographs, essay collections, and edited primary sources illuminates connections between war and society in Canada, focusing on military operations as well as the experience of civilians and non-combatants. It is supported by funding from the Laurier Centre for Military Strategic and Disarmament Studies (LCMSDS) at Wilfrid Laurier University.

MONTREAL
AT WAR
1914
1918
TERRY COPP
WITH ALEXANDER MAAVARA

UNIVERSITY OF TORONTO PRESS
Toronto Buffalo London

© University of Toronto Press 2022
Toronto Buffalo London
utorontopress.com
Printed and bound by CPI Group (UK) Ltd, Croydon, CR0 4YY

ISBN 978-1-4875-4154-5 (cloth)   ISBN 978-1-4875-4157-6 (EPUB)
ISBN 978-1-4875-4155-2 (paper)   ISBN 978-1-4875-4156-9 (PDF)

Library and Archives Canada Cataloguing in Publication

Title: Montreal at War, 1914–1918 / Terry Copp with Alexander Maavara.
Names: Copp, Terry, author. | Maavara, Alexander, author.
Description: Includes bibliographical references and index.
Identifiers: Canadiana (print) 20210287179 | Canadiana (ebook) 20210287217 |
    ISBN 9781487541552 (paper) | ISBN 9781487541545 (cloth) |
    ISBN 9781487541576 (EPUB) | ISBN 9781487541569 (PDF)
Subjects: LCSH: World War, 1914–1918 – Québec (Province) – Montréal.
Classification: LCC D547.C2 C575 2022 | DDC 940.4/0971428–dc23

LAURIER CENTRE
for MILITARY
STRATEGIC and
DISARMAMENT
STUDIES
WILFRID LAURIER UNIVERSITY

The Laurier Centre for Military Strategic and Disarmament Studies
generously provided financial assistance for the publication of this book.

University of Toronto Press acknowledges the financial assistance to its publishing
program of the Canada Council for the Arts and the Ontario Arts Council, an agency
of the Government of Ontario.

Canada Council **Conseil des Arts**
for the Arts **du Canada**

ONTARIO ARTS COUNCIL
CONSEIL DES ARTS DE L'ONTARIO
an Ontario government agency
un organisme du gouvernement de l'Ontario

Funded by the   Financé par le
Government   gouvernement
of Canada   du Canada   **Canada**

Contents

Acknowledgments

This project began as an attempt to write a book on the Canadian experience of the Great War inspired by Adrian Gregory's *The Last Great War: British Society and the First World War*. The decision to change the focus to Montreal would come to seem logical as I began my academic career writing about my city's history while teaching at Concordia and McGill. In fact the change developed as a result of the influence of two of my students: Geoff Keelan, who was writing his dissertation on Henri Bourassa, and Brendan O'Driscoll, who while completing his MA at McGill wrote essays on aspects of Montreal history that reawakened my interest in the social history of the city. Brendan subsequently provided research assistance and critical commentary.

The research became part of a Social Science and Humanities Research Council project titled "Through Veteran's Eyes" at the Laurier Centre for Military Strategic and Disarmament Studies (LCMSDS). The Centre's director and lead researcher for the project, Mark Humphries, supported the idea of a book on Montreal and encouraged me to make full use of the Centre's digitization resources to scan newspapers on microfilm. He also assigned a graduate student, Alexander Maavara, to me as a research assistant, and "Alec" soon became a close collaborator who scanned the newspapers and developed the research databases that the book relies upon. Alec also designed and administered a website that for several years carried an earlier version of this book. The website remains active to provide online supplementary materials, including documents and photographs. At various times other students contributed to the research, including Matt Baker, Caleb Burney, Mike Kelly, Garrison Ma, Anastasia Pivnicki, Eric Vero, and Ariadni Woodward.

Two anonymous readers offered comments, suggestions, and encouragement leading to revisions that have greatly improved the manuscript. My thanks to Len Husband for his continued interest in my work.

MONTREAL AT WAR

1914–1918

Introduction

Hindsight ... has been the curse of writing about the war ... we know how things turned out and can therefore attempt to explain why they turned out as they did ... We must remember that hindsight is unavailable to those who are living through the experience, and it cannot inform their decisions ... The First World War was not fought [or experienced] in retrospect and we must stop refighting [and re-writing] it that way.

Adrian Gregory, *The Last Great War*

This study of the impact of the Great War on Montreal describes the experiences of civilians, soldiers, and returned veterans. The work is based on a reading of primary sources, especially newspapers, journals, government reports, and archival records. The published and unpublished writings of other historians have been used as sources of information but the narrative avoids direct engagement with current historiographical debates. The purpose is to understand the war experience as it unfolded, leaving retrospective views about what it all meant to studies of post-war construction of memory.

Avoiding retrospective interpretations and viewing the wartime experience through the eyes of Montrealers of all backgrounds offers a different way of looking at history. War-related events and reactions take place in the context of a city struggling with poverty, a public health and housing crisis and, in the last year of the war, rampant inflation and the influenza epidemic. The war is just one of the challenges confronting citizens. Shifting the focus of research from Henri Bourassa and *Le Devoir* to enlistment statistics and the mass circulation press demonstrates that for the first two years of the war there was broad support for Canada's participation among all groups and considerable willingness for French Canadians to enlist in French-language battalions. Voluntary enlistment declined in the summer of 1916 in Montreal as well as the rest of Canada, but until the introduction of conscription opposition to Canada's war was confined to a small minority. Such contextual research also questions interpretations of issues like the impact of the "Ontario School Question" on attitudes to the war. The debate over the use of the French language in Ontario coincided with the period of voluntary enlistment and had ceased to be an issue before conscription was introduced. And there is much else to be learned. The research began with a systematic examination of the news reported in the *Montreal Star*, one of the city's two mass-circulation dailies. The *Star*, an evening newspaper with a circulation of 112,000[1] plus a weekend edition, *The Standard*, with 77,000 subscribers, was owned and directly influenced by Hugh Graham who, for his services to the Empire, became Lord Atholstan in 1917. Graham's passionate imperialism and aggressive political partisanship on behalf of the Conservative Party was of little consequence in the day-to-day coverage of events in the city, and the *Star* had the money to employ good reporters. The *Star* also provides extensive coverage of the war with particular attention to individuals and units from Montreal.

La Presse, an independent, popular daily with the largest circulation, 128,000, in Canada and a US edition claiming 23,000, was digitized and checked for specific issues. *La Presse* was owned by Trefflé Berthiaume, a pioneer of popular journalism, until his death in 1915; Berthiaume's sons shared control throughout the balance of the war. It included comics, a good deal of crime news, and many popular features, but also provided detailed reports on life in the city. Coverage of the recruitment and overseas experience of French Canadian soldiers was a major priority for *La Presse*. Pierre Vennat's two-volume *Les "poilus" québécois de 1914–1918* draws upon these reports, quoting verbatim thus providing a convenient source.[2]

Six other daily newspapers competed for readership in 1914. *The Gazette*, Canada's oldest newspaper, circulation 33,351, was closely linked with the Montreal business community and the Conservative Party. *The Herald and Daily Telegraph*, 19,279, was by 1914 controlled by Hugh Graham, offering a morning version of the *Star*. *La Patrie*, 21,000, owned by sons of founder Israel Tarte, imitated the populist approach of *La Presse* to news coverage, comics, and features while supporting the Conservative Party. *Le Canada*, 18,900, founded in 1903 as a Liberal Party newspaper, was initially edited by Godfrey Langlois, a radical exponent of secular, progressive ideals. Langlois's campaign for compulsory education antagonized the clergy, and he was replaced in 1909 by Fernand Rinfret, a less abrasive, moderate liberal. The *Montreal Daily Mail*, founded in 1913, had been largely forgotten, as it ceased publication in August 1917. An afternoon paper attempting to compete with the *Star*, it was a long shot financially but is an important source of city news.

The sixth daily, *Le Devoir*, founded in 1910 by the *nationaliste* icon Henri Bourassa, is said to have enjoyed an influence all out of proportion to its circulation, which declined from 19,000 to 14,000 during the course of the war. *Le Devoir* disdained features such as comics and popular entertainment. Its "ponderous signed editorials" resembling "papal pronouncements or legal briefs" were aimed at an elite trained in the province's classical colleges.[3] Bourassa's take-no-prisoners approach to politics drew equally aggressive responses from other newspapers, greatly enhancing his reputation.

Montreal's vibrant weekly newspapers provide other windows into the city during the war years. The *Montreal Witness*, a liberal, Protestant, temperance journal owned and edited by John Redpath Dougal, offers evidence of the difficulty of easy generalizations about the views of the city's Anglo-Celtic elite. The *Witness* began as the Saturday edition of the *Montreal Daily Witness* (1845–1913). It offered detailed American, international, and Canadian news stories during the war years. The *Witness* was accessed online through the website of the Bibliothèque et Archives Nationale du Québec (BANQ) along with a number of other weeklies, including *Le Nationaliste*, owned by *Le Devoir*; Jules Fournier's literary and political journal *L'Action*; and *Le Pays*, the paper founded by Godfrey Langlois after he left *Le Canada*. Another source for its war-years coverage was the *Canadian Jewish Chronicle*, the successor to the *Jewish Times*, available online at Google Newspaper Archive. Other journals were examined for specific topics, including the conservative Catholic and openly antisemitic *La Croix*; *L'Action Sociale*, which became *L'Action Catholique* in 1915; the satirical weekly *Le Canard*; and *Le Monde Travaileur/ Labour World*, founded in 1916 to represent the views of the Montreal Trades and Labour Council. The BANQ website offers the opportunity to search *Le Devoir*, *Le Pays*, *Le Nationaliste*, and *Le Canard* by topics and names. I have used this feature sparingly to avoid isolating issues out of context.

Montreal newspapers provided readers with detailed coverage of the war using official dispatches from London and Paris as well as semi-official reporting by war correspondents. Stories by Phillip Gibbs, a prolific author, were especially popular and frequently translated.[4] Gibbs spoke for all correspondents when he wrote that he "identified absolutely with the armies in the field," avoiding any words "that would make the task of officers and men more difficult or dangerous." Such self-censorship and, after 1915, official Canadian censorship has been seen as limiting knowledge of the horrors of war, but the publication of explicit letters from the front and the endless series of casualty lists carried in the daily newspapers brought the reality of war home to all who could read.

The *Montreal Standard* carried regular features on the war written by American journalist Frank H. Simonds of the New York *Herald Tribune*. Until America's entry into the war Simonds provided a more detached perspective on Allied and German strategy and claims of achievement. The *Standard* also offered anti-war activists such as George Bernard Shaw space in its pages. From March 1917 Stewart Lyon, former managing editor of the *Toronto Globe*, served as the first Canadian Press war correspondent, and his dispatches as well as those of his successors were reproduced in all the city's daily newspapers. Lyon certainly identified with the Canadian Corps, but his articles also illustrated the costs of battles like Passchendaele.

The book also relies on databases created by Alexander Maavara and our research assistants, including one that links the 1914 list of Montreal volunteers with their attestation papers and the sailing list of the First Contingent. We also analysed the nominal rolls of all battalions based in Montreal. The nominal rolls list each recruit's name, regimental number, rank, address of next of kin, and country of birth, allowing us to make accurate statements about the numbers of British- and Canadian-born and to distinguish between British-born with next of kin in the United Kingdom and those who lived with their families in Montreal. The nominal rolls also allow us to make a more precise estimate of the number of French Canadian volunteers from Montreal. These nominal rolls are accessible at the website associated with this book, montrealatwar .com.

Our approach to the war experience was influenced by Adrian Gregory's *The Last Great War: British Society and the First World War.* His chapter "Going to War" examines the ways in which people in Britain understood a war that had a beginning but no middle and no end until one was thrust upon them by the sudden collapse of the German army. Other chapters exploring issues with clear parallels to our work include "Atrocities and Propaganda 1914–1915," "From Voluntarism to Compulsion 1914–1916," "Religion and the Language of Sacrifice," and "The Inequality of Sacrifice." Gregory also explores the scale of sacrifice and the nature of public commemoration.

To consider these and other issues specific to Montreal, this book begins with a chapter, "Metropolis," describing the economic, social, and cultural characteristics of the city in the decade before the war. The chapter, while emphasizing the common experience of the vast majority of the population who survived on a marginal and uncertain income, also portrays a city that was ethnically diverse, residentially segregated, and politically divided before August 1914. The five chapters that follow examine distinct phases of the war, each shaped by responses to strategic, operational, and political decisions. A concluding chapter reflects upon our study of unfolding events and contrasts experience with constructed memory.

Chapter One

Metropolis

The city grew along the banks of the river and onto the terraces of the mountain until by 1914 more than 600,000 lived in Montreal and its adjacent suburbs.[1] The majority, 64 per cent of the population, were French Canadians, including large numbers who had recently arrived from rural Quebec. They found themselves in a divided city dominated by an Anglo-Celtic elite that controlled much of the national as well as metropolitan economy. Most of the Anglo-Celtic community, 24 per cent of the population, were wage earners or clerical workers sharing in the common struggle to earn a basic living. A growing number of Yiddish-speaking Jews, escaping Czarist Russia, made up the largest group of continental Europeans, 8 per cent, with Italians, 2 per cent, as the next largest immigrant community.[2]

Locational advantage at the head of navigation, tariff protection, aggressive entrepreneurs, and an abundant supply of cheap labour created a diverse, chaotic city grappling with too-rapid growth, widespread poverty, and an ongoing conflict between tradition and modernity. "All that was solid" did not "melt into air" until the second half of the twentieth century, but the transition to a modern, secular society was well underway before the outbreak of war.[3]

Montreal's economy was dependent on the river and the harbour. The Dominion government owned the banks and riverbed for a distance of some twelve miles, administering 350 acres of land through a Harbour Commission established by an act of Parliament. When Wilfrid Laurier became prime minister in 1896, the importance of the port and good politics led to a cabinet portfolio for Raymond Préfontaine, the member of Parliament for the riding of Maisonneuve and the political boss of east-end Montreal. Préfontaine accelerated the extension of the harbour east to Hochelaga and Maisonneuve with the construction of three new piers. The harbour railway system was expanded and the entire working area electrified to permit work to continue into the night.

After Préfontaine's death in 1905, Laurier appointed Louis-Philippe Brodeur to the post and placed him in charge of patronage for Montreal and the

Province of Quebec. Brodeur continued to encourage development of the port, funnelling "great dollops of capital" to the harbour and the vital St. Lawrence Ship Canal.[4] Brodeur was the minister responsible for the Canadian navy, created in 1910, with a commitment to build part of the fleet in Canada. It was the promise of naval construction that encouraged Vickers, the British shipbuilding firm, to establish Canadian Vickers in 1911. The Harbour Commission provided a thirty-acre site and a commitment to dredge the necessary deep basin. Vickers began construction of the shipyard and purchased a large floating dry dock, built in England and towed across the Atlantic. Canadian Vickers became a major employer in the city's east end.[5]

The most dramatic and consequential developments were the construction of new elevators. The first major project, Elevator No. 1, was completed in 1904, followed by No. 5. A project of the Grand Trunk Railway, No. 5 was situated at the mouth of the Lachine Canal so that grain could be easily transferred from inland rail or ship to ocean-going vessels. No. 2, completed in 1910, was twelve storeys high, looming over the harbour in front of Bonsecours Market. Constructed entirely of concrete, it was later featured in Le Corbusier's ode to functionalism *Vers une architecture*.[6] All of this activity helped to divert a growing proportion of the western grain trade to Montreal, though the Buffalo–Erie Canal route still handled more Canadian grain than Montreal as late as 1914. Competition with New York and Boston was a major reason that a delegation of a thousand businessmen, two hundred from Montreal, travelled to Ottawa in April 1914 to press for construction of the Georgian Bay Canal, a project that would allow ships to bypass the lower Great Lakes, using the new canal and the Ottawa River to reach Montreal. The Dominion government preferred a plan to widen and deepen the Welland Canal.[7]

The limitations of the St. Lawrence River canals offered railway builders the opportunity to compete for much of the bulk trade. Montreal had long been the managerial and maintenance hub of the Grand Trunk, which stretched from Chicago to Portland, Maine's ice-free harbour, before the Grand Trunk Pacific was built. The Canadian Pacific Railway, organized and financed by the city's capitalists, completed its line to Vancouver in 1885 and then built east to its own winter port at Saint John, New Brunswick. The CPR's Romanesque Windsor Station, built in the 1880s, was reimagined in 1909 with "an extension that would double the building's ground space while increasing its floor space dramatically, exploiting a downward slope on the site that would allow for 8 floors plus a massive 15 stories tower."[8]

The CPR was also directly responsible for the one of the city's largest enterprises, the Angus Shops. This vast twenty-two-acre complex built on the edge of the city created its own suburb, Rosemount, to house workers, one of the many examples of the movement of industry and housing to the urban fringe.

From 1903 to 1914 the shops produced 1,300 locomotives, 29,000 freight cars and 2,000 passenger cars. Together with Canadian Car and Foundry Company and the Montreal Locomotive Works, a subsidiary of the American Locomotive Company, the Angus Shops accounted for almost all of Canada's railway engine and rolling stock production.[9]

Canada's third transcontinental railway, the Toronto-based Canadian Northern, had a smaller footprint in the city until 1910 when William Mackenzie and Donald Mann, who controlled the railway, announced plans to build a tunnel under Mount Royal to reach the centre of the city and the harbour. Before publicizing the project they acquired a large tract of land north of the mountain that was to become a new garden suburb, the Town of Mount Royal.[10] Digging the tunnel turned out to be a major project not completed until 1916.

Locational advantage at the hub of the national distribution system and the national policy of tariff protection also explain the growth of Montreal's diverse financial and manufacturing industries. Two of the three largest financial institutions, the Bank of Montreal and the Royal Bank of Canada, were based in Montreal with branches across the country. The Bank of Montreal, founded in 1827, served as the Dominion government's banker, preforming many of the functions of a central bank. Montreal's insurance and investment firms made St. James Street the Wall Street of Canada. In 1914 the first stage of the Sun Life building, which, with the addition of a tower, would become the largest building in the British Empire, was under construction, a symbol of Montreal's response to Toronto's growth as a rival financial centre.

Redpath Sugar and Oglivie Flour were household names across Canada well before the turn of the century. Molson's Brewery, Macdonald Tobacco, Imperial Tobacco, Dominion Textile, and a long list of other firms founded in the nineteenth century were able to expand their activities in the first decades of the twentieth century. The Montreal Rolling Mills, Dominion Bridge, and other companies involved in the metal trades relied on the harbour to import their raw materials, using energy from coal-fired steam engines to shape the final product. The formation of the Steel Company of Canada in 1910 is usually associated with the primary industry in Hamilton, but the well-established Montreal firms that joined the "steel trust" provided much of the sales revenue that made the deal possible.[11]

By the turn of the century, electricity was becoming widely available to manufacturers and better-off households.[12] The Royal Electric Company, established in 1884 to both generate power and manufacture equipment, was transformed into Montreal Light Heat and Power by Rodolphe Forget and Herbert Holt, two of Montreal's most successful entrepreneurs. General Electric, one of the many American companies jumping the tariff wall to establish branch plants in Canada, bought the manufacturing side of the business while MLHP concentrated on generation and distribution of hydroelectricity. Holt and Forget also controlled the Montreal Street and Railway Company, electrifying the tram lines before selling the firm to a syndicate led by E.A. Robert and J.W. McConnell, who created Montreal Tramways as an island-wide monopoly, sparking years of controversy over the crucial means of mass transit. Montreal Light Heat and Power merged with Canada Light and Power to form an equally controversial private monopoly controlling the price of electricity.[13] As electric motors replaced stream-driven engines in the city's factories and workshops, the monopoly proved especially lucrative.[14] After General Electric left the city in 1907 the only major equipment manufacturer was Northern Electric, jointly owned by Western Electric and Bell Canada. The company's near-monopoly on telephone equipment encouraged the construction of one of the largest manufacturing establishments in Montreal, completed in 1914.[15]

Historian Paul-André Linteau notes that while the city's "traditional involvement in commerce was reinvigorated by the opening up of the Canadian West," the most significant development was the growth of the manufacturing sector. He concludes:

> The turn of the century brought exponential growth as many existing businesses extended their premises, sometimes relocating in the suburbs, and new factories sprang up. Montreal manufacturers embraced many sectors. Light industry was dominated by footwear, textiles, garments, tobacco and food products (such as beer, meat packing, sugar, flour, biscuits). Heavy industry began with the production of iron and steel products and rolling stock and expanded in the 20th Century to include petroleum and electrical products.[16]

The economic and political power of Quebec's Anglo-Celtic elite was evident in the negotiations leading to Confederation in 1867. The distribution of powers, outlined in the British North America Act, established a strong national government reflecting the views of the business and financial community. The questions of English-language rights and a guarantee of educational autonomy for English-speaking Protestants were also resolved in terms fully acceptable to the minority. The new province of Quebec was to be officially bilingual, and Protestant schools were protected by the provisions of Section 93 and the Quebec legislature's passage of the Education Act of 1869. The act delegated responsibility for education to separate Committees of Public Instruction, allowing Quebec's Anglo-Protestant communities to continue to live as part of English-speaking Canada and the British Empire.[17]

The BNA Act ignored the future of Roman Catholics who spoke English in Quebec or French in Ontario and the Maritime provinces. Montreal's Irish Catholics were easily accommodated in bilingual or English-language schools largely staffed by the Christian Brothers.[18] A similar situation developed in Ontario, where French was used as a language of instruction in specific schools until the issue was politicized after 1910. Language of instruction did not become a political issue in Quebec because the Catholic hierarchy had no wish to include Irish Catholics in their schools. The bishops preferred to protect their flock from the perceived dangers of Irish Catholic compromises with the secular, English-speaking world, creating a separate section of Catholic schools for the Irish.[19]

The Irish working class in Point St. Charles and Griffintown maintained a separate identity with their own Roman Catholic parishes, schools, and institutions. Middle- and upper-class Irish Catholics were, except on Sundays and St. Patrick's Day, indistinguishable from their Protestant counterparts.[20] The president of the Canadian Pacific Railway, Thomas Shaughnessy, and C.J. Doherty, the federal minister of justice, are but two examples of Irish Catholic grandees. A small but influential number of Irish Protestants were also part of the mix, though they lacked the passionate commitment to the kind of Orangeism that plagued Toronto and much of small-town Ontario.

After 1900 immigration from the British Isles brought thousands of new English-speaking residents to Montreal. The majority found work in low-wage jobs marked by seasonal and cyclical unemployment, but for many upward mobility was a realistic prospect in an economy where their language was privileged in both skilled-labour and clerical jobs.[21] When the industrial efficiency movement, inspired by Frederick Taylor, reached Montreal in the first years of the century, the dominance of English was reinforced. The Angus Shops introduced scientific management based on Taylorism in 1909, with each task timed and outlined in English-language instruction cards. Other manufacturers adopted similar methods, rationalizing production and deskilling workers.[22] Clerical work in the city's large financial, transportation, and manufacturing concerns also demanded literacy as well as fluency in English. This advantage carried over when the typewriter and changing attitudes towards the kind of work respectable young women could perform provided thousands of new jobs.[23]

French- and English-speaking Montrealers lived separate lives in separate neighbourhoods. After the tramway reached Notre Dame de Grace, the town was annexed to Montreal (1910) and developers provided both duplexes and detached homes for English-speaking clerical workers, craftsman, and professionals.[24] The city of Westmount, just east of Notre Dame de Grace, retained its autonomy as a separate municipality, with tree-lined streets, parks, and a magnificent public library. The city's Anglo-Celtic population had long enjoyed access to the Mechanics Institute and Fraser-Hickson libraries, both privately funded, but Westmount contained Montreal's first municipal public library.[25]

Most of the Anglo-Celtic community was Protestant in an era when religion appeared to matter a great deal. The non-conformist churches, Methodist, Presbyterian, Baptist, and Congregationalist, were all involved in the struggle to reconcile doctrines emphasizing personal salvation with the reform agendas of the social gospel.[26] Even the more conservative Church of England was changing. John Farthing, Montreal's Anglican bishop, allowed the vicar of Christ Church Cathedral, Herbert Symonds, a "Broad Church" liberal, to preach a modernist theology and become actively involved in civic reform movements.[27]

The jewel in the crown of Anglo-Celtic Montreal was McGill University. By the turn of the century McGill's transformation into a major North American research university was nearly complete. William Osler, who left Montreal in 1884, had done much to establish the reputation of the medical school, and after the opening of Royal Victoria Hospital in 1893 the faculty was able to attract outstanding staff and students from across Canada and the United States.[28] Lacking an endowment or government support, McGill depended on the generosity of men who had made their fortunes in the city. The most important of the many donors was Sir William Macdonald, who provided funds to build the physics (1890), engineering (1893), and chemistry (1898) buildings as well as Macdonald College (1906) in St. Anne de Bellevue.

Macdonald was Canada's leading manufacturer of processed tobacco, which "because of the simplicity of its ingredients and its growing popularity, owing to its addictive properties, lent itself to large profits."[29] By the 1880s Macdonald lost interest in running a mature business and turned his attention to philanthropy. A native of Prince Edward Island, he left the Roman Catholic Church of his childhood after "a traumatic experience apparently during his service as choirboy or acolyte." His "passionate aversion to the rituals and tenets of the church" extended to all organized religion, and McGill, a non-sectarian institution promoting science and practical education, fitted his values perfectly.[30] Macdonald wanted McGill to become Canada's Massachusetts Institute of Technology, and he provided funds to endow chairs in both sciences and the humanities. Ernest Rutherford, who won the Nobel Prize for Physics in 1908 for work done at McGill between 1888 and 1907, was the most famous Macdonald professor, but others made notable contributions to their fields.[31]

McGill was by no means a leader in the education of women until Donald Smith, Lord Strathcona, donated the money to build Royal Victoria College in 1899, providing classrooms and accommodations for women. They remained separated from men for classes, upholding the prevailing gender norms of the middle class. Not every female student accepted the limits of separate spheres, socially or intellectually. For example, Harriet Brooks, who graduated in 1898, joined Rutherford's research group, gaining a master's degree in science and developing a career in both research and as a lecturer at Royal Victoria College.[32]

McGill attracted students from all across Canada, becoming the country's leading university. Stephen Leacock, a political economist as well as the author of *Sunshine Sketches of a Little Town* and *Arcadian Adventures of the Idle*

Rich, set in "Metropolis," was the most famous professor, but McGill was best known for medicine and an engineering faculty that graduated most of the country's professional engineers.[33]

Large-scale immigration from Britain and continental Europe was offset by the internal immigration of French Canadians from rural Quebec to Montreal, allowing French Canadians to maintain their majority status. Most lived in the east end, finding work in unskilled and semi-skilled occupations, but a growing number joined the ranks of salaried workers. Employment with the municipal and provincial governments or the small and medium-sized commercial and manufacturing establishments owned by French Canadian businessmen provided opportunities to work in French. Wholesalers supplying the Quebec region and retailers such as Dupuis Frères, the city's third largest department store, required French-language clerical employees, including women in sales. There was also a large French Canadian bourgeoisie composed of doctors, lawyers, notaries, businessmen, journalists, teachers, and priests.

Much of the land on the fringes of the city was owned by French Canadians, and substantial fortunes were made by landowners, speculators, and developers. The town of Maisonneuve, carved out of Hochelaga in 1883, was developed by French Canadians like Oscar Dufresne, who promoted industry and the extension of the street railway to sell residential lots.[34] A second development project, the town of Montréal-Est, was the creation of Joseph Versailles who in 1910 persuaded the Quebec government to grant a charter after he purchased much of the land. His "garden city" plan did not survive the 1913 recession, but as mayor of Montréal-Est he presided over rapid industrial growth once the economy recovered.[35]

French-speaking Montreal appeared to be a city of spires, with sixty-four parish churches and a diverse array of clerically owned welfare and educational institutions. The full extent of those activities is outlined in the pages of *Le Canada Ecclésiatique*, an annual publication that includes detailed information on the clergy and specific institutions. The 1913 edition estimates the Catholic population of the diocese at 527,438 served by 765 priests. There were seven Collèges classiques, six Écoles classiques, and 731 public and convent schools. Seventy-two hospitals and welfare institutions are enumerated as well as 164 churches and chapels.[36] The church was heavily dependent on the thousands of women who joined religious orders, serving as teachers, nurses, domestics, and administrators. The majority of Quebec's 15,000 nuns worked in Montreal contributing much of the productive labour that maintained and financed diocesan institutions, as nuns employed as teachers and nurses did not earn direct wages; the state or individuals paid for their services through fees or contracted payment sent to the Mother House.[37]

The Montreal branch of Laval University, established in 1878, offered opportunities for graduates of the classical colleges to study theology, law, medicine, and arts as well as civil engineering and architecture in association with the École Polytechnique.[38] The Poly, which later developed into one of Canada's leading engineering schools, was small, underfunded, and unappreciated in a society where the classical curriculum held sway. Most graduates were civil engineers who found jobs in the provincial civil service or municipal government. The Quebec government was determined to create a second university-level institution offering practical education in the French language. The École des hautes études commerciales was established in 1907 to provide an advanced education in business and economics. Classes began in 1910 under a Belgian educator who modelled the school after similar institutions in his native country. It proved difficult to attract qualified students, and only nine of the thirty-nine who formed the first class in 1910 graduated in 1913.[39] This modest attempt at creating a secular educational institution did not please the archbishop, who insisted that the École des Hautes Etudes Commercials be placed under the authority of Laval, the city's Catholic university. The change did not translate into greater financial support for the school, albeit there was no obvious interference with its curriculum.

The diocese was led by Archbishop Paul Bruchesi, the son of an Italian father and a French Canadian mother. After studies in France and Italy, earning doctorates in theology and canon law, Bruchesi was ordained at the age of twenty-four. As one of the most promising French Canadian priests, he held a series of important appointments before his elevation to succeed Archbishop Edouard-Charles Fabre in 1897. Bruchesi was determined to maintain the conservative and ultramontane traditions of French Canadian Catholicism, establishing a reputation as an uncompromising opponent of all challenges, real and imagined, to the supremacy of the church in education, social welfare, and moral issues. Bruchesi believed that "philosophical errors" and "false doctrines" were undermining the faith of his people. His 1901 pastoral letter "The Weakening of the Christian Spirit and the Taste for the Pleasures of the World," which singled out foreign theatrical performances as a specific danger to young people, was the first of many failed attempts to preserve his flock from the modern world.[40]

Bruchesi's greatest moment came in September 1910 when Montreal hosted the Eucharistic Congress, attracting leaders of the Roman Catholic Church and tens of thousands of the faithful to the city.[41] The success of the congress reinforced the archbishop's determination to defend the prerogatives of the church in Quebec, particularly in the control of education, resisting all proposals that might endanger the church's monopoly over both public and private schools. The chief critic of the province's education system, Godfroy Langlois, was the editor of Le Canada and spokesman for the Lique de l'enseignment. Langlois led a campaign for compulsory education, uniform school texts, the medical inspection of school children, and a ministry of public instruction.[42] Naming the pressure group after the organization that was popularly understood to have banished religion from the public schools of France was bound to produce a reaction, and the church hierarchy dug in, refusing to accept any proposal, however constructive, that might be seen to weaken the authority of the church. Attempts to create a centralized school board for the Island of Montreal, which in 1910 had thirty separate school commissions, were vigorously opposed by local curés and Bruchesi's nominees on the Montreal Catholic School Commission. A Quebec Royal Commission failed to resolve the problem and further irritated the clergy, who insisted that Quebec possessed the best education system in the world.[43] Critics were simply part of the Masonic conspiracy.

Bruchesi was determined to punish his enemies, and after Langlois was outed as member of a Masonic lodge, affiliated to the Grand Orient of France, he was replaced as editor of *Le Canada*. Wilfrid Laurier and the premier of Quebec, Lomer Gouin, had tolerated Langlois as a means of keeping in touch with the Liberal Party's radical, *rouge*, wing, but membership in an organization known as a "declared enemy of the church" required Laurier to demand Langlois's resignation.[44]

Bruchesi was determined to further isolate Langlois, and in 1913 he issued a mandement forbidding Catholics to read his weekly newspaper *Le Pays*. When Langlois challenged Bruchesi to identify specific examples of anti-Catholic material in *Le Pays* the archbishop declined to reply. Langlois was effectively removed from the scene in 1914 when Gouin, perhaps at Bruchesi's request, offered Langlois the post of Quebec's representative in Belgium. *Le Pays* survived, but without Langlois as editor it was far less influential and could be ignored.[45]

The French-English duality, the famous "two solitudes," was altered after 1900 by the immigration of large numbers of Jews from Eastern Europe, who by 1914 made up 8 per cent of the population. Most of the newcomers were from the fringes of the Russian Empire and spoke Yiddish as their first language. They settled in the area adjacent to the existing garment factories and over the decade moved north with the industry, establishing the district known to Montrealers as "The Main."[46] The new residents quickly created their own mutual benefit societies, synagogues, public library clubs, and welfare associations. A Yiddish newspaper, the *Der Keneder Odler* (Jewish Eagle) was established in 1907, and a lively Yiddish theatre, connected to New York City, used the Monument National for performances. Relationships with the established "west-end" Jews were not always smooth, but common interest in Zionism and questions about the education of the young helped to connect the city's Jews across class and linguistic lines.[47]

Tension between these Yiddish-speaking immigrants and the existing population was no doubt inevitable, but it was complicated by outbreaks of antisemitism characteristic of Christian societies. Expressions of antisemitism predated large-scale Jewish immigration, especially during the Dreyfus Affair. Most French Canadian clergy, intellectuals, and journalists were outspoken anti-Dreyfusards during the long, drawn-out struggle to prove that Alfred Dreyfus, an Alsatian Jew, was innocent of the charge of treason. Antisemitism was kept alive in journals like *Le Croix, Le Nationaliste, L'Action Sociale,* and *Le Devoir,*[48] all of which published articles by men such as Edouard Drumont, France's most notorious antisemite.[49] A second, intense outburst of such prejudice occurred in 1910 after the mayor of Rome, Ernesto Nathan, a Freemason of Jewish ancestry, used the fortieth anniversary of the fall of the Papal State to deliver a provocative attack on the pope's "fortress of dogma" and "reign of ignorance."[50]

The pope and his secretary of state, Rafael Merry del Val, lashed out at Nathan, urging Catholics around the world to condemn his actions. The archbishop of Montreal willingly responded to the pope's request, organizing a well-advertised mass protest to take place at the Monument National. Montreal city council became involved when a resolution criticizing Nathan was introduced despite opposition from the Protestant Ministerial Association and spokesmen for the Jewish community. On Sunday, 17 October 1910, crowds estimated at 25,000 were diverted to the Champs des Mars where Bruchesi, Mayor James Guerin, and the nationalist leader Henri Bourassa addressed the crowd. The archbishop referred to Nathan as a Freemason, but Bourassa's coded reference to "an old attack which has existed since the time of Christ ... the same voice of hatred against Christ, the Church and the Papacy" was in tune with cries of "à bas les juifs" from the crowd.[51] The Nathan affair together with the grotesquely antisemitic address of Joseph Plamondon to the Quebec City branch of the Association catholique de la jeunesse canadienne marked a low point in relations between Jews and French Canadians. Plamondon was sued for libel in a case that was finally decided, for the plaintiffs, in December 1914.[52]

Relations between the Jewish community and the city's Anglo-Protestants were not free of difficulty or prejudice, but given the Roman Catholic Church's policy limiting school enrolment to church members, Jewish immigrants sent their children to Protestant schools. The responsibility for educating Quebec's Jews was formally assigned to Protestant school boards in 1903 after an agreement was enacted to have Jews pay their school taxes to the Protestant boards. A conscience clause exempted Jews from participation in Protestant religious exercises.[53] The schools retained their Protestant character, immersing immigrant students in a secular, English-language world. The board resisted appointing Jewish teachers until 1913, when a one-day student strike at Aberdeen School, called to protest a teacher's derogatory comments about Jews, persuaded the trustees to change their policy for the 1914 school year. By then Jewish students made up 40 per cent of those attending Protestant schools within city limits.[54]

The confessional character of Montreal's schools created a serious problem for immigrants from Eastern Europe who belonged to one of the Orthodox Churches, Greek, Syrian, or Russian. The Protestant school board, which was under pressure to educate this "foreign element," estimated that there were several thousand children of school age, but "practically none of them are in school."[55] Italians, after Jews the second-largest "foreign element," were able to send their children to either French or English Catholic schools. Most Italian children attended classes at their parish schools, Notre Dame de la Defense and Notre Dame de Mont-Carmel, where Italian was the language of instruction in the early years, then English.[56]

It is evident that pre-war Montreal was a complex, multicultural metropolis unlike any other city in Canada. There was, however, a common thread that ran through the experience of two-thirds of the population – workers locked into a low-wage economy. The organizers of the 1912 Child Welfare Exhibit examined the wages paid to unskilled workers and found that $1.75 a day was typical. This worked out to $550 per year, but "to get this much … a man must have continuous work six days a week, fifty-two weeks a year, with no sickness, no change of jobs, and he must not waste his money on drink or dissipation. Granted all this, he can give a family of five a mere existence … in unsanitary quarters sometimes below the street level."[57]

According to the 1911 census, adult male workers in manufacturing establishments averaged $10.55 per week, while a table entitled "Heads of Families in Specified Occupations" placed the average income of skilled building tradesmen at $13.70 per week, with construction labourers earning $10.20. Trainmen, traditionally among the highest paid workers, averaged $18.67 per week. By 1914, $2.00 per day appears to have been a more typical base wage, but it is clear that if either a modern definition of poverty – more than 70 per cent of total income spent on food, clothing, and shelter – or the Typical Family Budget developed by the Department of Labour in 1910 is used, then "poverty was the common experience of the majority of the population of Montreal" – unless there were additional sources of family income.[58] The average family in Montreal had 2.5 children most of whom would go to work by the age of fourteen. Girls employed in factories might earn $6.00 per week, boys a little more. Until such additional income was available, assistance from extended family members, taking in lodgers, and most importantly a wife who could improvise and manage the family economy were essential to survival.[59]

For women in an era before effective birth control, marriage and motherhood in their late teens or early twenties was the norm. This reality was no doubt reinforced by a patriarchal society that promoted an idealized version of "chaste young motherhood, spent in pure company, followed by a marriage blessed with numerous offspring."[60] Domestic service in the homes of the wealthy, which accounted for 15 per cent of the female labour force, was a possible alternative, as was entry into a religious order. In 1911 between 2 and 2.5 per cent of all women over twenty lived in religious communities, working as teachers, nurses, administrators, and domestics.[61]

Montreal's industrial structure provided extensive opportunities for the employment of women in the textile mills, the garment trade, and other enterprises. The large majority of women in the work force were unmarried and under twenty-five. This, together with the assumption that female employment was temporary until marriage, may account for women being linked with children in regulatory legislation. Both were to be protected from employment in "dangerous or unhealthy occupations." In 1913, their work week was limited to fifty-eight hours, though an exception could be made for a period "not exceeding six weeks." Women and children in textile mills were limited to a fifty-five-hour week, because conditions in the mills were "tiresome and depressing." The minimum age for children in the work force was raised from thirteen to fourteen in 1907. Those who could not read and write were supposed to attend night school until the age of sixteen, though as Louis Guyon, the chief factory inspector, pointed out, "in many cases there are no night schools and at best for boys only ... is it very practical to compel a child fatigued by ten hours of assiduous labour to spend even an hour and a half at school?" Guyon proposed that a certificate of elementary education be required for factory employment. In his 1913 report, he noted that "in many countries child labour has ceased to be a problem ... because every boy or girl is obliged to hand to his employer, with his age certificate, his school attendance book."[62] This was dangerously close to advocating compulsory education, a policy explicitly rejected by the church and the provincial legislature.

The child labour laws, Guyon added, did not apply to children who worked in shops or "the thousands of working children, errand boys and news boys ... seen shivering on the street until eleven o'clock at night."[63] Other loopholes existed. A *Star* reporter followed up news of underage children employed in the glass industry by visiting the Dominion Glass factory on Delormier Street, which employed 300 boys. "Entering the factory before midnight," he found the glass blowers at work placing "white glowing glass" into moulds "where it is blown up into bottles of various shapes ... At each pair of moulds sits a small boy whose duty it is to close the mould ... and remove the hot bottles when they are set." Other boys were involved in subsequent stages of the production. "Working as they do in grilling temperatures the boys wear very few clothes and the gauntness of their frames is painfully apparent ... There are youngsters who by no stretch of the imagination could be over twelve years old."

The boys worked alternate day and night weekly shifts, which violated a second law forbidding night work for anyone less than eighteen years of age. When approached by a reporter, Guyon explained that "small boys are necessary ... to get comfortably between the moulds." They also needed to be "fairly young in order not to rebel against the necessary discipline." Both Guyon and the works manager claimed that efforts were made to keep youngsters under the legal age out of the glass factory, but Guyon admitted that the order forbidding night work to those under eighteen would have to be held in abeyance. "There would be much hardship in the East End if these boys were thrown out of work."[64]

The *Star* followed the story for several days, quoting, among others, Mrs. Rose Henderson, a probation officer at the juvenile court. Henderson insisted that "factory child labour while technically under control is practically never interfered with … the law is broken every day, but there are no laws whatever to protect the street paper seller, the little shop assistant, the messenger boys and those engaged in some industry in their own homes." Mrs. Henderson thought that the solution was to have "the Government pay a certain sum to parents in need weekly for each child" so their children could go to school and lead healthy lives.[65]

These ideas for a family allowance, together with proposals to raise wages, were utopian dreams for economic as well as political and ideological reasons. Revenues available to all three levels of government under existing tax regimes could not support any significant transfer payments, and it is not easy to see where enough additional revenue for significant income redistribution could have come from. The inhabitants of the "Square Mile," Montreal's residential neighbour for the elite, could have paid slightly higher wages and taken lower dividends, but the amounts available for redistribution suggest that very large increases in gross national product were required before wage incomes could be significantly increased in real terms. GDP per capita, measured in 1900 dollars, reached $246 in 1911, rose briefly from 1916 to 1919, and then declined sharply between 1919 and the Second World War.[66]

This basic economic reality presented trade unions and socialist activists with a major dilemma. The Montreal Trades and Labour Council, affiliated to the Canadian Trades and Labour Congress (CTLC) and the American Federation of Labour, was the major workers' organization in the city. Its president, John T. Foster, a bilingual machinist, and secretary Gustav Francq, a Belgian-born printer, endorsed the kind of moderate craft unionism associated with Samuel Gompers and with Alphonse Verville, former CTLC president and member of Parliament for Montreal-Maisonneuve. Their proposals for an eight-hour work day, attempts to achieve union recognition, or strikes to achieve better living wages were unlikely to succeed in an economy flooded with immigrants and a manufacturing sector that relied upon a protective tariff to exploit a small transcontinental market. Even the best-organized workers in the American Federation of Labour craft unions had very limited bargaining power. This did not mean the workers were passive. A wave of strikes in 1903 involved street railway employees, longshoremen, teamsters, electrical workers, and building labourers, all searching for wage increases and hoping for union recognition. Two years later the machinists' strike against the Grand Trunk Railway and walkouts in the tobacco industry due to "reduction in wages and the employment of women and children" demonstrated their militancy but failed to achieve wage increases or union recognition. The growing importance of the garment industry with its piece-work rates and contracting out led to a series of strikes between 1910 and 1913, but the economic downturn and high levels of unemployment forced wage earners to settle for whatever they could get.[67] Disputes in Quebec's cotton factories prompted the creation of a royal commission, but the commissioners could only recommend minor changes in the conditions of employment for women and children.[68]

If the economy did not create enough wealth to overcome widespread poverty, there were certainly sufficient resources to work towards improving public health, housing, and education. The correlation between poverty and ill health was widely discussed among medical experts, and there was broad awareness that Montreal was said to have the highest infant mortality rate in the Western world. Babies born in the city's working-class wards were four times more likely to die before their first birthday than those born in the wealthiest parts of the city, and the toll of young lives continued between the ages of one and five. Two separate but related problems were involved. During the first year of life, breastfeeding would have prevented most of the premature deaths caused by gastroenteritis. Mothers in poorer neighbourhoods were less likely to nurse infants for the first year and appear to have relied on the city's milk suppliers for bottle feeding. The danger of this practice was demonstrated in 1914 with the publication of *The Milk Supply of Montreal*. Investigators from the Dominion Department of Agriculture visited all of the major dairy farms supplying milk to the city to acquire samples at the point of production. Of these samples, 30 per cent was grade "C," meaning unfit for drinking but still suitable for food processing. Another 20 per cent was labelled "'D' because it was five times worse" than grade "C" milk and unfit for any use. When the milk, shipped in ordinary, unrefrigerated freight cars, reached the city's distributors, 90 per cent was unfit for human consumption by the standard in use in American cities. Less than a quarter of the milk supply was pasteurized in 1914, and only one of the six dairies offering pasteurized milk was doing it effectively.[69] Two women's organizations tackled the problem, creating pure milk depots, or *gouttes de lait*, in working-class neighbourhoods. By 1914 these were supplying milk and counselling to the mothers of 3,101 infants, and deaths among this group were fifty per one thousand live births, one quarter of the city-wide average.[70]

The second important health problem in the city, tuberculosis, presented a more difficult challenge. Montreal's mortality rate, which was in excess of 200 deaths per one hundred thousand, was the highest in North America, and the link between poverty and disease was evident in the ward-by-ward statistics.

The campaign against the "white plague" was directed by physicians, private philanthropy, and the Catholic Church. The Royal Edward Institute, established in 1908, was initially funded by a gift from Jeffrey Burland, one of the city's millionaires who was active in numerous public health campaigns. Three years later the Sisters of Providence established a second hospital, L'Institute Bruchesi, offering treatment for TB patients and public education. Both institutions emphasized the dispensary method of treatment, first developed in Edinburgh, based on identification of the infected followed by home visits and instruction, written and verbal, on how to manage the disease. Both hospitals also opened small sanitariums outside the city to accommodate advanced cases. These commendable efforts, however, reached a very small part of the vulnerable population.[71]

Burland was a member of the Quebec Royal Commission on Tuberculosis, chaired by Dr. E.P. Lachapelle, which reported in 1910. The commissioners were surprised by "the almost general ignorance of the infectious nature of tuberculosis," the higher death rate among women than men, and the fact that "the death rate among our rural population too nearly equals that of the urban population." Their recommendations dealt with ways of educating the population and various means for isolating active cases. Dr. Lachapelle believed that Pasteur's revolutionary ideas on the transmission of infectious diseases were putting the field of hygiene "on a scientific basis," but tuberculosis might still be spread through the air. Improved ventilation of schools and industrial establishments as well as open-air schools, vacation colonies, and "preventariums" were therefore emphasized.[72] Almost all the recommendations required provincial funding as well as a considerable increase in the number of public health workers. Neither was forthcoming, and both mortality and morbidity rates were unchanged to 1914.[73]

Any city experiencing rapid population growth is bound to have a serious housing problem, and Montreal was no exception. The city's housing was in poor condition before the population doubled in a decade, so no one was surprised when the Board of Inquiry into the Cost of Living (1913) reported that "housing conditions in Montreal have degenerated and there is a decided lack of workingman's dwellings with proper conveniences at low rentals. Rents have increased by fifty percent in the last seven years leading to doubling up of families in the same apartment or house causing overcrowding and ill health."[74]

Over 80 per cent of the city's residents rented their dwelling, and while Montreal avoided the problem of tenement slums, the well-constructed duplexes and triplexes that would come to characterize much of the city were still a small part of the housing stock in 1913.[75] The shortage of rental housing was a frequent subject for the popular press. The *Montreal Star*'s survey of the situation in 1914 was typical. As people prepared for moving day, when leases expired, the newspaper reported that "houses and apartments ... are scarce and rent throughout the city will be raised twenty to forty percent" on May 1. Rates varied by district but "even at the lower end flats which rented for $15.00 a month have now increased to $19.00."[76]

Housing, like public health, was the subject of endless debate in Montreal as elsewhere. Herbert Ames, the owner of one of the city's largest shoe factories, had introduced the notion of "philanthropy plus five percent" by building "Diamond Court" as model housing. Neither Ames nor anyone else followed up on an initiative that remained an interesting exception to the duplexes lining the streets of the working-class wards. The Quebec Public Health Act in 1906 established a board with regulatory powers that issued regulations on housing, but two years later the chief inspector noted that "not one of our municipalities has established an effective supervision over the construction of dwellings."[77]

Given the limited financial resources of the municipal and provincial governments, the best that could be hoped for was a comprehensive building code with realistic mechanisms for enforcement. Instead Montreal was subjected to a number of schemes to build model tenements and garden cities. The Montreal Civic Improvement League, founded in 1909, lobbied for a metropolitan planning board, winning the support of Premier Lomer Gouin for an "Act to Establish the Metropolitan Parks Commission" in 1912. The commissioners seemed to possess sweeping powers to levy taxes, borrow money, expropriate property, and take other necessary actions "for the establishment of public parks, squares, promenades, boulevards, thoroughfares, recreation grounds, playgrounds, streets, baths and gardens as well as improvements in working class dwellings."[78]

These utopian proposals were presented to the public at the 1912 Child Welfare Exhibit, which related children's health to housing conditions as well as low wages. The exhibit was well publicized and well attended, but once it became clear that the Parks Commission was seeking a 5 per cent increase in the city's property taxes support dwindled and the provincial government declined to allocate funds even for administrative expenses. William Van Horne, who chaired the commission, suggested that the members "defray, by personal contribution, the costs they had incurred and then dissolve."[79]

The kind of tax increase sought by the Parks Commission would have been better applied to the city's failing public schools. The fundamental problem facing both school boards was financial. With minimal support from the province, schools depended on a property tax that proved inadequate to the needs of a rapidly expanding metropolis. The property tax was allocated from three panels, corporate, Catholic, or Protestant. Corporate taxes were divided on a per capita basis, but the greater wealth of the Protestant community meant that overall their board received roughly the same amount of money as the Catholic School Commission to educate half the number of students.[80]

Both public school systems were under enormous pressure to build new schools in an expanding city. The Catholic School Commission was unable to meet "the pressing needs of existing schools" where it was difficult to find space for children who were "more and more numerous" or to build the required number of new schools. The problem of too few schools and too little room also confronted the Protestant board, which constantly struggled to provide "sufficient accommodation for those who voluntarily attend."[81]

Charging monthly fees for those who attended school helped to close the funding gap, but the consequence was that few students stayed in school beyond the early grades. In 1905 the Montreal Catholic School Commission reported that while there were 3,442 pupils in first year, there were only 1,118 in fourth year and less than 500 students aged thirteen in the fifth year. As numbers increased the ratios did not improve. The provincial government resisted tax increases until 1908, when the Protestant board successfully lobbied for a modest increase in the mill rate for the Protestant and corporate panels. This compromise offered additional funds to the Catholic schools from the corporate panel while providing the Protestants with the opportunity to build new schools and improve accessibility.[82]

Those who defended the Catholic system of education in Quebec pointed to the contribution of the private schools and classical colleges, which were subsidized by the church and the contributions of the nuns and brothers who taught in the public schools, but the Montreal Catholic School Board's contract with the Christian Brothers called for the payment of $500 per teacher, while female religious orders received $350 per teacher, amounts roughly equivalent to lay teacher salaries.[83]

With wage and salary earners employed six days a week, there was little time for mass leisure except on Sunday, a day both Protestant and Roman Catholic clergy sought to control. In the late nineteenth century the major challenges to their efforts came from public spaces such as the Parc Sohmer, which opened in 1889, and the large municipal parks Mount Royal and Logan. Mount Royal was designed by Frederick Law Olmstead as an engineered natural space accessible by an inclined railway. Logan, renamed Lafontaine in 1901, provided a 160-acre green space in the east end. Parc Sohmer, which included a 7,000-seat pavilion for music and other entertainment, came alive each summer with scenes reminiscent of an Impressionist painting, and Sunday was the park's biggest day.[84] As well, in 1906 a new amusement park located between the river and Notre Dame Street opened; Dominion Park was built at the end of the tramway line and quickly became a major attraction.

The growing popularity of team sports, especially baseball, further challenged attempts to preserve the sanctity of Sundays in the city. Baseball, according to sport historian Alan Metcalfe, was the game most often played by Canadians of all backgrounds,[85] and this was certainly the case in Montreal, where as early as 1897 4,000 fans filled the stands at Atwater Park for the Montreal Royals season opening. A twenty-one-year-old local boy, Louis Belcourt, said to be the first French Canadian to play in the Eastern League, was the winning pitcher. The Royals won the league title in 1898, a feat they were unable to duplicate in the next two decades. By 1910 they were competing with a semi-professional City League as well as a number of amateur leagues. Baseball news from the American and National leagues as well as reports on the Royals and City League teams dominated the sports pages from April to September, when hockey took over.

The issue of Sunday sports plagued the Royals, as Atwater Park straddled the boundary between Montreal and Westmount. Both had by-laws prohibiting professional games on Sunday, but Westmount actually required observance of the rules, forcing the Royals to play at the National Club grounds in Maisonneuve. The City League, which included French and English teams, played a regular double-header on Sunday using the Shamrocks hockey club's field on St. Denis in Mile End. When "l'element puritain" protested, the league threatened to play outside the city limits and no attempt to enforce the Sunday by-law was made.[86]

Professional hockey gradually became an obsession among Montrealers during the second decade of the twentieth century. From its Victorian beginnings at McGill, where it was played as a "brutal game of rugby at high speed,"[87] to the emergence of the Montreal Shamrocks, who pioneered a more organized approach, hockey was transformed by the creation of professional teams playing at night in illuminated indoor ranks. By 1914 two Montreal teams, Les Canadiens and the Wanderers, successors to the Shamrocks, played in the National Hockey Association, forerunner to the National Hockey League.[88] Rivalry between the teams, portrayed as representing the French and English communities, provided newspapers with the kind of stories that built circulation, and since weekend games were played on Saturday there was no conflict with Sunday by-laws.

Arenas and parks were the main places for people to gather in large numbers until the movies came to Montreal. The city's popular vaudeville theatres remained closed on Sundays in response to pressure from the churches, but when Ernest Ouimet opened his 1,200-seat air-conditioned "Ouimetoscope" everything changed. Ouimet and his competitors were after large audiences, and with tickets priced at five cents the crowds came, especially on Sunday. Church leaders did their best to control the new medium, persuading the city to pass a Sunday closing by-law, but Ouimet and his rivals fought back. In 1912 the Supreme Court ruled against the city. Ouimet paid the legal costs, but it was the new "movie palaces," showing American films, that benefited. The Strand Theatre (1912), the Imperial (1913), and many smaller movie houses offered regular feature-length films that by 1914 attracted audiences estimated at 12,500 per day. The vaudeville theatres also began to show movies on Sunday and to include them in the weekly schedule. The Catholic hierarchy and the Protestant Ministerial Association were forced to accept Sunday movies, instead seeking to establish censorship and require children under the age of fifteen to be accompanied by an adult.[89]

Montreal was an important venue for American musical theatre productions. By 1904 John Bolingbrooke Sparrow, who began his theatrical career in the bill-posting business, had acquired control of the city's major live entertainment venues, the Theatre Royal, Academy of Music, Théatre Francais, and His Majesty's Theatre. As the Canadian agent of the New York Theatre Syndicate, he brought Broadway shows to Montreal. In the years before 1914 60 per cent of shows produced in Montreal originated in New York, and most of these were popular musical comedies or Victor Herbert operettas.[90]

French-speaking audiences were also drawn to musical revues, which used popular tunes and street language to poke fun at daily life in Montreal. Shows such as *La Belle Montréalaise* and *As-tu vu le R'vue* drew large crowds to hear songs satirizing life in the city. The seemingly endless debate over the construction of a municipal library, the poor condition of the streets, the tramway monopoly, the red-light district, and much else was lampooned in patter songs.[91] The construction of a modern French Canadian culture, irrelevant, audacious, and quite separate from the nationalist and Catholic ideas expressed elsewhere, was well underway before the outbreak of war in 1914.

This attitude was particularly evident when Archbishop Bruchesi sought to prevent Catholics from attending Sarah Bernhardt's performances in Montreal. The "Divine Sarah," the most famous international actress of the era, visited Montreal three times in the 1890s, attracting large crowds despite the warning that Catholics had "a rigorous duty to keep away from such plays." Before her 1905 tour all Catholic newspapers were asked to refuse theatre ads, and Bruchesi required his parish priests to read a letter from their pulpits denouncing Berhardt's performances as an "enemy of our Christian doctrine." Attendance by Catholics would be "an occasion of sin." The authority of both the archbishop and the church was undermined when Governor-General Lord Grey and his wife as well as leading figures in Montreal's French and English society attended the performance. When the program for a 1911 tour was announced Bruchesi successfully protested the inclusion of plays titled "Sapho" and "La Sorcière," but the "largest audience in the history of this Majesty's Theatre" flocked to performances of similar plays with less provocative titles.[92]

Church leaders who were unable to control popular forms of entertainment or prevent Sunday performances proved equally powerless when the city's Licensing Commission and the Quebec legislature addressed restriction of the number of liquor permits in Montreal. A coalition of church and temperance groups began a major effort to tackle the issue in January 1914, arguing for sharp reductions in the number of licensed premises. A proposal to cut the number of permits for hotels and restaurants from 473 to 350 and for liquor shops from 548 to 350 floundered when the cost of compensating those who would lose their livelihood arose. Attention was diverted by efforts to prevent the renewal of licences for four especially notorious "all-night cafés" where, according to a prominent Anglican minister, "boys and girls were sacrificed to Bacchus and Venus." The Licensing Commission agreed that the cafés "had been guilty of grave infractions … by permitting prostitutes of both sexes to resort there with a view to immoral assignations" while "allowing vulgar and immoral dancing," and announced that licences for the four cafés would not be renewed.[93]

The reference to "prostitutes of both sexes" points to another aspect of life in the metropolis. Montreal's red-light district, the area bounded by St. Lawrence and Saint Denis, Craig and Sherbrooke streets, was a long-established part of the urban scene tolerated by civic authorities.[94] The obvious collusion of the police with brothel-keepers was examined in a 1904 enquiry that included a commentary on ways of dealing with "the social evil." Justice Henri Taschereau condemned the policy of toleration practised in Montreal, noting that while the police were aware of the locations of "a hundred and eighty or two hundred houses of disorder or prostitution," raids were only carried out if there was a specific complaint.[95] He recommended a policy of "war without mercy, of energetic repression and complete suppression" along with reduction of the number of licensed restaurants and bars in certain sections of the city. No such war developed; five years later, the report was reprinted with additional recommendations from the recorder, the city municipal court judge.

The practice of tolerating heterosexual prostitution was not extended to its homosexual counterpart. After a raid on a club operated by a well-known doctor resulted in the arrest of a sixteen-year-old as well as men in their twenties, carefully worded newspapers accounts and further arrests kept the story of the "East End Club" and the "corruption of youth" alive.[96] One newspaper even compared the incident to the scandal surrounding the German emperor known as the "Eulenberg Affair," which had drawn transnational attention to homosexuality.[97]

Montreal was not yet the "open city" it would become during American prohibition, but the extraordinary range of leisure activities in the city was much commented upon. The *Montreal Standard* offered readers a full-page graphic description of citizens' quest for entertainment in May 1914. Under the title "Montrealers Spend Millions on Pleasure," the newspaper estimated that 2.5 million dollars had been spent attending the city's sixty-seven movie theatres with a further $600,000 for tickets to vaudeville and live theatre. Horse races at Bluebonnets and other venues attracted $160,000, hockey games $100,000, and baseball $60,000. Dance halls, a particularly popular form of winter entertainment, added a further $100,000 to the total. The *Standard* reported that Montrealers also spent 6 million dollars on liquor and beer as well as 2.5 million on smoking. Motoring, still seen as entertainment, was said to have cost $500,000 in the previous year. All of this the *Standard* noted despite "hard times" in the past twelve months.[98]

The contrast between life as experienced in the bars, brothels, and places of entertainment and the social teachings of the Roman Catholic and Protestant churches led a prominent *La Presse* editor to raise questions about the importance of religion in the city. Lorenzo Prince discussed the issue in his book *Montreal Old and New*, published in 1914. Prince estimated that "less than one in five Montrealers" attended church on Sunday, including "casual worshipers who go to church now and then." After deducting the very old and the very young, he concluded that "two hundred thousand people … did not go to church on a particular Sunday." Prince attributed the "declining influence of religion to a change that has come over the world." When men and women are asked "to flee from the wrath to come they say, save us from the misery which is present … They demand of Christianity a practiced application."[99] Prince, a Freemason active in liberal causes, may have exaggerated the decline of religious feeling, but it is evident that daily life in Canada's metropolis was breaking the boundaries prescribed by traditional authorities well before any disruptive effects of the war were apparent.[100]

The winter of 1914 never seemed to end. The snow began in November and there was no let-up until St. Patrick's Day, when the temperature rose above freezing, offering the first hint of spring. The next day a storm dumped six inches of snow on the city, providing a day's work for 3,000 unemployed men and a white cloak for the soot-covered snow banks. Montreal's Irish community had staged their annual parade, the second oldest in North America, the previous Sunday. On Tuesday, the St. Patrick's Day banquet featured William Redmond MP, brother of John Redmond, leader of the Irish Parliamentary Party, which had won the promise of home rule from the British government.[101] The Irish may have been the only Montrealers with anything to celebrate. An international financial crisis had begun in 1913, bringing an abrupt end to more than a decade of growth. The recession struck just as work on the two transcontinental railways neared completion and immigration from Europe and the United States reached an all-time high.[102]

The credit squeeze had an especially severe effect in a country that had financed much of its development on capital borrowed in London. As the president of the Canadian Manufacturers Association explained in his 1913 convention address, Canada's adverse balance of trade exceeded one billion dollars over the previous ten years. To cover this, he noted, "we have thrown industrial bonds by the millions, municipal bonds by tens of millions, and railway securities by the hundreds of millions." Eventually, "our credit abroad would approach its limit and in the past year the inevitable happened."[103] The *Wall Street Journal*, which ran a three-part series on Canada in early 1914, described the situation in similar terms: "There is a depression here, but there will be no crash. Canada is not going backwards, she is simply putting on the brakes until she catches up with herself." The real problem, the *Journal* insisted, was railway construction "ahead of requirements."[104]

Unemployment, estimated at 100,000 nationwide, was particularly severe in Montreal, where seasonal unemployment had always been high.[105] When the St. Lawrence River froze and the harbour closed, there was real hardship throughout the working-class wards. The winter of 1913–14 brought a further influx of unemployed "laborers and artisans from other parts of Canada," creating a situation described in the *Labour Gazette* as "worse than other places in Canada or in previous years."[106]

Those who read the daily newspapers in the first months of 1914 must have been depressed by the steady stream of bad news. On Christmas Day 1913 a break in the main conduit left the city without water for 193 hours. The enquiry that followed dissolved into a bitter dispute over responsibility, further diminishing the reputation of the civic administration. A five-member Board of Control had been imposed on the city after revelations of widespread corruption among aldermen were revealed in the 1910 Report of the Cannon Commission. The new system was supposed to offer honest and efficient government, but few believed either result had been obtained.[107]

Stories about unemployment, an increase in petty crime, the high cost of living, housing shortages, and the slump in real estate values dominated the news until the municipal election campaign began to catch fire in late March. The long-established tradition of alternating French and English mayors suggested that if the minority could find an acceptable candidate, the pattern would continue. When George Washington Stephens, the namesake son of a wealthy businessman and Liberal politician, returned from his Paris home to campaign, everything seemed to be in place. Apart from Hugh Graham's newspapers, which refused to endorse a Liberal, the French-language dailies and the *Montreal Gazette* supported Stephens, noting his contributions as chair of the Harbour Commission, fluency in French, and marriage to an Italian.

Henri Bourassa's decision to support Stephens was offered in the context of a series of four English-language articles printed on the front page of his newspaper, *Le Devoir*.[108] The tone was of an exasperated, kindly, but stern teacher reproaching the English-speaking community for its collective failure to behave like a minority. French Canadians, he noted, had accepted the convention of alternating mayors between the "races" despite the hypocrisy of the "English at large" who "talk of fair-play and broad-mindedness when and where they are in the minority, but seldom put these virtues in practice where they are the majority and when they can afford to assert their supremacy." The next day Bourassa characterized the entire English-speaking population of the city as a single community "confined in their opulent and closed quarter, proud of their factories, their shops, their bank, their stock exchange and their Board of Trade, strongly inclined to self-esteem and self-admiration." The tens of thousands of English-speaking Montrealers struggling to earn a living working sixty hours per week would have been surprised to learn about their "opulent and closed quarter," but since their newspapers largely ignored *Le Devoir* few learned of his views.

Bourassa complained that the "English-speaking residents of Montreal as a whole have made no effort to know their French-speaking fellow citizen, to learn their language, to understand their traditions and aspirations." In contrast, French Canadians had learned English and exhibited a "tolerant spirit," placing all citizens "on a footing of absolute equality in matters of civil rights." Bourassa's third article focused on the place of the French language in Montreal, where large companies headquartered in this city continued to resist using French, even in their contacts with customers. This well-documented argument was accompanied by a paragraph urging the English community of Montreal "to raise themselves above the inferior level of mercantilism and take rank with the cultured classes of all civilized countries who make use of the French language as the international vernacular of all superior thoughts and aspirations." The final essay dealt with the reaction of the English-speaking community to Regulation 17, the Ontario government's administrative order to restrict the use of French in that province's schools.

The question of the status of the French language in Ontario schools became one of the most discussed issues in the wartime relationship between French and English Canadians. The problem arose in the first decade of the century when the pattern of massive out-migration to the United States slowed. In 1900 the US census listed as residents close to 800,000 "Canadian-born first language English" and just under 400,000 whose first language was French.[109] After 1900 the southward flow was reversed and French Canadians, who had flocked to the mill towns of New England, sought employment in Montreal factories or opportunities in eastern and northern Ontario. By 1911 the French-speaking population of Ontario, barely noticeable ten years before, reached 202,442, or 10 per cent of the provincial total.[110] One considerable advantage Ontario offered over New England was a taxpayer-supported Catholic school system that, while requiring the study of English, allowed the use of French as a language of instruction. In practice this meant students in French Canadian areas of settlement were often taught exclusively in their native language.[111]

The growth of the Franco-Ontarian population challenged the dominant role of the Irish Catholic clergy, especially in Ottawa where conflict over control of the University of Ottawa and the city's separate schools became a major issue. The establishment of the Association Canadienne Français d'education de l'Ontario in 1910 sharpened the debate when a resolution demanding "that the French language be given a more official and prominent position in elementary and secondary schools and the teacher training institutions of the province" was passed.[112] This ambitious program provoked an immediate reaction from both Irish Catholics and militant Anglo-Protestants, forcing Ontario premier James Whitney, who had accepted a new grant formula improving funding for separate schools, to cancel the agreement because the resolutions "complicated matters" for him with the caucus.[113]

There were now three sides to the dispute: Protestants and secularists who were determined to protect the common school system from further erosion, Irish Catholics attempting to protect and extend their separate schools, and the French Canadians of Ontario who sought to establish a secure place for themselves in the province. Everyone believed that their values, cultural identity, and language were at stake, and "each group fought with all the self-rectitude of embattled justice."[114]

Questions about the future of the French language in Ontario and the rest of Canada were further inflamed by the controversy over the words used by British archbishop Francis Bourne at the September 1910 Eucharistic Congress held in Montreal. Bourne's vision of a "united Canada enunciating in French and English alike the same religious truths" included a statement on the necessity of using English in the "western provinces of the Dominion." Bourassa seized the opportunity to present a passionate defence of the value of the French language in preserving the Catholic religion, "wherever there are French groups living in the shadow of the British flag or the glorious star-spangled banner." Subsequently Bourassa and Bourne met to address their differences, but Bourne continued to argue that the church must give priority to English at least in the west, challenging Bourassa's vision of a bicultural and bilingual Canada.[115]

The language issue festered until 1912 when the Ontario government introduced Regulation 17, a circular of instructions that limited the use of French as "a language of communication and instruction" to the first two or three years of elementary school. The reaction among French Canadians in Ontario was swift and determined. A campaign of active resistance to Regulation 17 won broad support, especially in Ottawa where the French-language majority on the separate school board declared it would not implement Regulation 17. They continued to defy the government after funding was cut off for the 1913–14 school year.[116]

For Bourassa, whose interest in mass education was limited to ensuring that schools were Catholic and French, the future of the minority in Ontario was a major issue. He castigated the English of Quebec for failing to take a leading role in supporting minority rights in Ontario and warned that "the idea of retaliation was beginning to take root in the province." The minority should remember that "in matters of education, whether linguistic or religious," their rights "rest upon the same constitutional basis as those of the French in Ontario." Despite these grievances, Bourassa would continue to support Stephens, the "most qualified candidate."[117]

Stephens ran a well-financed campaign with meetings in all parts of the city. Placing himself firmly in the Citizen's Association, Board of Control, good-government camp, he argued for "real autonomy ... home rule for Montreal," honest civic administration, and a plan for a future Montreal with a population of 1.5 million citizens. Responding to comments about his wealth and year-long sojourn in Paris, Stephens recounted the story of his grandfather's journey north from Vermont and the hard work required to build the family fortune through three generations. This success allowed him to serve as chair of the Harbour Commission and now to offer to serve the citizens of Montreal.[118]

Initially the press paid little attention to Stephen's opponent, the flamboyant "cigar maker" Médéric Martin, but as Martin continued his populist campaign, taking over events organized by other candidates, the press began to cover his speeches. Martin was an experienced politician. A city councillor and member of Parliament for Ste. Marie, he was re-elected to both positions despite credible accusations of corruption outlined in the report of the Cannon Commission. Martin fought openly for the abolition of the Board of Control and the restoration of the old patronage system, criticizing Stephens as "the candidate of a clique, the candidate of the west end and of millionaires."[119] Martin's claim to represent the city's working class was challenged by John T. Foster, the president of the Montreal branch of the Trades and Labour Congress, who declared that Martin was not supported by organized labour. French Canadian trade unionists promptly criticized Foster, insisting he had no mandate to speak for local trade unionists on municipal elections.[120]

Martin took particular delight in responding to Henri Bourassa's attack on his candidacy. Bourassa had been on a speaking tour of western Canada and Ontario, where his ardent appeal for Canadian autonomy and recognition of the equality of the two founding peoples had been politely received. Martin poked fun at Bourassa, telling an east-end audience that "it is a queer thing for this hater of the English to do but then we are getting used to his somersaults." A week later he told a large audience that Bourassa was "an ambitious and destructive politician who had done more harm to his country than any other man in the Dominion" – a remark that the *Gazette* noted "was greeted with much applause." Martin also told his audience that Stephens had addressed a "meeting of suffragettes and millionaires at the Windsor Hotel," whereas he was opposed to women's suffrage and to their employment outside the home. "Workingmen," he argued, "are suffering by the fact that so many women are engaged in manufacturing."[121]

The suffrage question had taken on new meaning in Montreal after *La Patrie* reported that the charter of the city did not limit the vote to male ratepayers.

Women who were listed as owners of property or renters who paid water tax could vote, and as many as 13,000 women were eligible.[122] This news produced a further indication of a growing divide along linguistic as well as class lines. The Montreal Council of Women developed an energetic "Get out the Vote" movement aimed at eligible women. The Council had worked cooperatively with its French Canadian counterpart, La Fédération nationale Saint-Jean Baptiste, on social issues, but female suffrage was another matter.[123] Madame Caroline Béique, the wife of a prominent businessman and Liberal senator, who became the first president of the Fédération, had reached an accord with Archbishop Bruchesi to promote "good feminism." Bruchesi insisted that this mean "there will be no talk in your meetings of the emancipation of women, of the neglect of her rights, of her having been relegated to the shadows, of the responsibilities, public offices and professions to which she should be admitted on an equal basis with man."[124]

This agreement had not prevented the Fédération from working with the Montreal Council of Women to encourage spinsters and widows who owned property to vote in the 1910 municipal election, but after the 1911 visit of Emmeline Pankhurst and the formation in 1913 of the Montreal Suffrage Association,[125] the Fédération became much more cautious, refusing to become involved in controversial issues. The "Get out the Vote" campaign in 1914 was therefore dominated by women from the west end, English-speaking wards who established committee rooms, organized visits, and provided transportation to the polls – all in support of Stephens.[126]

If a large number of women from the west end voted, it made little difference. To the considerable surprise of the city's newspapers, Stephens and the "slate" backed by the Citizen's Association were overwhelmed by French Canadian voters who chose Médéric Martin, a new Board of Control, and a solid majority of traditional patronage-linked aldermen. The pattern of voting laid bare the class and ethnic divisions in the city. St. Lawrence Ward, the "city above the hill," gave Stephens 2,845 votes to 494 for Martin. Working-class St. Henri voted three to one for Martin. The equally working-class ward of St. Ann with its mixture of Irish, French, and English voters gave Stephens two-thirds of the vote. In the east end of the city, Martin won large majorities in all wards. Three of the five controllers elected in a city-wide vote were French-speaking Canadians, and only one, Joseph Ainey, was endorsed by the press and the Citizen's Association.[127]

The French-language dailies were unable to explain the voting pattern or the large crowds of Martin supports who filled the streets around the newspapers' offices on election night. La Patrie, which had supported Stephens, reported that after working hours, voters in the east end had arrived at the polls in large numbers to support Martin and then joined a crowd that grew to 40,000. The mayor-elect had barely mentioned minority rights in Ontario during his campaign, but Bourassa told the readers of *Le Devoir* that the voters had cast a protest vote against the humiliations inflicted on French Canadians in Winnipeg, Toronto, and Ottawa over the past twenty years.[128]

Spring came to the city gradually. A last snowfall was recorded on 20 April, but by early May temperatures averaged fourteen degrees and the more adventurous began to plant their gardens. The re-opening of Dominion Park was another sign of the change in seasons and moods. Destroyed in 1913 by "one of the most spectacular fires seen here in the past fifty years," the park was rebuilt in the style of Coney Island for the 1914 season.[129] For some Montrealers spring meant the start of a new social season, which began with the annual exhibition of the Arts Association. The association had moved into its magnificent new building on Sherbrooke Street West in 1913, offering Canadian artists a much-enhanced opportunity to display their recent work. The "stately stairway and finely proportioned hall of the gallery" also offered "an effective settling for the many fine dresses" on display for opening night. The 1913 exhibit had proven to be a popular success with more than 15,000 visitors, largely due to the controversy over a few post-Impressionist paintings that scandalized critics. *The Montreal Herald* led off by demanding to know if the selection committee endorsed "the Infantist School" with its "peculiar colour effects" represented by the nude paintings of Randolph Hewton and the works by John Lyman, whose paintings the *Herald* declared were "contemptuous of all precedent." Not to be outdone, the *Star*'s arbitrator of good taste, S. Morgan Powell, deplored "the faddish and inartistic fetish for bad draughtsmanship" of the two artists, who were insincere disciples of the school "founded by a couple of Montmartre cranks, Van Gogh and Gaugin."[130]

If the Arts Association hoped for an equally invigorating and attendance-building controversy in 1914, they were disappointed. The *Gazette* reported that "Sanity, Sincerity and Progress" characterized the majority of paintings at the exhibition. Hewton's painting "Fons Solis" of nymphs dancing around a fountain was said to feature colours that were "high but harmonious." Lyman, a friend and admirer of Matisse, submitted one of his more conventional Bermuda pictures, which *La Presse* described as "un bon poem en coleurs." The prize-winners in an exhibit that included a number of major artists were Marc-Aurèle Suzar-Coté and the Impressionist painter Mabel May. Without controversy, the press coverage was thin and attendance down.[131]

The lateness of spring postponed the opening of the harbour, idling more than 2,000 longshoremen for an additional month. By May there were signs of a partial recovery. Mayor Médric Martin, responding to his electorate, provided employment to several thousand labourers at $2.50 a day. The Angus Shops and other large companies added workers, but on "short time." Overall unemployment remained high; the estimate for June was 25,000 to 30,000 men, though demand for women willing to work as domestic servants was "fair."[132]

News of the assassination of the Austrian archduke in Sarajevo, 28 June 1914, was featured prominently in the city's daily newspapers, but the story was soon overshadowed by events in Mexico, a new crisis in Ulster, and the dramatic confrontation prompted by the arrival of the *Komagata Maru* in Vancouver. The Mexican revolution and the Unionist revolt in Northern Ireland were covered through syndicated reports, but the story of the would-be immigrants from India produced detailed reporting and numerous opinion pieces, especially in the English-language press. The Sikh and Hindu immigrants aboard the Japanese-registered ship were British citizens who had the right to enter Canada if they found their way around a 1908 exclusionary statute requiring immigrants and visitors from within the British Empire to reach Canada on a continuous voyage from their country of birth. Gurdit Singh, a wealthy Sikh resident of Hong Kong, decided to challenge a law designed specifically to prevent immigration from India by assembling potential immigrants at Hong Kong before crossing the Pacific. The politicians, press and, as far as could be told, the residents of British Columbia were outraged.[133]

The *Komagata Maru* incident prompted the vicar of Montreal's Christ Church Cathedral to preach a sermon questioning how Christians could reconcile the exclusion of Asiatics with their professed doctrines.[134] The Reverend Herbert Symonds was well known for his liberal views, but he was not the only one to protest government policies. *The Montreal Witness* was consistently sympathetic to the "Hindus," questioning the exclusionist policy and the government on humanitarian grounds. One editorial asked, "Is it possible that if we could see the events of our time through the eyes of historians writing in 2014 we should find the most significant thing to be seen in the world today is the *Komagata Maru* ... is it possible that the assumption of white superiority is already out of date?"[135]

A hunger strike, angry public meetings in Vancouver, and an appeal to the courts kept the standoff on the front pages. After the Appeals Court upheld the 1908 statute, an attempt to board the ship was "repulsed by a shower of coal, iron bars, clubs and pieces of machinery." The prime minister, Robert Borden, then decided to send the militia and *HMCS Rainbow* as "extreme measures were now necessary." On 23 July, the day of the Austrian ultimatum to Serbia, the Sikhs decided to avoid further violence and return to Hong Kong. Borden and his wife promptly left Ottawa for a Muskoka vacation.

Chapter Two

War

The prime minister, an avid golfer, was on the greens when Austria declared war. He did not return to Ottawa until summoned on 31 July.[1] By then the minister of militia, the irrepressible Sam Hughes, had decided to ignore existing mobilization plans and raise an expeditionary force for rapid deployment overseas. Measures outlined in a War Book, prepared in response to advice from the Committee on Imperial Defence, were being implemented and both militia and permanent-force soldiers were moving to guard places that might be liable to sabotage.[2]

Borden had long been devoted to the idea that Canada should have a voice in imperial foreign policy without ever explaining how this might be achieved. The basic absurdity of the position was cruelly evident during the first days of August. The British cabinet was involved in a serious internal crisis that was not fully resolved until the German invasion of Belgium. No consideration was given to consulting Canada, and no attempt was made to provide the Dominions with information about British intentions. Two days before the British cabinet decided on war, the Canadian government offered "a considerable force for overseas service" with volunteers enlisting as "Imperial troops."[3] Neither the possible violation of Belgian neutrality nor any other specific issue was discussed. Borden's cabinet and caucus had framed their view of international relations through the lens of the naval race and Anglo-German rivalry for so long that no thought was required. As for Borden's "voice," the cabinet and later Parliament learned that "Canadians have nothing whatsoever to say as to the destination of the troops once they cross the water, nor have we been informed as to what their destination may be."[4]

Left without guidance from their government, Canadians learned about events in Europe from the daily newspapers. The initial reports from Vienna and Berlin explained the content and purpose of the Austrian ultimatum and the crisis atmosphere created by the forty-eight-hour time limit. It was evident that the Austro-Hungarian Empire was determined to go to war, and although no one knew the details of the "blank cheque" provided by Berlin, commentators assumed that Vienna would not have acted on its own. On 24 July, an editorial in *The Star* warned that "we may find ourselves listening to the thunder of Armageddon before we had time to realize its approach."[5] The editors still believed that Sir Edward Grey, the British foreign secretary who had successfully mediated previous conflicts, would find a way to prevent war. But when the Austrian ultimatum expired on 25 July, news that Russia would stand by Serbia and a report from Berlin that Germany would support its ally made a European war seem inevitable.

On 29 July, *The Star* proclaimed that if Britain acted "Canada is ready to do her duty." *La Presse*, *Le Canada*, and *La Patrie* joined *The Star* in featuring bold war-related headlines. Other newspapers and public opinion leaders were more cautious. A lead article in *The Montreal Witness* warned against "the jingo press howling for blood."[6] *The Christian Guardian* and *Presbyterian Record*, the leading Protestant weeklies, went to press before the violation of Belgium neutrality and Britain's declaration of war. As a result, their issues, dated 5 August, maintained their commitment to what imperialists called the "peace school of thought."[7]

All the daily newspapers reported the German ultimatum to Belgium, requiring free passage through the kingdom to attack France, in return for a guarantee of post-war independence. King Albert and his cabinet rejected this pro forma offer and prepared to defend the frontier forts. The majority of the British cabinet, including the prime minister and foreign secretary, favoured war in support of France, but it was the ultimatum to Belgium that persuaded a large majority in the country and Parliament that war was both inevitable and necessary. When Germany failed to heed the demand to withdraw its troops from Belgium, Britain and thus Canada were at war.

The German emperor, his chancellor, Bethman-Holweg, and the German General Staff were gambling on a plan that called for rapid destruction of the French army before turning east to deal with the Russians. No one in Berlin was willing to raise questions about the weakness of their Austro-Hungarian ally, the possibility of effective Belgian resistance, logistical problems in an advance beyond Paris, or the significance of British intervention, which was bound to include a naval blockade. The war would be won, and won quickly – any other outcome was unthinkable. The decision-makers in Paris and St. Petersburg reacted to events according to equally well-established, unexamined assumptions. Despite much pre-war discussion on the possibility of a German advance through Belgium, the French commander-in-chief, Joseph Joffre, was determined to take the offensive and force the enemy to conform to his plan to recover Alsace-Lorraine. The czar's semi-trained, poorly equipped armies began a general advance with no clear idea of how an offensive strategy could be transformed into operational success. The British army, commanded by men of limited experience and less understanding of industrialized warfare, sent six of its seven regular army divisions to France with only the vaguest instructions about their role.[8]

Historians now debate the question of just how much enthusiasm for war ordinary citizens demonstrated in early August, noting, for example, that the crowds who filled the streets of London on 3 August were there because it was a "fine August bank holiday." News of the war and the sound of a military band drew people to Buckingham Palace, but there was little evidence of war fever.[9] In Montreal signs of popular enthusiasm were first evident on the night of 3 August after news of the British ultimatum reached the city. According to *The Star*, a crowd of "thousands" marched through the west end singing and cheering. They invaded the Windsor and Ritz Carlton hotels, and demonstrated their support in front of the French consulate by singing *La Marseillaise*. The Royal Highland Regiment added to the drama by parading north from their Bleury street armoury to the "weird, wild, strains of bag pipes." The next morning many of those who did not need to be at work gathered in front of newspapers bulletin boards waiting for definite word of war. The Grenadier Guards announced that they would parade their band, guaranteeing another raucous evening.[10]

The commanding officer of the 65th Carabiniers Mont-Royal struck a more cautious note. Lieut.-Colonel J.T. Ostell, who had joined the regiment in 1881 as a bugler and served during the North-West Rebellion, told a *Star* reporter that "we are prepared to do our duty" but "the Canadian military has much work to do here in Canada … Canada's highest duty it seems to me is to be prepared to feed Great Britain."[11] Nevertheless, the 65th organized a parade for the night of 5 August, attracting large crowds.

There were other, different reactions to the prospect of war. The usual Sunday meeting of socialists in Philips Square featured speakers who denounced the coming conflict as "a war of the capitalists … who desired larger markets." A "great demonstration" to be held in honour of Jean Jaurès, the assassinated French socialist leader, was announced.[12] Elsewhere in the city, all Catholic parishes followed the archbishop's instructions to include "prayers for times of calamities" in the mass. If the city's Irish Catholics were hesitant, Irish parliamentary leader John Redmond, who agreed to suspend the implementation of home rule for the duration of the war and promised support for the war effort, removed any doubts.[13]

The Anglican bishop, John Farthing, led prayers for peace, but his sermon included words of support for Christian men "who must take up arms to defend the weak" and if necessary go to war "to relieve those oppressed." Ministers at St. James Methodist and other non-conformist churches stayed with their anti-war traditions, praying for peace.[14] The weekly edition of *The Montreal Witness* appeared on 4 August with a series of commentaries on the war, which the editor assumed had become a reality. John Dougal agreed that "Britain must fight," but described the war as a "midsummer madness ... nothing but the very highest sense of duty could be an excuse for joining in the war." An editorial titled "Power of the Press" argued that the conflict between Austria and Serbia "is largely a newspaper war ... newspapers the world over, living by sensation ... have not ceased in each country to exasperate the people of rival countries ... peace and prosperity are too humdrum and do not make news that will sell extras."[15]

All the city's newspapers carried news of the battles fought in Belgium. The burning of Louvain and its historic library was widely reported, but the deliberate massacres of Belgian civilians were not yet known.[16] The siege of Antwerp, 28 September to 10 October, prompted fears of an invasion of England, though the *Standard* quoted the *Times* of London, which claimed the loss of the city was "always reckoned upon," reminding readers that the British navy will see that they will make no effective use of the sea route.[17]

One voice was missing from the discussion. Henri Bourassa was in Alsace on the last stage of a European trip that included the study of minority-language practices in Wales, Belgium, and German-occupied Alsace-Lorraine. His investigation was cut short when his host, who planned to flee to France, reminded the Canadian journalist that he was a British subject and faced internment. Bourassa escaped this fate, arriving without his luggage in Le Havre on 9 August. Omer Heroux, who had been left in charge of *Le Devoir*, suggested that Canadian troops should defend their own territory and concentrate on raising wheat to export to England. The next day his editorial focused on the Ontario school question, arguing that Ontario had established a regime analogous to that imposed by the Prussians in Poland. The repeal of Regulation 17 was, he declared, the best method of promoting "la rapprochement necessaire entre Anglo et Franco-Canadiens." Heroux did not suggest that such a rapprochement would lead the nationalists to support Canadian participation in the war.[18] Henri Bourassa's first public statement after returning from Europe praised the unity of the French people, the patriotic response of the clergy, and the revival of the Catholic faith evident in the "full confessionals." The article, in the form of an interview with Omer Heroux, included the comment that "in France and England one has the sense that it is a peoples' war."[19]

Bourassa's first signed editorial, 8 September, surprised his admirers by its apparent endorsement of limited Canadian participation.[20] He clarified his position in a commentary on the British White Paper. To Bourassa, Edward Grey was praiseworthy because he had pursued British interests and had been willing, Bourassa believed, to sacrifice France if the Germans respected Belgian neutrality. Canadians too, he argued, should follow Grey's example and pursue their national interest, not that of Great Britain. *Le Canada*'s editor, Fernand Rinfret, responded immediately, "profoundly deploring" Bourassa's views and offering his own detailed analysis.[21] This debate was far too complex to attract much interest or have any effect on recruiting, though it did mark the beginnings of Bourassa's efforts to limit Canadian participation in the war without openly opposing enlistment.[22]

Le Canada and the other mainstream French-language dailies could not ignore Bourassa, but they were far more interested in promoting enlistment and the work of the Comité de secours national de France, established on the outbreak of war. Raoul Dandurand, president of the Montreal branch of the Comité France-Amerique, was a prominent member of the business community as well as a Liberal party senator. He led an energetic campaign to encourage his compatriots to raise funds to assist the displaced women and children of France and to inspire French Canadian support for the French war effort. The women's section of the Comité France-Amerique established a parallel organization, L'Aide à la France, under the leadership of Madame Marie Thibaudeau and Anne-Marie Huguenin, the editor of the women's pages of *La Patrie*. Thibaudeau sought the support of Archbishop Bruchesi, who encouraged his fellow bishops and parish priests to assist L'Aide à la France as a work of Christian charity.[23]

The fate of Belgium was a common and recurring theme in all the city's newspapers. Stories of Belgian bravery and German ruthlessness did more to make the war seem real than accounts of great battles. The honourary Belgian consul in Montreal, Clarence de Sola, a prominent member of the business community, and Gustav Francq, the Belgian-born labour leader, helped to make sure that the plight of Belgium and its people was not forgotten. The arrival of a Belgium delegation in Montreal, sent to North American to win moral support and raise funds for Belgian relief, produced an exceptionally strong response. The Monument National was filled to capacity on 24 September to hear the Belgian minister of justice, Henri Carton de Wiart, deliver an impassioned address in his native language. He denounced Germany's violation of Belgian neutrality and the campaign of terror conducted by the German army. Describing the burning of Louvain to an audience that had just learned of the shelling of the Reims Cathedral roused intense feelings, keeping the issue of Belgium and its refugees at the centre of public discourse.[24]

Belgium's cause was increasingly linked with the actions of Cardinal Mercier, Belgium's Roman Catholic primate, who publicly resisted the German occupation of his country. Mercier, who was in Rome for the papal conclave that elected Benedict XV when the war began, was shocked by the pro-German sentiments of those who surrounded the new pope. He returned to Belgium via London, where he was received by the king and welcomed by the leaders of all political parties. Addressing "50,000 London Irish," with John Redmond at his side, Mercier's declaration "God Save Ireland, God Save Belgium" was greeted with thunderous applause.[25]

Clarence de Sola, the honorary Belgian consul, was also president of the Zionist Federation of Canada and a member of the city's most prominent Jewish family. His father Abraham and brother Meldola both served as rabbis at Shearith Israel, the Spanish and Portuguese synagogue and the oldest in Canada. Clarence de Sola was fully behind the war effort, as were other members of the Sephardic Jewish community, a position not easily shared by the more recent Jewish immigrants who had fled Eastern Europe in the wake of Russian pogroms. For them the British alliance with Czarist Russia raised questions that were not easily answered.[26]

The *Canadian Jewish Chronicle* carried one of many stories on "the dangers of blood pogroms" in Russia on 31 July, and on 7 August reported the vehement protest of the *London Jewish Chronicle* "against England associating with Russia." As the German Army marched into Belgium opinion among Jews in both England and Canada quickly changed, however, and both communities debated the issue of establishing a separate "Jewish Brigade" to support the Allies or encouraging Jews to enlist in established units.[27]

Montrealers of all backgrounds responded to appeals to assist Belgian refugees, creating relief committees and raising funds. English-speaking Montrealers contributed generously to Belgian relief, but the campaign to raise money for the families of those who volunteered for overseas service soon took precedence. Montreal's members of Parliament included two unusual backbenchers: Robert Bickerdike, a Liberal who was devoted to the cause of prison reform and the abolition of capital punishment, and Herbert B. Ames, a Conservative social reformer and author of *The City Below the Hill*. Ames had expected to be included in Borden's cabinet, but the prime minister opted for a personal friend, George Perley, the member for Argenteuil, as the Protestant counterpart to C.J. Doherty, the Irish Catholic MP from Montreal St. Anns. Independently wealthy and very ambitious, Ames moved to revive an organization created during the Boer War, the Canadian Patriotic Fund, which was to become a nation-wide concern, raising millions of dollars to assist the families of men who had volunteered.

Archbishop Bruchesi offered a personal donation of $1,000 to the Patriotic Fund and tried to rally French Canadians behind the war effort. In a widely published public letter he argued that "Britain is engaged in a terrible war, which it tried to avoid at all costs … we owe her our most whole-hearted co-operation." He asked for victory for the Allies, "who defend at the cost of their blood the sacred causes of justice and honour."[28] Bruchesi also agreed to obtain the support of the other Quebec bishops for a joint pastoral letter to be read in all parish churches on 11 October. A special collection was arranged, with half the proceeds going to the Patriotic Fund. Not all the bishops shared Bruchesi's commitment to the Allied cause, and the letter on "the duties of Catholics in the present war" reflected the new pope's determination to remain neutral and focused on the responsibility of loyal subjects to their sovereign rather than the "sacred causes" pursued by Britain and France.[29]

Montreal's Church leaders, both Protestant and Catholic, paid little attention to the fate of people classified as "enemy aliens" due to their birth in Germany or the Austro-Hungarian Empire. Under the provisions of the War Measures Act the government was free to regulate most aspects of life in Canada, and on 15 August 1914 subjects of enemy countries were forbidden to leave Canada. During the fall of 1914 unemployment and growing fear of sabotage prompted a second order-in-council requiring all enemy aliens to register and carry identification cards. Those "considered dangerous or indigent along with those who failed to register" were to be interned as "prisoners of war."

Most of Canada's enemy aliens were to be found in western Canada, where Ukrainians with the misfortune to be born under Austrian rule had settled in large numbers. Montreal, with perhaps 12,000 immigrants from enemy countries, was also thought to be a problem area. The first 364 men from the city to be interned were regarded as prisoners of war and sent to Petawawa, where the military base had been converted to an internment camp. The American consul general in Montreal, who as a representative of a neutral power was made responsible for Austro-Hungarian interests, estimated that in February 1915 there were "9,000 men, 500 women and 1500 children" in the city who were largely destitute as a consequence of both discrimination and lack of work. Four thousand of these registered with the consulate, seeking assistance.[30]

New internment camps at Kapuskasing and Spirit Lake in northern Quebec were built in 1915. Spirit Lake, which housed most of the internees from Montreal, could accommodate up to one thousand persons, both single men in ten thirty-by-seventy-eight-foot bunkhouses and families and married couples who lived nearby in a second encampment. A tall wire fence surrounded the encampment "in the interests of the prisoners on account of the peril to those who attempt" to escape. The American vice consul and a representative of the Roman Catholic Ukrainian Church who visited Spirit Lake in 1915 both reported favourably on conditions in the camp, a view not always shared by those who had to live there.[31]

The popular French-language press focused on events in France and Belgium and the departure of their reservists assembling in Montreal. On 3 August *La Presse* reported that the French consul had received numerous requests from French Canadians who wanted to enlist in the mother country's army. Two days later, with a drawing of the Union Jack and the Tricoleur prominent on the front page, *La Presse* suggested that French Canadians regiments be authorized to enrol under the flag of France, greatly increasing their enthusiasm to serve in the military and their effectiveness as a fighting unit. This "magic effect" would be produced if orders were given in French instead of English. The editors were convinced that Great Britain would grant this "exceptional authorization"; the problem was with the minister of militia and the Canadian government.[32]

This proposal was made in the context of the long, unhappy relationship between the Militia Department and French Canadians. Well before Sam Hughes became the minister in 1911 the militia, above the regimental level, functioned in English, offering few concessions to Canadians whose first language was French. The Royal Military College was resolutely unilingual, and apart from a few candidates from bilingual, essentially assimilated families, French Canadians avoided the college. Since English-speaking cadets were not required to gain fluency in the other official language, RMC graduates had little contact with French Canadian regiments. A 1912 list of the 271 Permanent Force officers who were at least in theory professionally trained and capable of providing instruction and leadership included just 27 French Canadians, 20 of whom were below the rank of lieutenant-colonel.[33]

Hughes compounded the situation. Despite his oft-repeated demands for military preparedness and willingness to continue building armouries in communities that might favour Conservative candidates, French Canadian regiments were left to wither away. One exception was the 65th Carabiniers Mont-Royal, a regiment that had served in the North-West Rebellion. The 65th had its own armoury on Pine Street and included a number of prominent Montrealers among its officers. It especially benefited from the patronage of Sir Rodolphe Forget, an honorary colonel. Forget and his father, Louis-Joseph, were wealthy members of the financial elite and prominent Conservatives. As a member of Parliament, Rodolphe Forget might have expected special consideration for his regiment instead of the hostility exhibited by Sam Hughes. The minister's June 1914 decision to forbid the Carabiniers to continue the tradition of carrying arms in the annual Corpus Christi procession created a completely unnecessary conflict that played out in Quebec as another example of Orange Ontario bigotry.[34] The city's other French Canadian regiment, the 85th had a much lower profile, sharing the Craig street armoury with English-language artillery batteries.[35]

The contrast between the status of the city's two French Canadian regiments and the extraordinary number of prestigious, well-organized Anglo-Celtic units could not have been much greater. At the top of the list was the 5th Royal Scots, or Royal Highlanders. Closely tied to the Scottish Presbyterian community, the Highlanders drew their officers from among the wealthiest, most influential families. The Grenadier Guards, who had moved into a splendid new armoury facing Fletcher's Field and the mountain in April 1914, were, along with the Victoria Rifles, close competitors for recruits and the favours of the establishment. Two cavalry regiments, the 6th Duke of Connaught's and the 17th Duke of York's Hussars, as well as the Montreal Artillery Brigade, also attracted large numbers from an English-language community that was deeply involved with the militia.[36]

Montrealers were also drawn into the excitement generated by the news that Hamilton Gault, one of the wealthiest men in the city, had obtained permission to raise a regiment of veterans of the British army living in Canada. The Princess Patricia's Canadian Light Infantry was to mobilize at Landsdowne Park in Ottawa with Lieut.-Colonel Frank Farquhar DSO, a British army officer, in command and Gault, who provided $100,000 to equip, feed, and maintain the regiment, as second-in-command. More than one hundred other Montrealers joined the battalion, including Talbot Mercer Papineau, an American-educated lawyer who was the direct descendant of Louis-Joseph Papineau and first cousin to Henri Bourassa. Papineau was one of the 10 per cent of the regiment's volunteers born in Canada.[37]

At the Royal Highlanders armoury there were far more volunteers than could be processed, and a similar situation existed at the other English-language units; Major Andrew McNaughton told a reporter that "recruits were applying by the hundreds" to join the artillery, but the Montreal Field Batteries "were already above war strength." Officers and men "were wildly enthusiastic," and only those who had seen actual service would be considered.[38] New instructions from Ottawa limited the number of men that "rural regiments and those from small cities" could enlist to 125 officers and men. Officers from this vaguely defined category were told that they "must be prepared to accept rank in the contingent junior to that at present held by them in the militia." The situation in larger centres was dealt with by allocating quotas. The Highlanders were allowed to recruit a full battalion, but the other three principal infantry regiments were informed that each was to contribute one third of the number required to form a second battalion.[39]

This decision ended any possibility of including a French Canadian battalion in what was to become the 1st Canadian Division. The commanding officer of the composite battalion, Lieut.-Colonel Frank Meighen, was bilingual but his second-in-command, William Burland, and the adjutant, A.P. Holt, were drawn from the English-speaking upper class and spoke little French. This left the two companies allotted to the 65th Regiment isolated in what was now called the "Royal Montreal Regiment."[40] The 85th Regiment received even less consideration. According to the list of those from Montreal who volunteered to serve in the first contingent, 251 men were from the 85th, but by 3 September the number training at Valcartier was down to 7 officers and 143 men. All were serving in the 12th Reserve Battalion, which included men from twenty-one Quebec, New Brunswick, and Prince Edward Island regiments. A month later when the contingent sailed, just 71 men from the 85th were still with the battalion. The others had been dispersed to other units, had been medically rejected, or had simply gone home without attesting for overseas service, severely limiting the pool of reinforcements for the two French Canadian companies in 14th Battalion.[41]

The decline in the number of French Canadians at Valcartier was proportionate to the overall pattern, as more than 5,000 men were struck off strength before the contingent sailed. The largest number, 2,164, were declared medically unfit, an indication of the chaos created by Hughes's decision to rush the enlistment process. Another 1,530 left the camp in September with "no reasons stated." The minister's insistence that married men could only serve with their wife's permission led to 379 men returning home, while another 282 left at their own request.[42] A steady influx of new volunteers replaced those who left Valcartier, bringing the total in camp to over 33,000 not counting the Princess Patricias. Hamilton Gault was determined to keep his elite battalion as far away from Sam Hughes and Valcartier as possible, and when the British Admiralty refused to allow the Princess Pats to sail independently Gault arranged to use the militia camp at Lévis, away from the chaos unfolding across the river.[43]

A debate over exactly how many French Canadians enlisted in the first contingent developed quickly in 1914 and continued to produce controversy throughout the war. The issue was complicated by Sam Hughes, who declared that French Canada had done its duty, suggesting with typical hyperbole that more than 2,000 French Canadians had volunteered. Jules Fournier, who opposed sending any Canadians to Europe, calculated that since 80 per cent of the recruits were British born, almost half of the Canadian-born recruits must be French Canadian.[44]

Numbers aside, what really mattered was the absence of a distinctly French Canadian unit in what became the 1st Division. Throughout 1915 stories about the experience of the Canadian Division established an image of heroic battalions linked with specific cities, towns, or regions. The role of Montreal's 13th Royal Highland Battalion at Second Ypres won enormous prestige for the regiment, while the less dramatic accounts of the 14th Royal Montreal Regiment included only passing reference to the French Canadian companies. Once the 22nd "French Canadian" battalion reached the front lines in late 1915, Quebec newspapers sought out stories. But until the Battle of Courcelette in September 1916 there was not enough blood or glory for the journalists to celebrate in lead stories.

French Canadians who supported participation in 1914 were well aware of the problem that the makeup of the first contingent posed for voluntary enlistment. La Presse, which had tried hard to promote battalion status for the 65th, began a campaign to persuade the government to establish a purely French Canadian battalion to serve in the second contingent. Dr. Arthur Mignault, the medical officer of the 65th, who had made a fortune selling patent medicine, and Lorenzo Prince, the editor of La Presse, organized a bipartisan committee of notables and arranged a meeting in Ottawa with the prime minister. Borden, who had allowed his militia minister complete freedom to recruit and (dis)organize the first contingent, approved the proposal after Arthur Mignault offered to contribute $50,000 to recruit and equip the regiment.[45] Neither the prime minster nor Sam Hughes seemed the least bit embarrassed at their own failure to take such an obvious initiative. The 22nd "French Canadian" Battalion began recruiting in October in the aftermath of the German advance, the Battle of the Marne, the withdrawal to the River Ainse, the siege of Antwerp, and the "Race to the Sea." These events were reported in as much detail as the censors would permit.

Despite broad public support and a further increase in unemployment due to "the uncertainties of war,"[46] recruiting Canadian-born volunteers was a considerable challenge in 1914. Fully two-thirds of the first contingent were born in the United Kingdom, and only the Royal Montreal Regiment could claim to include more Canadians as a result of its Carabinier companies.[47] The composition of the second contingent proved to be similar, with more than 60 per cent born in Britain. Raising a full Canadian-born battalion, 1,100 men, required considerable effort. *La Presse*, and to a lesser extent *La Patrie*, provided free publicity for the 22nd Battalion, including a coupon for readers to use as the first step to enlistment. The climax of the campaign came on 13 October with a vast assembly at Parc Sohmer, featuring patriotic music and emotional appeals from Sir Wilfrid Laurier and other prominent figures. Laurier avoided the typical British Empire rhetoric, arguing that French Canadians should fight for eternal France; "La France existe toujours," he declaimed, urging young men to volunteer.[48] This unofficial recruiting drive came to an end on 19 October when authority to mobilize the battalion was finally received. The departure of the Royal Canadian Dragoons as part of the first contingent freed up their barracks at St. Jean and the 22nd moved in.

The campaign to enrol and retain enough volunteers to constitute a French Canadian battalion has been thoroughly documented by Jean-Pierre Gagnon in his "socio-militaire" study *La 22e battalion (Canadian-français) 1914–1919*. Gagnon notes that by 30 November there were 34 officers and 937 men in the battalion, but after 200 men were struck off strength as "unsuitable" the campaign for volunteers continued. The 22nd was also plagued by absence without leave and the outright desertion of more than 100 men.[49] Georges Vanier, who joined the battalion as a lieutenant, recalled that with the approach of Christmas and New Year's "most of our men gave themselves leave … the climax came on New Year's Day when family spirit was so strong that practically everyone went home."[50]

The 22nd was not alone in struggling to enrol and retain active service volunteers. Military District 4, centred on Montreal, was required to raise a second battalion for the new contingent as well as an artillery brigade and a number of ancillary units such as a sixty-man ammunition park. Given the large numbers of men who were said to have enrolled in the city's militia regiments, observers assumed that the 24th Battalion (Victoria Rifles) could pick and choose.

Initially Lieut.-Colonel J.A. Gunn insisted that recruits were to be five feet, seven inches tall with a thirty-seven-inch chest,[51] but it soon became apparent that the supply of such men was limited. The "Vics" found that many of those who had signed up to serve in the militia were unwilling or unable to go overseas. On 30 October, the Victoria Rifles had enlisted just 189 men. The 5th Royal Scots provided 220 more, and the 53rd Sherbrooke Regiment, an English-language unit, another hundred.[52] Further volunteers came forward slowly, and as late as 22 January 1915 Lieut.-Colonel Gunn noted that there were still "vacancies for 100 soldiers." He hoped "they would come forward soon as the time for departure of the second contingent approaches."[53]

The Militia Department tried to raise a third Quebec battalion for the Second Contingent, from Military District 5, centred on Quebec City. Hughes believed that no French Canadian was qualified to lead the battalion, and he appointed Lieut.-Colonel F.W. Fisher, a Grenadier Guards officer who was currently commanding the Westmount Rifles. Fisher was told to recruit two companies for the 23rd Battalion in Eastern Quebec and two in Montreal, but it was soon evident that Quebec City and district would produce few volunteers. The French Canadians who came forward were needed to complete the ranks of the 22nd Battalion, and the 23rd quickly became a Montreal-based English-speaking battalion. Two-thirds of the five hundred men recruited in Montreal were Canadian born, but drafts of men from western Canada, largely British immigrants, were required to bring the 23rd to full strength.[54]

The challenge of securing recruits for active serve was complicated by the ambitions of various members of the Anglo-Celtic elite who lobbied for the right to create new militia regiments. The suburban city of Westmount supported the 58th regiment, Westmount Rifles quickly attracting a cadre of officers and senior NCOs. A third cavalry regiment, the Scottish Light Dragoons, also competed for recruits in Montreal alongside the two Hussar regiments. The new units were told that no arms or equipment would be available until the second contingent had sailed, but recruiting continued.[55] Irish Catholic community leaders were also determined to demonstrate their support for the war effort, establishing the 55th Irish Canadian Rangers as a militia regiment for home service. They lacked weapons, uniforms, and experienced officers, but Lieut.-Colonel H.J. Trihey, their commanding officer, was a local hero who had captained the Montreal Shamrocks to two Stanley Cups. With C.J. Doherty, the minister of justice, as honorary colonel and Father Gerald McShane, pastor of St. Patrick's Cathedral, offering strong support, the regiment drew over 500 recruits in the fall of 1914.[56]

Montreal's major university was also determined to participate on its own terms. McGill had established the first Canadian Officer Training Corps unit in 1912, and in the first months of the war McGill students and recent graduates flocked to the colours, providing many of the junior officers for the Montreal regiments. The university also formed a provisional battalion, enlisting 350 undergraduates who continued to attend classes while training under the command of Professor Auckland Geddes, a veteran British officer.[57] The McGill medical faculty was equally committed to the war. Most of the medical officers serving with the 5th Field Ambulance, a militia unit mobilized as part of the first contingent, were from McGill. Later, Dr. Herbert Birkett, the dean, who had recently retired from the Canadian Army Medical Corps, proposed the formation of what became No. 3 Canadian General Hospital (McGill). It took the intervention of Sir William Osler to persuade the British War Office to accept their offer to serve with the expeditionary force, and the unit – 33 doctors, 73 nurses and 205 other ranks – reached France in June 1915.[58]

A parallel effort to establish a French Canadian hospital was initiated by *La Presse* in September 1914. The newspaper sought contributions from the twelve hundred municipalities in the province for a twelve-hundred-bed hospital in Paris administered by the French Red Cross. The campaign failed to attract significant support,[59] and in March 1915 Arthur Mignault won Ottawa's approval for a hospital that he would command. Mignault recruited the medical staff from Montreal hospitals, and on 6 May 1915 No. 4 Stationary Hospital embarked for England. Mignault succeeded in transforming the hospital into a larger, general hospital and persuading the prime minister to offer it to the French government. No. 8 (French Canadian) General Hospital opened in a Paris suburb in November 1915, receiving its first patients, French soldiers wounded at Verdun, in March 1916.[60]

Montrealers responded to the initial challenges of the war in ways conditioned by their pre-war identity and experience. Those born in Britain, both men who had come to Montreal with their families as boys and large numbers of recent arrivals, rallied to the defence of their homeland, seeking to enlist in whatever units would accept them. Large-scale unemployment in the aftermath of the boom years no doubt contributed to this rush to the colours, as did the general belief that the war would be brief and glorious. Native Canadian-born Montrealers, with the exception of those involved in the militia, were far more cautious, and relatively few enlisted in the ranks. French Canadians who volunteered to serve in the first contingent found themselves isolated and ignored in a unilingual army that stressed its British imperial connection. Once the opportunity to serve in a French language unit was made available a battalion, made up exclusively of men born in Canada, was quickly recruited and Montrealers could imagine that a new *entente cordiale* was being forged in their city.

Chapter Three

Ypres

While recruiting for a second and then a third division continued at home, the first contingent, 33,000 men and 7,600 horses, arrived at Salisbury Plain, a ninety-square-mile training area south-west of London. British engineers had supervised the erection of "thousands of bell tents, marquees and kitchen shelters" in four large camps, and the first Canadians to reach the area were impressed with the preparations for their arrival. Then it began to rain. As the official history notes, "It was the beginning of a period of abnormally heavy precipitation which brought rain on 89 out of 123 days, the fall of 239 inches between mid-October and mid-February almost doubled the 32-year average."[1]

The war diaries[2] kept by Montreal's two infantry battalion offer little insight into their experience in England apart from frequent entries reporting "rain" or "heavy rain." Official reports, letters home, and stories filed by newspaper reporters tell stories of the flooding of Salisbury Cathedral and "the great wind storm" of 11 November when many of the leaky tents were blown down during "a solid month of dirty weather." Complaints were frequent but, as one group of soldiers told a journalist, only the "chicken hearted" were protesting conditions.[3] *The Montreal Daily Mail*, responding to such stories, urged readers to send comforts to the troops, including "cholera belts, sleeping caps, socks, mufflers, cigarettes, pipes and Christmas presents." Cholera belts were cummerbunds of flannel or silk which were used to protect stomachs from chills that were popularly associated with cholera in previous wars. On 25 October the divisional commander, General Sir Edwin Alderson, announced his decision to override the minister of militia's insistence on dry canteens for Canadians. Henceforth, Alderson declared the "wet" canteen customary in the British army would make beer available within the division. The news prompted widespread protests in temperance circles in Canada, but "amongst the troops, who were after all the most vitally concerned, the move was a popular one."[4]

Despite the weather, training continued at Salisbury, and the expeditionary force was organized into a standard British infantry division of 18,000 men

with reserve or depot battalions theoretically able to provide trained reinforcements. The division was composed of twelve infantry battalions, each of
roughly a thousand officers and men grouped into three brigades. Each brigade
was supported by its own field artillery, four batteries of four eighteen-pounder
guns. Each gun was towed into position by a team of four draft horses. A second horse team, towing a steel-bodied wagon, added thirty-eight rounds to the
twenty-four carried with the gun. Resupply depended on wagons and the 600
horses of the ammunition column. Engineers, a company of cyclists, and one
of signallers, service corps teamsters, a cavalry squadron, and medical corps
personnel plus a mobile veterinary section were also attached to the division.[5]
British battalions relied on the sturdy Lee-Enfield rifle and a Vickers machine
gun section for fire power, whereas the Canadians were equipped with the more
delicate Canadian-made Ross Rifle and Colt machine guns. The attempt to
use unique Canadian equipment extended to different webbing; the McAdam
shovel, which was supposed to serve as a bullet-proof shield; and boots manu-
factured in Canada to specifications that took little account of English roads or
weather. All would have to be discarded, to the dismay of Sam Hughes.[6]

Hughes, who had sailed to England from New York in time to meet "his
boys" at Plymouth, returned to Canada to organize a second contingent, leaving Col. John Carson behind as his personal representative. Carson, a wealthy
Montreal financier, had commanded the 5th Royal Scots before his age-forced
retirement. Carson loved everything about the military, and with the support of
his friend Sam Hughes he helped finance the transformation of a failing militia
regiment into the Canadian Grenadier Guards.[7] The job in England was his
reward, but given the attitude of the British officials towards colonials and an
uncertain relationship with the acting high commissioner, George Perley, no
one knew what the job was. Lines of authority became even more confused
when Col. J.C. Macdougall was promoted and told that he was in command
of all Canadian troops, with the responsibility to ensure that jobs were found
for all the Canadian officers in England. Since 1st Division was under War Office control and the Canadian Cavalry Brigade had been given to J.E.B "Jack"
Seely, the former British secretary of state for war, there was little for either
Carson or Macdougall to do, and few jobs for unemployed officers made sur-
plus by the new battalion organization that called for four large instead of eight
smaller companies.[8]

One positive development was the result of the determination of Julia Drummond, who travelled to England in November 1914 seeking to play a role in
the war. As Lady Drummond, the widow of Sir George Drummond, one of
Canada's wealthiest men, she was able to employ both money and influence,
establishing the Canadian Red Cross Information Bureau in February 1915.
Known initially as the "Information Department, Casualties and Prisoners,"
the bureau's mandate was to "collect and distribute information concerning the

sick, wounded, missing, and prisoners of the Canadian Expeditionary Force." Volunteers were recruited throughout the United Kingdom to visit Canadians in hospitals and convalescent homes. Drummond, who had helped establish the Victorian Order of the Nurses and much else in Montreal, was a superb manager who recruited a cadre of highly skilled women to run an organization that grew to include scores of workers and visitors.[9]

Another influential Montrealer, Hamilton Gault, was able to free his battalion from Salisbury and the Canadian army. The Princess Patricia's Canadian Light Infantry, known to some as the "Princess Pets," was assigned to the 27th British Division, and despite their lack of combined arms or brigade-level training they crossed to France in December 1914. Ready or not, they entered the trenches south of Ypres in January. The trenches were "ditches dug across a sea of mud, too wide for protection from shellfire and too shallow to be bullet-proof." When they rotated out three days later "swollen feet, dysentery and severe colds were the chief troubles."[10]

The regiment next moved a few miles north to take over trenches at St. Eloi. It was here that Francis Farquhar, who was proving to be a superb commanding officer, organized a sniper section to curb the enemy's use of this tactic. Unwilling to stand on the defensive, he ordered what many believe was the first large-scale trench raid of the war. Farquhar called it a "reconnaissance in force," and at 5:15 a.m. on 27 February one hundred men of No. 4 company set out to do some damage to an enemy that the war diary noted that "had become very aggressive." They crossed no-man's-land without rousing the enemy. "Lieut Crabbe then led the company down the trench whilst Lieut Papineau ran down the outside of the Parapet throwing bombs at the enemy." Lieut. Talbot Papineau was awarded the Military Medal for his actions.[11] During the withdrawal Gault was wounded while assisting the stretcher bearers and was evacuated to England. During their weeks in the line 85 Patricias, including Francis Farquhar, were killed, and losses due to wounds, sickness, and shell shock further reduced their numbers.

By February 1914 the Canadian Division was considered to be "well trained and able to take their place in the line." Captain Emile Ranger, who was now second-in-command of the French Canadian company in the 14th Battalion, and a journalist in civilian life, provided *La Presse* with a running account of his impressions after the division reached France. These well-written articles offered human interest stories quite different from the official dispatches. He described the enthusiastic crowds at St. Nazaire, where the battalion entrained for northern France in freight cars marked "40 hommes – 8 chevaux." Officers, of course travelled in first-class compartments. Two days later, they reached their billets in the small village of Flêtre, where "the principle industry was beer."[12]

After a move to Armentières, which was close to the front lines, the Canadians were introduced to trench warfare through the simple method of attaching a section to a British platoon. "In this way newcomers learned trench routine. Almost before they were aware of it they knew the posting of sentries, the screening of fires, the establishment of listening posts. The issuing of rum … ration pouches, wire cutters, loop holes … and all the score of things that are of vital import when men gather in opposing ditches to do one another to death."[13]

The two Montreal battalions were part of the 3rd Infantry Brigade, which, with the rest of the division, took over its own sector of the front line near Fleurbaix, south-west of Armentières. Shallow trenches, overlooked by the enemy on Aubers Ridge, and inexperience led to numerous casualties from enemy snipers, part of the regular "wastage" of trench warfare. Ranger's description of the new daily routine included the story of an entente, or informal truce, with the enemy that ended when the Saxons warned, "look out Sunday, Prussians," and an account of his first fighting patrol.[14] After their second four-day tour in the line, the 13th Battalion "enjoyed a bath and change of underclothing" before moving into reserve well behind the front. During the seven-mile march a new song, with verses that would survive the war, emerged:

I want to go home, I want to go home
The Germans shoot dum-dums / I don't like their roar
I don't want to go to the front anymore.[15]

Instead of home they found themselves in the Ypres salient, a legacy of the determined defence of the only major town in Belgium to escape occupation by the enemy. The battle known as First Ypres ended in November 1914 with the Germans in control of much of the high ground, able to observe and shell the salient from three sides.

Wars fought by coalitions are never free from politics, and the French government, determined to control all aspects of strategy, had taken over defence of the salient, inserting a small French army between the British and the Belgians.[16] This attempt to limit British influence with the Belgians had serious military consequences when the French commander-in-chief, Joseph Joffre, began preparations for his spring offensive aimed at Vimy Ridge. Joffre persuaded Sir John French, the British commander, to take over defence of the southern half of the salient, leaving a much-reduced French corps, the Détachment de l'armée Belgique, in the northern half. As the British Official History notes, this change was made without any arrangement for unity of command among the three national armies.[17]

Sir John, who needed his veteran divisions and most of the available artillery for their part in the spring offensive – the Battle of Aubers Ridge – sent the Canadians and two recently formed British divisions, the 27th and 28th, to Ypres. The Canadian Division was deployed next to the newly arrived 45th Algerian Division, and General Alderson placed the 3rd Canadian Infantry

Brigade, with its two Montreal battalions, on the Algerian flank, hoping to overcome the language barrier. The 2nd Brigade was next in line, while 1st Brigade was in reserve behind the Ypres-Yser canal.[18] British and Canadian officers were sharply critical of the state of defences left by the French army, but the situation was partly the result of the very different doctrines the two armies followed in 1915. The French practised defence-in-depth, with lightly held forward trenches backed by their quick-firing 75-mm guns. Most of their own infantry was held in reserve to counterattack. The French had also begun construction of a well-sited position with barbed wire and deep dugouts in case a withdrawal was required.[19]

British doctrine called for full occupation of the front, which was to be held to the last man. Local reserves were to be committed to regain lost forward trenches, while artillery assisted the infantry with observed fire at relatively short ranges.[20] Implementing this doctrine in the salient proved to be a difficult task, as the 14th Battalion discovered when daylight revealed the contours of the position they were supposed to defend. The regimental historian described the scene:

A parapet of sand bags stretched along the Battalion front, but this was flimsily construction, was not bullet proof, and was broken by one gap approximately 100 yards wide. Some value attached to the parapet as a screen from view, but danger signs gave warning that Germans sniped through the protection repeatedly. No parados had been built on the trench; few traverses existed, and no shell proof dugouts at all. Water, and bodies buried but a few inches beneath the surface, had rendered the construction of underground shelters impossible. Many bodies had been buried in the parapet of the trenches; scores lay unburied between the lines; large rats wandered everywhere; and unsanitary arrangements were, from a Canadian point of view, inadequate. Consequently the line was dangerous and possessed of the most sickening smell imaginable.[21]

After five days and twenty-two casualties, including seven killed, the regiment was replaced by the 13th Battalion. The 13th, which increasingly advertised its connection with Scotland's prestigious Black Watch (Royal Highland) Regiment, went into the line wearing their customary kilts.[22] Lieut.-Colonel Frank Loomis established his headquarters in the village of St. Julien, where he was made garrison commander. Three Black Watch rifle companies, with 200 men each, went forward to assume responsibility for 500 metres of trenches between a small creek and the Ypres-St. Julien-Poelcappelle road. To their right the 15th Battalion, Toronto's 48th Highlanders, occupied a similar stretch of low ground, linking up with Brigadier Arthur Currie's 2nd Brigade. The situation on the left flank was less certain. The 45th Division had arrived in the salient in mid-April and was just settling in. However, the 1st Battalion

Tirailleurs, known to the British as "Turcos," were professional soldiers and readily agreed to a request to adjust the boundary so the Black Watch could occupy both sides of the road. Canadian engineers had constructed a series of machine gun emplacements "roofed with arched sheets of heavy corrugated iron, with loopholes for crossfire." With two additional machine guns on loan from the 14th Battalion, the Black Watch was as well prepared as possible.[23]

The Canadians were part of the 5th British Corps commanded by Lieut.-General Sir Herbert Plumer, who appeared to believe his troops would soon be ready to attack the enemy. A "Memorandum on Offensive Action" required his three divisional commanders to make "definite plans" as to where such actions should be carried out.[24] To the Germans, on the high ground, the bulging salient presented an opportunity to carry out an experiment that had been suggested by a German scientist. Fritz Haber, a chemist who would later win the Nobel Prize, though not for peace, argued that if chlorine was released from pressurized cylinders, a favourable wind would carry the gas cloud into the enemy lines, forcing a withdrawal. The Hague Convention outlawed the deliberate use of poison gases in munitions, but it did not mention asphyxiating gas clouds. Haber left the question of legality to the army but told his fellow scientists that gas might shorten the war and save lives.[25]

The prevailing winds in France and Belgium were westerly but north winds were common enough, so hundreds of gas cylinders with simple hose extensions were installed on the north face of the salient in early April. Shortly after the cylinders arrived a young German soldier deserted his post and provided the French army with a detailed account of the plan to use "asphyxiating gas."[26] He brought one of the packets of gauze distributed as a primitive mask with him, but no one in authority knew what to do with the information. Was it a ruse to force withdrawal? Would such a gas be more than a nuisance? Information about the possible use of gas was passed on to the British army. By the time it reached the senior Canadian medical officer on 15 April the intelligence was characterized as a "rumour that this evening the enemy will attack our lines with an asphyxiating gas to overcome our men in the trenches. Arrangements for the handling of 1000 wounded tonight."[27] When the "threatened attack" did not occur, the warnings were ignored. No one thought to ask a British or French scientist about the kind of gas that might be used, its effects, or possible counter-measures.

German artillery began shelling the salient on April 20. A siege gun firing a "42 cm shell, five feet long and a ton in weight" targeted Ypres. "The first of them, landing in the Grand Place ... killed a captain and about forty soldiers and civilians."[28] The artillery assault continued through the next several days until the late afternoon of 22 April, when a shift in the wind provided the opportunity to open the gas cylinders. Clouds of greenish-yellow smoke were reported, but it was not until hundreds of French soldiers streamed through the

Canadian lines that the full extent of the danger was recognized.[29] The result was a forced withdrawal of the French divisions to the west bank of the Yser Canal, exposing the Canadians' left flank and threatening encirclement of the divisions still in the salient.

The Algerian battalion closest to the Canadians was on the edge of the gas cloud and held on until it was outflanked. The nearby Black Watch company, commanded by Major Rykert McCuaig, sent a platoon to assist the Algerians, buying time for McCuaig to turn his company to the north. The Black Watch reserve, a half company, led by Major Edward Norsworthy, extended the new line using the ditches along the Ypres-Poelcappelle road. His second-in-command, Captain Guy Drummond, who spoke fluent French, encouraged and cajoled the retreating Algerians into joining the Black Watch. "He walked up and down the road, cheering and jollying us up and speaking to each one of us." Without artillery support the position was quickly overwhelmed, both Drummond and Norsworthy were killed, and McCuaig was wounded and taken prisoner along with more than one hundred men.[30]

The Black Watch line, which now bent back towards St. Julien, was bound to be outflanked unless reinforcements arrived. The situation was temporarily stabilized by a battery of eighteen-pounder guns firing shrapnel at the German infantry advancing into the gap. Shortly afterwards reinforcements advanced from St. Julien, an Royal Montreal Regiment company and a Black Watch machine gun section led by Lance-Corporal Frederick "Bud" Fisher.[31] The gunners, who were under fire trying to move the guns, were saved by Fisher and his men, who checked the German advance with suppressive fire. Fisher, a nineteen-year-old McGill engineering student who had enlisted at the outbreak of war, fought until most of his detachment was killed. He then recruited volunteers from the Royal Montreal Regiment company to carry the heavy machine guns, moving them forward to support the Black Watch. Killed in action the next day, he was awarded the first Great War Victoria Cross won by a Canadian.[32] His comrades held onto the apex of the salient until the next morning, but they were out of water and unable to evacuate the wounded. A withdrawal across open terrain produced more casualties. New trenches "about two feet deep" were dug and links established with the 7th British Columbia Battalion, which had reached the crossroads at Keerselaere to close part of the gap. Machine gun ammunition and food was brought forward "but with no water, eating biscuits was like chewing sand."[33]

Elsewhere in the salient the 10th and 16th battalions had suffered heavy losses in a hastily improvised counterattack ordered in support of a promised French advance that failed to materialize. The Germans had originally planned to cross the Yser Canal and advance to Poperinghe, but by the afternoon of the 23rd a lack of reserves led the 4th Army to limit the objective to "the closing of the Ypres Salient."[34] This decision produced continued pressure on the

Canadians holding positions along the Ypres-Poelcappelle Road. One company of the Royal Montreal Regiment, tasked with defending St. Julien, lost all its officers and most of the men to heavy shelling and probing attacks. Captain Wilf Brotherhood, a twenty-eight-year-old electrical engineer and pre-war Grenadier Guards militia lieutenant, reported that "enemy forces were advancing on his left and front … should the enemy force him to retire to the right he would contest every traverse of the trench."[35] Brotherhood was killed that afternoon.

After two more Canadian battalions attacked across open country in support of another failed French advance, it was surely time to reconsider ways of defending Ypres. Instead of a prepared withdrawal under cover of darkness, however, additional troops were brought forward to hold the narrowed salient.[36] As dawn broke on the 24th, the German artillery burst into action, firing for close to an hour before "men wearing mine-rescue helmets appeared over the German parapet. They seemed to have hoses in their hand and immediately there was a hissing sound, and a heavy greenish-yellow cloud rose slowly like a thick fog moving across no-man's land."[37] By mid-afternoon roughly 800 Canadian soldiers, some shell-shocked, some slightly wounded, many simply unwilling to remain in exposed positions under continuous fire, made their way back to the rear, where an engineer officer organized them to form a new defensive line.[38]

The next day attempts to hold St. Julien and Gravenstafel Ridge were abandoned as German artillery blew apart the shallow trenches. The Canadians, who had suffered close to 6,000 casualties, were gradually withdrawn west of the canal to be placed by British and Indian army troops. The Black Watch lost 511, men including 69 known dead and 236 missing. It was later learned that 130, many of them wounded, were taken prisoner. Royal Montreal Regiment casualties were concentrated in the Grenadier Guards company; overall the toll was 29 killed, 84 missing, and 122 wounded.[39]

One of the many soldiers who had endured the prolonged battle war Major John McCrae, a medical doctor who had served with the artillery in the Boer War. In 1914 he was forty-two years old, a pathologist, and a professor at McGill, where many of his colleagues were working to establish what became the army's No. 3 General Hospital. McCrae was unwilling to wait and volunteered to become the surgeon for the 1st Canadian Field Artillery Brigade. The brigade was in reserve when the German attack began but was soon fully committed to the defence of Ypres and the canal line. McCrae's advanced dressing station was just west of the Ypres-Yser Canal within sight of the Germans on Mauser Ridge. The rough dugouts, built into the mounds of earth left over from digging the canal, were later enlarged and protected by concrete. Visitors to the Western Front who make the pilgrimage to "Essex Farm Dressing Station" need to remember how primitive conditions were in 1915 when, during a lull in the battle, McCrae composed the best-remembered poem of the war, "In

Flanders Fields." He described the rough wooden crosses placed over just-dug graves, not the neat, orderly rows of tombstones at nearby Essex Farm Cemetery. His third verse, which begins "Take up our quarrel with the foe," was written in the context of the horrors of Second Ypres and the death of his close friend, Lieut. Alexis Helmer.[40]

The Canadian Division's ordeal ended on 27 April, but one Canadian infantry battalion closely identified with Montreal remained in the salient. The Princess Patricias, like other battalions left in action, were to be the victims of the uncertain leadership of Sir John French. Sir John, under pressure from the French army, rejected the advice of his army commander and authorized further attempts to regain ground lost to the gas attacks. As losses mounted and the French withdrew artillery to support the spring offensive, Sir John belatedly agreed to a withdrawal. A new line apparently selected without reference to the ground offered little protection from the overwhelming firepower the enemy would bring to bear. The Patricias occupied a sector in front of Bellewaerde Lake, working all night to build fire trenches to add depth to the position. Of necessity, these were located on a forward slope open to direct observation from the higher ground to the east. The British Official History describes the trenches of the new line as "narrow and only three feet deep – they were difficult to improve, even with slight evacuation, reached water level. The soil was treacherous; the trenches fell in even without bombardment and there was a great lack of sandbags to repair them … the position, though defensible, was a framework on which much still required to be done. Without deep dugouts to shelter men during bombardment, it does not seem possible that any troops could have held out for long."[41]

Hamilton Gault, who had returned to the regiment, bringing a draft of 47 reinforcements, assumed command after Lieut.-Colonel H.C. Buller was wounded. He ordered everyone available, "Signalers, pioneers, orderlies, and servants[,] into the support trenches" prepared to fight to the last man. The shelling began again, and Gault was among the severely wounded. Command was passed to Captain Agar Adamson and, when he was wounded, to the senior lieutenant, Hugh Niven.[42] The Patricias would not give ground even after the battalion on their left flank was overrun. The war diary notes the arrival of a platoon from the King's Shropshire Light Infantry bringing small arms ammunition and reinforcements. "Another attempt by Germany to advance was stopped by rifle fire although some reached the fire trench on the right … none of our men there were alive at this point." At 11:30 p.m. the Patricias were relieved, handing over their support trenches to a reserve battalion "who gave us assistance to bury our dead … it was impossible and imprudent to attempt to reach the fire trenches" where most of the dead lay. For the Patricias the battle, designated "Frezenberg Ridge," was over. They had lost 10 officers and 375 other ranks, including 93 killed in action with 79 missing, presumed dead.[43]

The thirty-three-day bloodletting at Ypres was "a new kind of battle in which the enemy infantry would merely occupy ground" from which artillery and poison gas "had driven every living creature."[44] The French and British armies were totally unprepared for this kind of warfare. They lacked reliable air observation, signals equipment, and above all heavy artillery able to disrupt the enemy through counter-battery fire. The opening of the French army's Artois offensive and First British Army's attack on Aubers Ridge brought no relief to the battered battalions in the salient. What was left of the British Divisions fought on for another week before exhaustion and ammunition shortages forced the Germans to pause. Ten days later, with favourable wind, clouds of chlorine gas rising to a height of forty feet drifted towards the British lines, forcing a further withdrawal. The new line held long enough to persuade the enemy to declare victory – the battle known as Second Ypres was over. Close to 60,000 British, Canadian, and Indian army soldiers were killed, wounded, or missing in defence of the salient.[45]

A British officer, Sir Morgan Crofton, who served with a dismounted cavalry regiment at Ypres kept a diary throughout the struggle in the salient. His words on the gallantry of the Canadians who "were never broken ... their steadfastness saved the day" recognized the difference between the initial crisis and the attritional bloodletting that followed. Crofton's entry for 5 June reads: "There is no doubt that the Salient at Ypres is simply an inferno. It is not war, but murder, pure and simple. The massacre that has been going on there since 22 April is not realized at home. From May 1–16 we were losing men at a rate of 1,000 a night ... we cannot conceive of why the Salient is not straightened and given up."[46]

News of the fighting in Flanders reached Canada on 24 April when the morning newspapers reproduced Sir John French's dispatch reporting an attack "preceded by a heavy bombardment" in which "the enemy at the same time made use of a large number of appliances for the production of asphyxiating gas." The scale and quantity of the chemical used "indicates long and deliberate preparation, contrary to the terms of the Hague Convention." Later on the same day the War Office provided the first indication of Canadian involvement, noting that the loss of part of the line at Langemarck "laid bare the left of the Canadian division which was forced to fall back ... The Canadians had many casualties but their gallantry and determination undoubtedly saved the situation."[47] On 25 April the *Montreal Star* published a free "Special Edition" on Langemarck, and for the next week the daily newspapers provided regular accounts of the ongoing battle, reporting rumours, second- and third-hand accounts, and the first news of heavy casualties. A United Press story dated 26 April described the Canadian counter-attacks in heroic terms, with the *Star* adding dramatic subheadings such as "Though Terribly Sick, Half Blind and Weak from Poisonous Fumes and German Bombs, They Drive Their

Charge Home – Magnificent Dash and Spirit."[48] Details of the gas attack were published on 27 April when a British scientist explained that the gas cloud was undoubtedly chlorine, an asphyxiating gas outlawed by the Hague convention. A British war correspondent reported the impact in graphic terms:

> Among those who escaped nearly all cough and spit blood, the clorine attacking the mucous membrane. The dead were all turning black at once. The effect of this poisonous gas was felt over about six kilometers away.[49]

One of the most dramatic and heroic reports was credited to a "Canadian Highlander." He paid tribute to the Algerian troops, "among the finest soldiers in the world," who had been transformed into "a mass of dazed and reeling men … they bore upon their faces masks of agony." His battalion, the 16th Canadian Scottish, was, with the 10th Battalion, committed to the night attack on Kitcheners' Wood, which was described in vivid terms: "Overcoats, hats and even equipment was [sic] dropped and we immediately advanced in light order. Scarcely had we reached the low ridge in full view of the wood when a perfect hell of machine gun fire was hosed on us … instantly the order was given to charge and on we rushed cheering, yelling, shouting, screaming, for the foe."[50]

By the third day the newspapers began to describe the personal, city-wide tragedy that was unfolding, identifying those killed, wounded, and missing who had listed a Montreal address for "next of kin." This meant that large numbers of British-born who had enlisted in Montreal and provided a next of kin address in the United Kingdom were not identified, but more than one quarter of the 320 names published in the *Star* were British-born residents of the city. Of those born in Canada, 71 were French Canadian and 169 English-Canadian.[51] Inevitably stories focused on the officer casualties, especially the death of Guy Drummond. The *Gazette* story was titled "It Will be Difficult for the People of Montreal to Realize the Death of Lieutenant Guy Drummond … He Was Only Married a Little Over a Year Ago and Was the First to Give His Life for His Country." His wife, "pregnant with child," was in England with her sister and her mother-in-law, Lady Drummond. Both of the young women, the daughters of A.D. Breithwaite, the assistant manager of the Bank of Montreal, were widowed on the same day.[52]

All the daily newspapers carried stories about Drummond, including a tribute from a friend, Gonzalve Desaulniers, president of L'alliance Française. Desaulniers, a journalist, lawyer, and poet who was a leading figure in the Ecole litteraire de Montréal, wrote: "His death brings grief not only to his own family but to all French Canadians and French people."[53] The newspapers used the Drummond family tragedy to personalize the bereavement of all women, describing Lady Drummond's continuing charitable work in London as an example for all.

The two major English-language weeklies offered detailed and emotionally charged coverage of the first major Canadian action. The *Witness*, in a lead editorial, noted that "Montreal could hardly have been hit harder in a single battle than by the loss of such a group of her younger leaders … The achievement of the Canadian force will rank in history with the great deeds of war from Marathon to Waterloo, but glory will not give us back these men."[54] The *Standard* maintained its heroic approach to the conflict with dramatic stories and subheadings on the "giant struggle" in which "Canadians made themselves immortal." Stories of "the heroic fight made by the boys from the Dominion" were interspersed with accounts of the horrors of the "German murderer's fiendish act." The flagrant breach of the rules of civilized warfare "led one officer to state that he now believed "the Germans actually did massacre the Belgian people."[55]

A news report from Berlin that noted the capture of 1,000 Canadians encouraged many to believe that there was hope for those missing, but as the list of confirmed casualties grew the mood darkened. Memorial services were organized to take place at the five largest Protestant churches, with Roman Catholics gathering at St. Patrick's. Anglican bishop John Farthing and the non-conformist ministers preached sermons that reflected their commitment to victory in a necessary and righteous war.[56] Hugh Pedley, the minister at Emanuel Congregational Church, declared that the "highest honour we can do them is to push on this war until their work is complete." He then quoted from the Gettysburg address: "we here highly resolve that these dead shall not have died in vain; that this nation, under God, shall have a new birth of freedom." The Crescent Street Presbyterian Church was crowded with soldiers from the new Black Watch battalion, the 42nd. The minister spoke of the "sacrificial heroism" of those being honoured, who were fighting against an enemy "threatening not a Dominion, not an empire even, but liberty herself."[57]

The city's two largest Methodist churches were the setting for particularly patriotic, total-war messages. The sermon at Dominion Methodist "breathed a spirit of lofty religious patriotism." The Rev. Dr. S.P. Rose told his congregation that it would be most unwise to emphasize the sadder or more painful aspect of affairs: "old age is not necessarily a distinction while an early death may well be a crown of honour." He then expressed a germ of an idea that would come to dominate and disfigure Protestant discourse for the balance of the war: "When therefore a man, from motives of patriotism turns his back upon home and comfort, and offers his life in devotion to the good of his Empire, he shares no slight measure, in the same purpose that brought Jesus to the cross." Dr. Rose concluded his address with an appeal for volunteers. "From the unmarked graves of France," he intoned, "the cry comes to us, who will take our places and carry forward what we died to achieve?"[58]

La Presse, *La Patrie*, and *Le Canada* all gave prominent coverage to the death of Guy Drummond and other English-speaking Montrealers, though much of their reporting was naturally focused on French Canadian volunteers. Three French Canadian officers, Major Hercule Barré, Lieut. Adolphe Dansereau, and Lieut. Henri Quintal, were among the wounded. Barré's story in *La Presse* explained that he was wounded early in the battle, suffering two of the most terrible hours of his life waiting for assistance. Dansereau was the son of the political editor of *La Presse*. He attended Royal Military College and joined the Corps of Guides in 1911. Dansereau's transfer to the 48th Highlanders, a Toronto regiment, was one of the many inexplicable decisions made at Valcartier.[59]

A letter from Dansereau, written from hospital in England, provided a graphic account of the second day of battle. Dansereau was struck by shrapnel from a "whiz-bang" and briefly lost consciousness. Awakening, he recalled making an act of contrition, as he "was covered with blood. One of my men put a bandage on my head with a field dressing to stop the blood." As he was being evacuated Dansereau was again struck by shrapnel, but he reached the dressing station and was sent to Boulogne for transfer to England.[60]

Montreal was still mourning the men lost in Belgium when a German U-boat sank the *Lusitania*. A debate over the circumstances surrounding the loss of the Cunard liner and her 1,153 passengers and crew began almost immediately and has continued for a hundred years. The German consulate in New York had issued a warning that all Allied ships sailing into the war zone were liable to be sunk, but no one believed the giant, 32,000-ton passenger liner could or would be attacked. After the *Lusitania* was torpedoed Berlin declared that the ship was armed and carrying munitions and was therefore a legitimate target.[61] The ship was not in fact armed but was carrying war material. In 1915 few people in the Allied or neutral nations cared about such issues. What mattered was the terrible loss of civilian lives, men, women, and children.[62]

The city's English-language newspapers outdid each other in describing the "most stupendous act of piracy in human history." The best answer to "Prussian treachery" was to recruit more volunteers to serve overseas. The *Standard* appeared on 8 May with headlines declaring "World Will Hate the Baby Killers More than Ever" and "Awful Scenes as Lusitania Sank with Passengers."[63] The *Gazette* and the *Star* provided detailed coverage of the fate of Hugh Montague Allan's daughters Anna and Gwen, sixteen and fifteen, who were with their mother and the family maids when the *Lusitania* sank beneath them. The Allan girls were lost when suction from the ship's sinking drew them under. Gwen's body was recovered on 16 May but Anna's was never found. Lady Allan suffered serious injuries but she and the two maids, Annie Wallar and Emily Davis, were saved. Dorothy Braithewaite, who was on her way to London to join her two sisters, widowed at Second Ypres, was with the Allans, and she too was drowned, as was her eighteen-month-old grandson, her maid, and the baby's nurse. The story of the survival of Herbert Holt's teenage son, who was said to have given his life jacket to a woman before swimming for over an hour towards shore, added to the drama that played out for the next several weeks.[64]

The city had barely processed these events when a report that the "Reinforced Canadian Division Again Suffered Severely in Recent Fight" was published. Few details about the battle were available given the control over information exercised by the British War Office, but the long lists of killed, wounded, and missing, often accompanied by personal stories, made the war seem all too real.[65] The battle, known as Festubert, was the British army's second attempt to support the French offensive in Artois. The first action, Aubers Ridge, ended in defeat, swift, bloody, and complete, with British losses of 10,000 men. Douglas Haig, the army commander, who had tried a brief "hurricane" barrage the first time, now proposed to experiment with a sixty-hour preparatory artillery program, hoping to observe the effects of fire and attack through gaps created by the guns. Few gaps were created, as a high proportion of dud shells and problems with observation and accuracy plagued the gunners. This did not stop Haig from ordering repeated infantry attacks that over ten days resulted in close to 16,000 casualties.[66]

The Canadian Division was in reserve when Festubert began, attempting to absorb several thousand replacements. There were not enough men in the first contingent's reserve battalions, so company-size drafts from Montreal's 23rd Battalion were sent to the Patricias as well as the 13th and 14th Battalions. The 23rd had recruited a large number of British army veterans and men who had served in the militia, but less than six weeks had passed since their arrival in England. Haig's decision to employ such men in a failing operation suggests how determined the British were to meet French demands to support their spring offensive. The full story of the Canadians at Festubert has never been told, but there are indications that in the initial advance across flat west fields intersected with ditches the 14th Battalion, Royal Montreal Regiment, stopped and dug in to avoid annihilation. This early example of officers and men at the sharp end exercising agency and finding a middle ground "between mutiny and obedience" left the 16th Battalion, which continued forward, in difficulties, but they too soon ceased to advance. Other battalions were then ordered forward, completing the capture of what came to be called the "Canadian Orchard." The casualty toll reached 2,468 men.[67]

The casualties from Festubert reinforced the sombre mood in the city, marked by seemingly endless memorial services for those killed in action. The Protestant clergy, who had offered support for the war in terms of Christian duty, tried to explain how God could permit such horrors to occur and how the faithful were to reconcile the command to love your enemies with German war crimes. Ephriam Scott, the editor of Montreal's *Presbyterian Record*, told his readers that loving your enemies referred to "an attitude of mind and heart with which men do the duty of life, even though it be the duty of stopping evil and death by stopping the life that is wrongfully causing evil and death."[68] A McGill classics professor, John MacNaughton, provided a different message in a tribute to Guy Drummond and Edward Norsworthy, "those twin stars that have annexed Langemarck to Canada." The "Scotch Catechism," MacNaughton declared, "tell[s] us that the souls of believers are at their death made perfect in holiness and do immediately pass into glory." He did not elaborate on the fate of non-believers.[69]

The nationalist newspapers took a very different approach. *Le Devoir* provided basic news-service coverage of events, but Bourassa's editorials deplored the attitude of "everything for the Empire and nothing for Canada." The tenth anniversary of the death of Jules Tardival prompted a lengthy essay lauding the achievements of the icon of clerical nationalists and antisemites, whom Bourassa described as the founder of independent journalism in Canada. *Le Nationaliste* emphasized the heavy losses and the likelihood of conscription. Editor Georges Pelletier questioned the failure of the English to come to the aid of the Canadians during the battle and deplored the "Jingos" who wanted to send more men to the battlefields.[70] On 19 May Bourassa delivered a two-hour address at the Monument National offering a defence of French language rights and the necessity of maintaining a bi-ethnic and bilingual country. There was no reference to Ypres or the *Lusitania*; the focus was on the plight of the Franco-Ontarians.[71]

By the summer of 1915 the French Canadian bourgeoisie was split between Bourassa nationalists and those who continued to support Canada's participation in the war. The pro-participation popular press argued that the future of France and the fate of Belgium justified Canadian involvement. The newspaper carried stories about the Canadians in battle, emphasizing the contribution of French Canadians, and provided detailed war reports from Paris. German actions in Belgium were the subject of frequent comment, and Cardinal Mercier's defiance of the German occupation authorities was a major story. *La Patrie* published the entire text of Mercier's declaration denying the legitimacy of German rule, and both *La Presse* and *Le Canada* provided detailed coverage of his actions.[72] The nationalist press did not ignore these issues but chose to isolate events in Europe from Canadian affairs. Was the stage now set for a great crusade, a surge of Canadian-born volunteers motivated by a desire to ensure the heroes of Langemarck had not died in vain? Or would nationalist opposition, casualty lists, and graphic images of soldiers choking on poison gas discourage enlistment?

Chapter Four

Mobilizing

At the beginning of 1915 an overwhelming majority of Canadians of all backgrounds appear to have supported Canada's participation in a just war that Britain had tried to prevent. Atrocities such as the burning of Louvain demonized the enemy, but after the German defeat at the Battle of the Marne, the race to the sea, and the successful defence of Ypres in November 1914 the war seemed less urgent. Most people believed France and Britain would take the offensive in the spring of 1915 and expel the Germans from French and Belgian soil. Canada was doing its part, raising a force that would join in the Allied offensive.

The Dominion government reflected this optimistic view. The budget address presented by the minister of finance, Thomas White, recognized that war expenditures would greatly exceed revenue but proposed to raise additional funds by borrowing in London and New York. An income tax, he told the House of Commons, was not required.[1] The prime minister, who was content to leave financial issues to White, was equally willing to allow the minister of militia to shape the military effort. Hughes continued to favour a policy of creative chaos, authorizing new battalions that competed with each other for volunteers.

On 10 April 1915, the prime minister presented a report on the country's war effort, claiming that the government's policy of keeping 50,000 men "continuously in training" was being met. He informed the House of Commons that, in addition to the 22,272 men of the second contingent "on their way to England," there were now twenty-four "reserve battalions in various stages of development" that could constitute the core of a third contingent. Borden also noted that the Canadian Mounted Rifles now consisted of thirteen regiments of 7,411 officers and men. The CMR had been created in response to pressure from the cavalry colonels and the governor general, the Duke of Connaught. Since there was no apparent role for more cavalry in the trenches of Belgium and France, Borden suggested the CMR might join the British forces in Egypt.[2]

Two of the twenty-four reserve battalions Borden referred to were based in Montreal: the 41st "French Canadian" Battalion, associated with the 65th Regiment, and the 42nd, a Black Watch Battalion. With the financial support of Arthur Mignault, the 41st got off to a good start, enlisting close to 500 men in the first three months of 1915 before it was transferred to Quebec City under a new commanding officer, Lieut.-Colonel Louis-Henri Archambault. A militia veteran who had served as an inspector of cadets, Archambault proved to be poor leader, unable to impose discipline on his officers or men. The morale of the battalion suffered accordingly, with desertion becoming a major problem.[3] The contrast between the experiences of the 41st and 42nd battalions could not have been much greater. The 42nd, with ample funds and officers drawn from the city's Anglo-Celtic elite, was able to rely on hundreds of British immigrants to fill the ranks. Fewer Canadian-born joined the 42nd than the 41st, and when the battalion sailed for England in June 1915 just 21 per cent of those on the nominal role were born in Canada.[4]

Relatively few Canadian-born Montrealers had volunteered during the long winter of 1914–15 though unemployment was "so widespread" that local citizens as well as single men "coming from outside the city to find work" were homeless. The Meurling Refuge, which had opened in 1914, increased its capacity to 675 beds, and was frequently full. The Board of Control appropriated $100,000 to support various charitable institutions in December and another $50,000 in January 1915 when unemployment was estimated at "around 30,000." The Saint Vincent de Paul Society, with 75 per cent of the parish's reporting, supported 1,192 families, a total of 10,528 individuals. Apparently $1.10 a day and support from the Patriotic Fund for dependants, averaging $20 a month, was not sufficient inducement to join the army.[5] It is also likely that physical requirements and medical standards stood in the way of enlistment. The height and chest-size requirements together with strict guidelines for dental and vision exams led, according to some estimates, to the rejection of one in every three volunteers.[6]

French Canadians may have had other reasons for rejecting calls to enlist in the first months of 1915. The issue of French language rights in the schools of Ontario had been eclipsed by the outbreak of war in Europe and the dramatic battles of 1914, but beginning in December 1914 a new wave of protests began. The renewed focus on the Ontario language question developed after the Ontario Supreme Court rejected a challenge to Regulation 17. In response, the Association catholique de la jeunesse canadienne on 21 December organized a mass rally for the wounded of Ontario ("les blessés d'Ontario"). Two Franco-Ontarian senators, Conservative Phillipe Landry and Liberal Napoléon Belcourt, were the main speakers, but Archbishop Bruchesi, Henri Bourassa, and Liberal senator Raoul Dandurand also participated. Le Nationaliste, in promoting the event, had called attendance at the Monument National "une devoir patriotique," and a large crowd was in attendance.[7]

Archbishop Bruchesi began the evening with a brief introduction whose opening words were "We are loyal subjects of the British Empire"; he continued with a statement about the "undeniable rights of the French language in Canada." Belcourt's lengthy address reviewed the history of the conflict and outlined the ambitious goals that Franco-Ontarians were pursuing. Belcourt wanted much more than the repeal of Regulation 17. The recognition of the right to maintain existing bilingual schools and establish new ones wherever the majority of students were French speakers was crucial to the future of the French language in Ontario, Belcourt insisted. New Ontario, the mining and forestry region in the north, was, he argued, destined to become an area of French Canadian settlement, doubling their share of the province's population. Bilingual schools and inspectors as well as a normal school to train bilingual teachers were required.[8] All of the speakers, perhaps in deference to the presence of the archbishop, avoided any reference to the role that Bishop Michael Fallon and other Irish Catholic clergy played in opposing bilingual schools, with Belcourt blaming *les orangistes* for the problem. Bourassa, who had just returned from Ottawa where a mob, including a number of men in uniform, had prevented him from speaking, could not resist a comparison of Prussian tolerance of French rights in Alsace-Lorraine to the "Prussians" of Ontario.[9] The meeting received considerable coverage in the nationalist press and in *Le Canada*, but the other dailies, French and English, largely ignored the event and the subsequent campaign for "Le fond patriotique Franco-Ontarien."[10]

The confrontation with Ontario was further escalated when Cardinal Bégin added his voice, declaring that "if, which God forbid, the trial imposed upon our brethren in Ontario be prolonged, it will be the noble duty of the French and Catholic province of Quebec to assist with all its influence and all its resources those who suffer and struggle until full justice can be rendered them."[11] The cardinal's intervention prompted the Quebec premier, Lomer Gouin, to make a statement in the legislature calling, "in the name of the whole population of Quebec, English, Scottish and Irish-Canadians as well as French Canadians," for "justice and generosity" to the minority. Two English-speaking members then moved a motion urging respect for "one of the cardinal principles of British liberty throughout the Empire ... regard for the rights and privileges of minorities."[12]

English-speaking Montrealers were aware of the debate over French language rights in Ontario and generally supported the quest of the Franco-Ontarian minority. The Montreal *Star*, for all its fervent imperialism and opposition to the nationalist cause, insisted that Ontario's policy was "a mistake in statesmanship, a blow at brotherhood and practical violation of the pact on which this country was established." The editorial continued with a reminder that the educational clauses of the BNA Act were intended as a bargain between the majorities of Upper and Lower Canada to ensure that the minorities representing them in other provinces would enjoy educational autonomy.[13]

The controversy over Regulation 17 and French language rights is often seen as a catalyst in the development of French Canadian attitudes towards the war and enlistment. The evidence for this is mixed. The mass circulation dailies covered the unfolding conflict in Ontario, but a survey of *La Presse*, *La Patrie*, and *Le Canada* suggests that the issue received relatively little space in pages crammed with war news, sports, entertainment, advertisements, and local events.

For example, newspaper coverage of the 1914–15 hockey season and the playoffs in March told the story of the struggles of the Montreal Canadiens, who won just six of twenty games. The Montreal Wanderers, the English-language team, tied for the league lead but lost to the Ottawa Senators in a two-game, total-goals playoff. The rivalry between the two city teams was great for sports reporting, but when the Canadiens broke the language divide, hiring the best players available for the 1915–16 season, this too was good for newsstand sales. When George Kennedy, the owner of the club, agreed to a new contract for Newsy Lalonde the Canadiens were on their way from last place to their first Stanley Cup.

At the end of the hockey season attention was focused on other sports, including Edouard Fabre's first-place finish in the Boston Marathon. *La Presse*, described by *Le Pays* as "notre trombone nationale," had sponsored Fabre, a well-known distance runner and snowshoe racer. *La Patrie* was equally enthusiastic about an achievement that displayed "the virility of our race."[14] It is not easy to gauge the importance of such events in the lives of people, but we should not assume the war or fate of the Ontario minority loomed larger than the Stanley Cup.

The linguistic divide in Montreal was carried over from politics and hockey to the very different war reporting. The English press was focused on the British Expeditionary Force, while the French papers provided extensive coverage of the French army with reports from Paris instead of London. Much of this was no doubt due to the costs of translation, but it is evident that the editors selected material they believed would appeal to their readers. One common ground was the fate of Belgium and the ongoing story of the resistance offered by Belgian primate Cardinal Mercier. All the dailies published stories about Mercier's defiance of the German occupation authorities, and most reprinted his Christmas letter.[15] The *nationaliste* press did not ignore Mercier but refused to draw a connection between Belgium and Canada. The major dailies also provided extensive coverage of the man who still drew the support and affection of the large majority of French Canadians – Sir Wilfrid Laurier. To take but one example, on 7 August 1915 Laurier was greeted by crowds estimated at twelve thousand when he returned to St. Lin, the village north of Montreal where he was born. Laurier's speech included an endorsement of Canada's war effort and encouraged enlistment. French Canadians, he argued, had a double duty to both Britain and France.[16]

When the popular press focused on minority language rights it adopted a position similar to the one expressed by the Franco-Ontarians' leader, Senator Belcourt, who was determined to separate the schools issue from the war. Beginning at the Parc Sohmer meeting to promote enlistment in the 22nd Battalion, Belcourt urged enlistment in the "sacred cause of Freedom" and argued that "our pacifist spirit must not compel us to become doctrinaire Pacifists … Canada, no more than other civilized nations, has no right to remain a silent witness to the terrible and barbaric drama played out on the devastated fields of Belgium and France."[17] Belcourt continued to argue against "isolationism" throughout the war, as did Sir Wilfrid Laurier and Rodolphe Lemieux, his senior Quebec lieutenant. Lemieux actively supported recruiting at dozens of rallies, and his son was one of those who enlisted.

By the spring of 1915 economic conditions had begun to improve. The opening of navigation and the resumption of construction were traditional signs of recovery from winter, but there were also new war-related orders for the textile, garment, and leather industries. One of the most remarkable developments occurred in the east end of the city, where on 1 January the British Admiralty took direct control of the Canadian Vickers shipyard to begin construction of submarines for the Royal Navy. The Canadian government was not consulted. This stunning example of British imperial arrogance troubled Ottawa, but the shipyard provided hundreds of jobs to both skilled and semi-skilled workers and delivered the first "H-Class" submarines to the Royal Navy in May 1915.[18]

Despite employment opportunities at Vickers and a few other firms, large numbers of skilled and semi-skilled workers were still unemployed in the spring of 1915. A British Board of Trade delegation seeking skilled workers for the British munitions industry recorded the names of five hundred men "willing to enter into a six month contract to work in British factories and shipyards."[19] There was no such demand for labourers, and organized protests, including one in early June that involved "close to 1000 men," led the city to increase the budget for paving streets from $200,000 to $500,000. The *Star* claimed that this action "was not a moment too soon" as there were "rumours of serious rioting" if work was not available.[20] The *Labour Gazette* correspondent for Montreal was equally pessimistic, reporting that while war orders were beginning to stimulate the economy and machinists were in demand, there was little change in other trades and no sign of a recovery in building construction. Apart from the tunnel under Mount Royal, railway construction was at a standstill, and the much-heralded orders for munitions production had not materialized. The Angus Shops were still offering "short term employment" to a limited number of workers.[21]

The news of the Canadian action at the Battle of Langemarck in the Ypres Salient transformed perceptions of the war for many Canadians, including Montrealers, but the challenge confronting those who favoured a more energetic commitment to the Allied cause was considerable. Herbert Ames spelled out the problem in a speech to a patriotic rally. "We Canadian born," he declared, "take unto ourselves too much credit. We call the first contingent Canadians, we glory in its achievements but save that the battalions are under Canadian officers it is in great part a British army recruited on Canadian soil. From two thirds to three quarters are British-born."[22] Ames suggested that the supply of British-born recruits would soon be exhausted and Canadians would have to step forward. The immediate problem confronting Montreal's Anglo-Celtic citizens was to find men to fill the ranks of the 60th Battalion allocated to Military Districts 4 in May. Lieut.-Colonel Frederick Gascoigne, a forty-nine-year-old militia veteran and senior official in the Canadian Pacific Railway who commanded the Victoria Rifles, was charged with raising the 60th as part of the third contingent. He drew upon men who were already in the militia for the core of the unit, with one company from his own regiment and one each from the Grenadier Guards, Westmount Rifles, and Irish Rangers. Gascoigne was able to select officers and NCOs from the four regiments and to raise sufficient funds for recruiting and additional equipment. His CPR connection proved invaluable, particularly after Captain Alfred Shaughnessy, the second son of the president of the CPR, joined the battalion.[23]

The 60th began recruiting in earnest in June 1915, and by early July a "whirlwind week," with meetings in various city parks scheduled for each night and special Sunday services, was organized to complete the battalion. City boy scout troops participated, carrying banners declaring, "If you don't go, we will have to."[24] The English-language press offered free publicity, including full-page ads. When the battalion moved to the Valcartier close to fifteen hundred men were on strength.

After several hundred volunteers were "weeded out" and a reinforcement company sent to England to provide replacements for those lost at Festubert, there were still enough men to form a full battalion. There were, however, relatively few Canadian-born, less than 30 per cent of the total.[25] The continuing predominance of British-born recruits was reflected in a recruiting poster created by the battalion with the heading "Kitchener Calls for Men." The wording suggested that the 60th, "Montreal's Crack Regiment," was to be part of Kitchener's New Army being raised in Britain. There was no specifically Canadian reference.[26]

The heavy casualties suffered by the Princess Patricias prompted letters, editorials, and an energetic campaign to rebuild a battalion that was said to be in "danger of extinction." One letter to the *Star* recalled that "Montreal in August last had turned out en masse to bid farewell to the Princess Pats." It was now time to prove that Montrealers "are as good at fighting as in cheering." The anonymous writer suggested that a small percentage of the young men, "white collared, well dressed, well fed, of athletic appearance" that "fill and adorn Montreal's 9 A.M. street cars" would save the Patricias from extinction.[27]

Two days later the *Star* published a graphic account of the Battle of Frezenberg provided to the paper by the uncle of a young Patricia officer.

> For eight hours the Germans shelled us ... soon the groans of the wounded and dying men rose upon the air. Men lay half-buried, with legs and arms gone, slowly dying ... Two hundred and thirty paid the toll that day ... our own artillery were apparently out of action for they hardly replied ... Saturday dawned and then came the worst day of all ... They tore our trenches to pieces.[28]

Percival Molson and other prominent McGill graduates proposed sending the university's Canadian Officer Training Corps volunteers to replace the Patricias lost in the Ypres Salient. The majority of these were Canadian-born, as were the hundreds drawn from other university companies who joined the battalion in the months that followed. This extraordinary misuse of university students, most of who would serve as riflemen rather than junior officers, was yet another indication of the government's failure to think through the challenges of mobilization.[29]

The most organized response to the events of April 1915 came from the city's upper- and middle-class women who possessed both the wealth and leisure time to undertake voluntary work in support of the war effort. These "elite women,"[30] drawn from both language communities, had been engaged in such activities from the outbreak of war, but as the editor of the Montreal *Standard*'s Society page reported, "The pall that was cast over the social world by the appalling casualty list which was published after the Langemarck engagement has lifted only very slightly. No entertainments which could be regarded as strictly social have taken place during the week although each day has been productive of one or more functions ... of a charitable or patriotic nature."[31]

The columnist noted that a "large number of country houses have been offered to the government for the use of convalescent soldiers" and activities intended to raise funds for the Queen Mary's Needlework Guild and other organizations were being planned. The guild was one of the many organizations involved in knitting and sewing for soldiers as well as women and children displaced by the German occupation of northern France and Belgium. The Red Cross and its French-language counterpart Le Croix Rouge organized volunteers in Montreal and throughout the province.[32] For English-speaking women the Imperial Order of the Daughters of the Empire[33] and seemingly every Protestant church in the city were focal points of activity. The St. John Ambulance Society concentrated on recruiting and training scores of young women who volunteered to serve as Voluntary Aid Detachment nursing assistants in hospital and convalescent homes both overseas and in Canada.[34] News of the fate of horses in the Flanders battles inspired a group of Montreal women to establish the first Canadian branch of the Purple Cross Society, an international organization dedicated to animal welfare. They prepared "bandages for horses made of flannel and soft cotton in lengths of five to eight yards each with a double tape sewn in to simplify the task of the soldier or veterinarian trying to staunch a wound."[35]

The Montreal Branch of the Canadian Patriotic Fund attracted the largest number of committed volunteers, with 150 women devoting an average of three half-days a week to various administrative tasks. By the end of 1915 more than six hundred other volunteers were working as "visitors" to families receiving assistance.[36] Since a third of those registered with the Patriotic Fund were French Canadians, attracting volunteers who could visit these families was a priority, and with help from the Féderation nationale St. Jean Baptiste, seventy-two French-speaking volunteers were recruited to carry out "friendly" visits.[37] This army of unpaid labour was directed by Helen Reid, a member of the first class of women to graduate from McGill, who had forged a career as a social worker and public health activist. Reid, co-founder of the Charity Organization Society, was a firm believer in the virtues of "friendly visiting" for hospital outpatients and families receiving financial assistance.[38] The system, Reid argued, was the most effective way of preventing fraud as well as offering advice and support to worthy families. To be worthy, women who had suddenly become heads of families were required to avoid bad behaviour, defined in terms of sexual impropriety and alcohol. Reid and her volunteers do not appear to have been greatly concerned about the meagre sums distributed by the Patriotic Fund when counselling or investigating families. A soldier's wife with two children received a "Separation Allowance" of $20.00 a month from the government in addition to fifty cents a day of "assigned pay" deducted from their husband's $1.10 a day. The Fund normally added another $15.00, bringing the total to $50.00 a month.[39] Since many of the men and women active in the Montreal Branch of the Patriotic Fund had been involved in the 1912 Child Welfare Exhibit, they knew that $600 a year in 1915 condemned a typical family to "a mere existence" in "unsanitary quarters, sometimes below street level."[40] Herbert Ames argued that the absence of the father reduced the amount needed by the family, justifying the policy, but no evidence of actual costs was presented.[41]

Upper- and middle-class French Canadian women were mobilized by stressing the importance of assistance to France and Belgium. While the Canadian Red Cross urged women to donate money or to knit and sew on behalf of the soldiers of the British Empire, Montreal's Croix Rouge, established in September 1914 by the Féderation nationale, encouraged support for the women and children of France by raising money or joining one of the many sewing circles springing up in the city. By September 1915 the Croix Rouge, working in "perfect harmony" with the Red Cross, had made 100,000 articles of clothing for soldiers and civilians.[42]

Madame Gleason-Huguenin, president of the Croix Rouge (section Canadienne Francaise), was a regular contributor to the Féderation nationale's newspaper *La Bonne Parole* and as "Madeleine" was the editor of the women's page of *La Patrie*.[43] During the summer of 1915 Madeleine began to organize a Canadian version of the popular French movement to encourage women to write to soldiers serving at the front. The *marraines de guerre* (wartime godmothers) began as a patriotic attempt to sustain the morale of the French *poilu* by writing letters to men who had no family. It was to be a connection between a soldier and a mother or sister figure, but as newspapers picked up the story, romance and flirting at the front became a major preoccupation of the press.[44] Madame Hugenin did her best to prevent her *marraines* from flirting, urging French Canadian women to "exercise a moral influence,"[45] but as their numbers grew supervision became impossible. Late in 1915 Madeleine extended her program to French Canadian soldiers.

One Montreal community that had kept a low profile during the first year of the war also mobilized during June of 1915. Italians, the third largest minority in the city, had followed the political situation at home since the outbreak of war. Italy insisted that membership in the Triple Alliance did not require participation in a war sparked by Austrian aggression, and declared neutrality on 2 August 1914. In the months that followed there was much speculation about the prospects of Italy gaining Trieste and other Italian areas within the Austro-Hungarian Empire by war or diplomacy. Would Berlin persuade Vienna to compromise or would London and Paris persuade Rome to open a new front? The British foreign secretary, Sir Edward Grey, won the day, negotiating a treaty that promised to meet Italian territorial demands when the war was won. The Italian government also gained a promise that the Vatican would be excluded from any peace conference, a commitment the British and French were only too willing to make.[46] The declaration of war was far from universally popular in Italy, but in North America Italians rallied to the cause and hundreds of young men gathered in Montreal, where arrangements to send reservists and volunteers to Italy were being organized.[47]

Montreal's mass circulation newspapers naturally endorsed the actions of the Italian government, hoping that opening a new front would shorten the war. Their endorsement drew a heated response from Henri Bourassa, who attacked the "servility" of the press in supporting an extension of the war that would threaten the Vatican and the policy of neutrality advocated by Pope Benedict.[48] This editorial essay appeared in *Le Devoir* just as the Italian community was organizing a mass meeting at the Champs de Mars. The principal speaker at the evening rally, the Reverent Liborio Lattoni, a poet and passionate Italian nationalist who was also a Methodist minister,[49] was later to claim that while he criticized Bourassa he tried to prevent the crowd from demonstrating in front of *Le Devoir.* If so, few listened. A chanting mob stoned the building, breaking most of the windows, an event Bourassa described in an editorial the next day as "le sac du Devoir." The editorial added fuel to the fire with its description of a "brutal attack" by a band of "Calabrais et Napoltains" who paradoxically were said to earn better salaries than French Canadians while relying on "our" convents and St. Vincent de Paul society to get through the winter. Bourassa claimed the attack demonstrated that French Canadians now had to fear for their freedom of expression in Quebec as they did in the rest of Canada. French Canadians, he insisted, had the right to support the policies of the Vatican against those of Republican Italy.[50] *La Croix* agreed with Bourassa but predictably saw "Italy's treason" as a plot by Freemasons.[51]

Bourassa's confrontation with the Italian community was largely ignored by the other daily newspapers, who continued to minimize the significance of a man they regarded as a provocateur. *La Presse* reported the incident but the newspaper, which Bourassa had been singled out for "servility," devoted considerable space to Italy's war effort and carried a daily war summary, in Italian, on its front page. *La Patrie* offered a mild defence of free speech deploring violence but continued to applaud the Italian intervention and the patriotism of the city's Italian community. The editor of the Montreal *Witness* best expressed the views of English-speaking Montreal in an editorial condemning the attack in principle while emphasizing that the proper course of action was to avoid giving Bourassa any prominence as "nothing better suited him."[52]

In July 1915 the decision to add fourteen new battalions to the Canadian Expeditionary Force (CEF) was announced. The Militia Department feared that finding the additional men would not be easy. The height requirements for recruits were lowered so that men under five feet, three inches could enrol. An even more important measure was the creation of the Canadian Dental Corps, which permitted men with bad teeth to be treated after enlistment.[53] Vision standards, another major cause of rejections, were also modified. The rules requiring a wife's consent for husbands and a parent's consent for eighteen-year-olds were dropped, as was the escape clause that permitted men who had attested from changing their mind and leaving the army.[54] The new standards increased the pool of potential recruits, especially if men who had previously volunteered and been rejected could be persuaded to volunteer again.[55]

Another measure designed to encourage attestation was a card designed by the Canadian Patriotic Fund to be distributed to potential recruits. The answer to the question "What will my wife receive during my absence?" was "$20.00 a month separation allowance (also part of your pay) and if this is not enough to comfortably maintain your family the Canadian Patriotic Fund will further assist your family." Recruits were also told that if they died there would be "an adequate pension, that will enable the family to live comfortably, until the children are old enough to look after themselves."[56] Both of these promises would prove to be empty, but they may have played a role in encouraging enlistment.

The changes may help to explain the rapid recruitment of a new English-language unit, the 73rd Royal Highlanders of Canada.[57] Montreal's Highland Regiment had already raised two overseas battalions, the 13th and 42nd, but when Sam Hughes proposed creating a third Black Watch battalion the regimental seniors quickly agreed. The 73rd Battalion was commanded by Lieut.-Colonel Peers Davidson KC, the son of Sir Charles Peers Davidson, former chief justice of the province of Quebec. With an Imperial Guards veteran as regimental sergeant major, sergeant-instructors from the Permanent Force, and ample funds to aid enlistment, the battalion quickly took shape. By 30 September, after less than a month of recruiting, eight hundred men had attested. At the end of 1915 the 73rd was at full strength, but just 377 of the 1,155 men on the nominal roll were born in Canada.[58] Trying to train in a rainy autumn at Valcartier made little sense, and both the 73rd and 60th returned to Montreal for the winter, residing in rented buildings hastily converted to barracks. Both battalions left for England in March 1916 to be greeted with the news that they would be broken up to provide reinforcements. Gascoigne and Davidson fought an energetic and ultimately successful battle to reverse this decision, replacing less influential battalions in the 4th Division order of battle.[59]

French-language battalions could not draw upon the British-born to fill the ranks or to provide experienced sergeant-instructors. They also lacked a reservoir of trained militia officers. This problem was compounded for the 41st when five of the most experienced officers were selected to serve with the 250-man "reinforcing draft," which all battalions forming in Canada were required to send overseas in the summer of 1915.[60] Since the 41st had already provided 100 men to the 22nd Battalion, the new battalion commander, Louis-Henri Archambault, had his work cut out for him. Unfortunately Archambault proved to be a specially incompetent and corrupt individual who made little attempt to discipline or train the men quartered in the immigration sheds at Quebec City.[61] Historian Desmond Morton's detailed description of "the short unhappy life of the 41st Battalion" suggests that the army's experience with the 41st, which included two separate murder cases while the unit was training in England, may have been a factor in rejection of requests for additional French-language combat battalions. Perhaps, but as Morton himself argues, "long before the outbreak of war in 1914 the Canadian militia had become predominantly English-speaking in composition and British in tradition."[62] This reality better explains the decision to limit French Canadian participation in the first contingent to a single company and then to abolish it, disbursing the men throughout the battalion.[63] Political pressure forced the army to accept the 22nd Battalion, but there was no desire to add the 41st or any other French-language battalion, never mind a French Canadian brigade.

The problems facing the 41st Battalion were further complicated when the Militia Department decided to create a new French Canadian battalion, the 57th, with headquarters at Valcartier. Hughes selected Lieut.-Colonel Etienne-Theodore Paquet, a Quebec City lawyer from a prominent Conservative family, to command the new battalion. Paquet had reached the rank of major in the Regiment de Lévis while serving as an Inspector of Cadets.[64] He received permission to recruit throughout the province and promptly established a depot in Montreal under Major Henri-Thomas Scott, a man of extraordinary talent and energy. Scott was in charge of physical education for Montreal's Catholic School Commission and had organized gymnastic competitions throughout Quebec, taking his best students to Rome in 1908 and 1913 as well as France and Belgium in 1911. The success of his young athletes attracted international attention and made Scott a well-known personality in Montreal. According to his biographer, many of those who enlisted were his former students.[65]

The 57th had barely begun to get organized when the order to provide a 250-man reinforcement draft arrived. Those men, together with five officers, all with militia experience, left for England in July 1915, leaving the 57th vulnerable when the Camp Valcartier commandant recommended the merger of the 41st and 57th. After vigorous protests the 57th was allowed to continue recruiting, but only after transferring more than 600 men to the 41st.[66] This allowed the 41st to embark for England with a full complement of officers and men, but did nothing to solve the chronic problems caused by the poor leadership of Lieut.-Colonel Archambault and some his officers.[67]

According to Major-General Sam Steele, who had to deal with the 41st in England, "at least 17 of the battalion's officers were unfit" but the men, including a company of Russians who spoke little French or English, simply needed a few more competent junior leaders. Steele noted that after Archambault's dismissal Major R.C. Bouchard took charge of the training. Bouchard asked for "twelve good NCOs," insisting "it did not matter what language they speak."[68] Despite signs of improvement, the 41st was disbanded in March 1916. Many of the men and a few of the officers would later serve in Belgium and France, including 428 who fought with the 22nd.[69]

Scott was determined to rebuild the 57th, seeking recruits in rural Quebec as well as Montreal. One of his projects, a "festival" at Parc Sohmer to raise money for recruiting and instruments for a band, attracted "thousands" of supporters. The Parc Sohmer rally occurred one night after a group of young men had disturbed a recruiting meeting in Lafontaine Park. This time when the heckling began, Major Scott and some of his comrades confronted them. According to the *Gazette*, "he told them if they wanted trouble it was waiting for them but if they wished to address the crowd they could wait their turn and would be given a chance ... but nothing more was heard from them."[70]

Scott's real challenge came from Hughes's decision to authorize another Montreal-based French-language battalion, the 69th, commanded by Adolphe Dansereau, the young veteran of Langemarck. A locally famous twenty-four-year-old might serve to attract recruits, but was he a suitable commanding officer? It mattered little to Sam Hughes, who was now fully committed to raising as many battalions as he could. Did Hughes believe that these units would, as he frequently promised, stay together overseas in an ever-expanding army, or was this a "confidence trick" designed to produce reinforcements?[71] Either way the initial reaction to the 69th was positive, eclipsing the efforts of the 57th Battalion, which sailed to England as a detachment of 419 men.[72]

The 69th was actively supported by both *La Presse* and *La Patrie*, both of which provided recruiting facilities and much publicity. Dansereau's father, an editor at *La Presse*, also provided modest financial assistance, though there was never the kind of money available to English-language units. By October the battalion was training at Valcartier. The normal wastage of recruits deemed medically unfit or unlikely to become effective soldiers, together with the constant problem of men absent without leave, meant that recruiting continued after the battalion moved to winter quarters in Saint John, New Brunswick.[73] The 69th was at full strength when it left Canada in April 1916. Once in England the battalion became part of the 40,000-strong "reserve division" commanded by Major-General Steele at Shorncliffe. Steele noted that both the battalion and its commanding officer were exceeding expectations, but it was too late to include the 69th in the 4th Division's order of battle.[74] After Courcelette more than 400 men were sent to reinforce the 22nd Battalion and the remainder were merged with the 23rd Reserve Battalion. Dansereau returned to Canada.[75]

The 1st Regiment, Canadian Grenadier Guards had already contributed a large number of men to other local battalions, but Hughes allowed it to recruit a new unit, to be known as the 87th Canadian Grenadier Guards. Lieut.-Colonel Frank Meighen, who commanded the 14th Battalion at Second Ypres, returned from France to lead the 87th and brought two senior warrant officers home with him. There were scores of officer candidates; more than one hundred applied for thirty-four positions. There was no shortage of money or energy for the recruiting campaign, with scarlet-dressed drummers from the regimental band joining the recruiting teams, but relatively few Montrealers proved able or willing to join the 87th, which sought Guardsmen who were at least five feet, seven inches tall. Competition with a new Eastern Townships battalion, the 117th, limited recruits from that area to 219 men, so the campaign was extended to Ontario and the west. Fewer than one-third of the battalion's other ranks were from Montreal, but for the first time British-born volunteers were in a minority, just over 40 per cent of the rank and file.[76]

During the summer and fall of 1915 a steady flow of volunteers joined the army, which grew beyond its authorized strength of 150,000. Borden agreed to raise the total to 250,000 in late October, and Hughes began to plan a further expansion, boasting he could raise ten divisions, half a million men.[77] As the second winter of the war loomed and the new medical standards took full effect, 1,000 men a day were said to be enlisting.[78] By years' end 212,690 men were enrolled in the CEF with 120,000 overseas. Enlistment in the fall of 1915 may have been influenced by the public response to the execution of Edith Cavell. Cavell, a British nurse who worked as the matron of a Brussels hospital, joined the Belgium Red Cross on the outbreak of war, treating wounded soldiers but also assisting the escape of some 200 British soldiers into the Netherlands. She was arrested and charged with the crime of violating the rules of war by aiding the enemy. During her two-month imprisonment her case was widely publicized in Britain, Canada, and the United States. After weeks of solitary confinement without access to a lawyer, she and a Belgian colleague, Phillipe Bracy, were tried, found guilty, and executed by firing squad. All popular Montreal newspapers followed the case and expressed outrage at her execution.

The issue was kept alive throughout the early months of 1916 partly because of an interview with the German military governor of Belgium. Baron von Bissing was unrepentant and tone deaf. He told a *New York World* reporter that he could not understand why the world was so interested in the case, as "the Cavell woman" was guilty of aiding soldiers to escape. "With all the thousands of innocent people who have died in the war why should anyone become hysterical over the death of one guilty woman?" When told that even in Berlin the execution was viewed as a political blunder, von Bissing replied, "Sometimes people make mountains out of molehills and sometimes molehills turn out to be mountains."[79] Revenge for the death of Nurse Cavell became a rallying cry that is said to have influenced men to volunteer in Canada as well as Britain.[80]

The surge of enlistments and broad public support for Canada's war effort encouraged the minister of militia to propose the formation of a fifth and then a sixth Canadian division, creating a two-corps Canadian army.[81] He announced that eighty-two new battalions would be authorized and encouraged unit officers to believe that if they recruited to full strength they would serve together on the Western Front. Since two new divisions could only absorb twenty-four battalions, Hughes was encouraging a ruinous competition between units in the same city or region. The prime minister, who ought to have known better, endorsed Hughes's plans and issued a New Year's statement pledging that Canada would now seek to enlist 500,000 men.

The decision to raise the authorized strength of the CEF to half a million men caught everyone by surprise. As the *Montreal Witness* noted, "what has been done in the way of enlistment since the beginning of the war will now have to be duplicated." This "gigantic task" will require that "between six and seven percent of the total population will be rendering military service."[82] Borden's New Year's statement did not indicate whether he wanted a total of half a million volunteers or was establishing the strength of the CEF at half a million men. Borden was still delegating such details to Hughes, and neither man seems to have understood what exactly they were proposing.[83] Normal "trench wastage" and sickness required a steady flow of replacements to maintain a 70,000-man Canadian corps without considering the impact of casualties from a major battle. Continuing to create new battalions each with its own cadre of inexperienced officers who would add to the already large number of unemployed officers in England was not the best way of responding to the challenges the Canadians would face in the last six months of 1916.

The plan to add 250,000 men to the CEF led a number of business leaders to demand a more rational system of recruiting to limit the enrolment of skilled workers. Canadian employers were concerned that the flood of volunteers would jeopardize both the farm and factory economies. Before monthly enrolment peaked in March 1916 at 33,900 men, fears of labour shortages led the president of the CPR, Thomas George Shaughnessy, to challenge the government's approach to recruiting.[84] His warning was given at a meeting of the Montreal Board of Trade called at "the request of local military leaders ... to learn what further should be done to carry out the present scheme of warfare and improve recruiting." Board of Trade president H.B. Walker introduced the speakers, suggesting that "the time had come to consider how far we can go in this without in some measure depleting our ability to carry on the necessary business of the country and especially the supplying of stores and munitions of war. There must be a point where we cannot send any more men without impairing our position at home."

Sam Hughes then rose, greeted by "applause which speedily broke into cheers." The minister of militia avoided Walker's question, delivering one of his typical recruiting speeches declaring that "with proper presentation" and the cooperation of business men with the Citizen's Recruiting Association "not 50,000 men but 70,000" could be secured from the Montreal region. Introduced as the country's "first businessman," the CPR president, recently elevated to the peerage as Lord Shaughnessy of Montreal, expressed his admiration for Hughes's "enthusiastic energy and earnestness." However, Shaughnessy bluntly rejected the notion that Montreal could enrol 70,000 men, 10 per cent of its population, and doubted that raising 500,000 men nationally was "a practicable suggestion":

We have many duties to perform. First we have our contribution to the Army of the Empire. Then we have our work as manufactures of munitions ... Then we have our agricultural work – we must help to feed the British nation – Then there is another thing of little less importance – finance. If we were to raise 500,000 or add 225,000 to our present army, we would be making a draft upon the working population of this country that would be seriously felt.

Shaughnessy argued for an immediate slowdown in recruiting, concentrating on "units approaching completion rather than starting more new battalions every day, a competition that cannot have but bad results."[85] Hughes dismissed the speech as "piffle," while Borden saw it as a direct attack upon his government, already under pressure from an opposition bent on exploiting the "Shell Scandal,"[86] but Shaughnessy knew whereof he spoke. The rapid growth of the munitions industry and war orders for other sectors of the economy meant that the days of large-scale unemployment were coming to an end, and as Canada's leading transportation and manufacturing centre Montreal was ahead of the curve. Production of shells, fuses, and an array of war-related items was absorbing all available male and female labour.

Beginning in November 1915, the Montreal correspondents of the *Labour Gazette* reported heavy demand for both men and women in a wide variety of industries. There was "general prosperity" in steel and large orders for other firms, so much so that in January 1916 Dominion Textiles gave its 7,000 employees a 5 per cent wage increase in hopes of retaining workers who might flee to the munitions plants.[87] May 1916 was described as "one of the best months for Montreal manufacturers and for all classes of labour."[88] One study of employment patterns estimated that by mid-1916 20,000 men and 10,000 women were employed in the city's munitions plants while other industries were seeking additional workers,[89] especially after the new Imperial Munitions Board opened its factory in Verdun.[90]

Shaughnessy's view received a polite hearing but few were convinced, and a motion encouraging employers to cooperate with recruiters by supplying lists of eligible employees was proposed. When Leo Doyon, a French Canadian member, sought to amend the motion by proposing that "no further action be taken to accelerate Canada's share in the war," his intervention was met with "hisses and cries of dissent." The chair refused to consider the amendment, which he declared was "an insult to any man of intelligence."[91]

Doyon did not mention the tense situation in Ottawa in the preamble to his amendment, but the ongoing struggle between two sisters and the Ontario government dramatized and personalized the school question as never before. Béatrice and Diane Desloges, lay teachers at the Guignes school, simply ignored the rules imposed by Regulation 17, teaching exclusively in French. When, in October 1915, they were removed from the school the young women taught their students in improvised classrooms; then in early January 1916, hundreds of mothers and other local women surrounded the school and occupied it. The defence of the school and the Desloges sisters were frequently front-page news in January, forcing Laurier and the Quebec Liberals to assume leadership of a movement that was uniting French Canadians of all political persuasions.[92]

Laurier encouraged one of his most promising Quebec MPs, Ernest Lapointe, to introduce a resolution that read:

> That this House, especially at this time of universal sacrifice and anxiety, when all energies should be concentrated on winning the war, would while fully recognizing the principle of Provincial Rights and the necessity of every child being given a thorough English education, respectfully suggest to the Legislative Assembly (of Ontario) the wisdom of making it clear that the privilege of the children of French parentage of being taught in their mother tongue not be interfered with.

Lapointe and after him Laurier made the case for a compromise that would permit the use of French in Ontario schools. Quoting Egerton Ryerson, the father of public education in Ontario, they endorsed Ryerson's view that "it is quite proper and lawful for the trustees to allow both languages to be taught in their schools."[93] Asking for acceptance of the French fact in Ontario without claiming a constitutional right did not satisfy the nationalists, but did allow Laurier to take control of the issue in Quebec, providing a "sheet anchor" in his struggle with Bourassa. As he told his former colleague W.S. Fielding, "If I were to remain silent under such circumstances I would certainly lose my own self-esteem and respect."[94] The debate over the Lapointe Resolution illustrated the deep divisions in the country, but Laurier was able to retain the support of almost all his Ontario MPs and prepare the ground for the decision of the Judicial Committee of the Privy Council in London. The Law Lords declared that while Regulation 17 was within the powers of the province, the takeover of the Ottawa Separate School Board was unconstitutional. This apparent compromise, together with the papal encyclical requiring Canadian Catholics to maintain unity and place religion ahead of language, ended the legal battle and diffused the conflict.[95] Bourassa was unwilling to publicly challenge the pope and remained silent.[96] The Lapointe Resolution led directly to the Bonne Entente movement initiated in June 1916 by Ontario Liberals, who proposed sending a delegation of prominent citizens to Quebec to establish "friendly intercourse and mutual respect." The delegation arrived in Quebec in October and was well received. A Quebec delegation then travelled to Ontario.[97]

Another attempt at friendly intercourse was initiated by Captain Talbot Mercer Papineau,[98] an officer in the Princess Patricias, who sent a letter to his law partner Andrew McMaster, a prominent Liberal, and asked him to forward it to the addressee, his cousin "Henri." Papineau, a grandson of the *patriote* leader Louis Joseph Papineau, criticized Bourassa's attitude towards the war and presented a defence of Canadian participation. McMaster asked Papineau to change the original letter.

You speak of an Imperial War ... that is not the keynote of all the appeals made
for patriotic purposes here – very often it is the Canadian note that is sounded and
that the war is for civilization and liberty.[99]

McMaster was right: Laurier and other Liberals were countering the Tory-imperial rhetoric with arguments about Canada's responsibility to participate in a just war against German aggression and help liberate Belgium and France. Papineau agreed to revise the letter and asked McMaster to send it to Bourassa, but if there was no reply to arrange for publication elsewhere. The letter, written in English by a man who had been raised as a Protestant by his American mother and attended the High School of Montreal and McGill University before winning a Rhodes Scholarship, restated the basic Liberal view of the war, provoking the dismissive comment from Bourassa that he barely knew his cousin and doubted he had written the letter. Bourassa, who declined to publish Papineau's letter, used the occasion to restate his oft-expressed views on the evils of British imperialism and Ontario jingoism, but there was nothing new in either letter.

Bourassa's reply to Papineau was published on 5 August when the other newspapers reported on ceremonies marking the second anniversary of the outbreak of war. All across Canada crowds gathered to hear speeches "expressing Canada's determination to persist to the war's successful conclusion."[100] The campus of McGill University was the setting for the Montreal meeting, and thousands gathered to hear the prime minister and Laurier's lieutenant, Rodolphe Lemieux, declare Canada's resolve. Lemieux's fiery speech, demanding to know "how can there be neutrality when the honour of humanity, all the noble liberties and all the rights of the innocent are at stake," was widely reported. As usual, *Le Devoir* had different reactions, describing the leaders of the two parties kneeling at the altar of the British Empire to mark the end of the second year of military imperialism.[101]

Throughout late July and early August the question that dominated the international news was the trial and execution of Roger Casement. The Easter Rebellion in Dublin had been presented to Montrealers as German inspired, with Sir Roger Casement as the prime villain. The *Montreal Star* headline "Twelve Killed in Riots Fathered by the Germans in Dublin" was followed by stories outlining Casement's attempts to recruit Irish prisoners of war in Germany to join a rebellion and his efforts to provide arms to the rebels.[102] The *Standard* provided photographs and detailed coverage emphasizing the German connection, Casement's links to Irish Americans, and John Redmond's statement urging "true Irish nationalists" to support the authorities.[103] The French-language popular press told a similar story, but *Le Nationaliste* published an editorial cartoon titled "Riel and Casement" linking the two treason trials.[104] Montreal's Irish were disturbed by Casement's execution, but the leadership remained loyal to John Redmond and the moderates of the Irish Parliamentary Party.

The year 1916 proved to be one of the most prosperous in the city's history. The Dominion government's decision to finance the war through borrowing meant that inflation was inevitable once the country's unemployed and underutilized industrial capacity was put to work.[105] This became evident in 1916 as rising prices began to gradually erode wage gains. For most, however, full-time employment and strong demand for women and children's participation in the work force increased family incomes.[106] The increasing employment of children under fourteen was noted by the provincial government's factory inspectors, who seemed powerless to prevent it. Louis Guyon's 1916 report declared that "child labour remains the same unsolvable problem we have encountered … since 1886," but the war was adding immeasurably to it.[107] The thousands of fourteen- to sixteen-year-olds in the work force were of course not officially children.

Apparently, full employment in a city where sports, entertainment, alcohol, and sensual pleasures were readily available did little to encourage enlistment or focus attention on a distant and seemingly endless conflict. On a typical summer weekend, track meets, baseball games, lacrosse, soccer, and horse races captured the attention of young men. Both Parc Sohmer and Dominion Park were in full swing with attractions, concerts, and vaudeville acts. King Edward Park, reached by boats from the Pie IX pier, added horse races to its summer schedule. Sports rivalry between French- and English-speaking Montrealers added spice to contests such as a lacrosse match between the Shamrocks and Nationals that drew 5,000 spectators in July.[108]

Movies were more popular than ever, with stars like Charlie Chaplin and Lilian Gish featured in performances across the city. Montreal's appetite for movie palaces led American theatre chains to invest heavily in the city. Construction of the Theatre St. Denis, at a reported cost of $200,000, was finished in time for a March 1916 opening. With 3,000 seats, it was the largest and most luxurious theatre in Canada. Owned by the Keith-Albee company, the St. Denis was aimed at an east end audience, with both signage and subtitles in French. Le Pays described this as an innovation in Montreal theatres. A second American company, United Amusement, opened the 1,100-seat Regent in the same month to attract audiences from the rapidly expanding Plateau area.[109] Movie theatres required music, and Montreal pianists and composers played ragtime and two-step for silent films and the dance halls that were especially popular. The less savoury such halls offered "private lessons at all hours," but during the city's long winters dances were regular features at the Ritz Carlton as well as the downtown dance palaces. Weekly newspapers such as *Montreal qui chante* and *Passe temps* provided news, gossip, and above all the sheet music that allowed composers to get their work before the public.[110]

Despite the best efforts of the Roman Catholic hierarchy and Anglo-Protestant temperance advocates, prohibition, which was drying out the rest of

Canada, made little headway in Montreal.[111] One merchant boasted that he had acquired stocks of liquor from Manitoba and Ontario to sell at bargain prices.[112] Alcohol helped to fuel the city's flourishing nightlife, with hotels, cafés, and retail stores competing with blind pigs and brothels for customers at all hours. Housing hundreds and sometimes thousands of soldiers in improvised barracks helped to ensure there were customers for the bars, the vaudeville shows, and the city's red-light district. Civic and religious authorities were deeply divided over what to do with a growing sex industry and rising rates of venereal disease. In the summer of 1916 both Mayor Méderic Martin and the leading English-speaking member of the Board of Control argued for the recognition and regulation of the red-light district to protect public health. Controller Ross insisted that "the social evil will always exist, the best we can do now is limit the field of action, limit contamination, regulate and inspect." *Le Pays*, which supported regulation, criticized opponents for claiming that "segregation does not segregate" while insisting that "prohibition will prohibit."[113]

Montreal's tolerance for illegal activities was tested the same month when complaints about a private club operating on St. Hubert Street, "one of the smartest French Canadian residential sections of the city," forced the police to raid the premises. The club was said to have operated on Notre Dame Street for at least three years before moving uptown, where after complaints it was placed under surveillance. Two "secret service men" from New York were brought in to mingle with members and gather evidence. On the night of the raid a visitor accidentally tripped a warning bell on the third step, allowing a "dozen or so, young men, all in their teens" to flee before the police arrived. Eight men, including the organizer, E.L. Carreau, a well-known proprietor of a religious supplies store, were arrested and charged with "gross indecency." The Carreau affair became the talk of the town, particularly after the men paid $50.00 bail and were set free, allowing Carreau to flee to the United States. Most of the French-language newspapers reported the bare bones of the story, leaving the juicy details to the *Star* and *Standard*. *Le Canard*, the satirical weekly, could not resist exploiting the story and kept it alive for some weeks, while *Le Pays*, in full anti-clerical mode, tied Carreau to the church.[114]

Montrealers clearly had other things on their mind when Sam Hughes authorized a number of new battalions to begin recruiting in Montreal during 1916. The English-speaking population, which had provided several thousand men in 1915, were now asked to fill the ranks of the 148th Battalion. It was affiliated with McGill University, in the hope that students and recent graduates would come forward. Lieut.-Colonel Alan Magee, a McGill graduate and Canadian Officer Training Corps instructor, was given command, and he drew twenty of his thirty-one officers from the university's Officer Training Corps.[115] Otherwise, recruiting proved to be a difficult and lengthy task. By late February 1916 less than half the required numbers had enlisted, and Magee told an audience gathered at His Majesty's Theatre that "we have tried to stir up the patriotism of Montreal but it seems as though we must give up because there is nothing left to stir." Montreal's recruiting record, Magee insisted, "is simply rotten."[116] When the battalion left Canada in September 1916 there were 36 officers and 951 other ranks on the embarkation list, just 40 per cent of whom were born in Canada and less than half of which were from the city. After drafts of 250 men were sent to reinforce three of Montreal's front-line battalions, the 148th was disbanded and absorbed by the 20th Reserve Battalion. Magee served as a staff officer for the balance of the war.

Four French Canadian battalions also began recruiting early in the new year. The 150th, affiliated with the Carabiniers Mont Royal, was commanded by Lieut.-Colonel Hercule Barré, who had been wounded at Langemarck and then survived the sinking of the ship returning him to Canada. Barré had helped save women and children found waiting in their cabins as the *Hesperian* went down and was lauded as a hero in Montreal.[117] Unfortunately, the battalion lacked capable officers and NCOs, while Barré himself was said to be "unstable" and unwilling to involve himself in the details of training and the maintenance of discipline.[118] The 150th never came close to full strength, and despite "very bad feeling" between the units it was merged with another new battalion, 178th.[119] The 178th was originally based in Victoriaville with orders to recruit in Athabaska, Nicolet, and Drummond counties but later concentrated on Montreal, which provided most of the recruits.[120] The 515 men eventually enrolled provided reinforcements to the 22nd and four English-language battalions.[121] Barré protested the decision to send his men to English-language units as they had a "very poor command of English" and will "risk punishment for inadequately carrying out orders, the full purport of which they do not understand."[122] This was not an issue the military was prepared to address.[123]

The history of the 163rd Battalion, known as "*poil-aux-pattes*" or "Hairy Paws,"[124] is intertwined with the story of Olivar Asselin's personal decision to enlist and to take the lead in raising a battalion for overseas service. Asselin, one of the founders of the nationalist movement, was until December 1915 devoting his considerable energies to supporting the cause of the Franco-Ontarian minority. During the fall of 1915 he published a series of articles in Jules Fournier's newspaper *L'Action* criticizing the editor of the *L'Action Catholique* for "seeking to make the French-Canadian bishops popular at London and Rideau Hall" by urging moderation on the Ontario school question and endorsing the war effort.[125] All of this was in tune with Asselin's anti-clerical views, opposition to the government's war policy, and commitment to French-language rights.

Asselin's nationalist and anti-clerical credentials were beyond dispute, but he was also an ardent Francophile who had earlier offered to enlist in the Canadian army as an interpreter. When Ottawa ignored his request he tried to enlist in the French army.[126] By December 1915 Asselin was determined to go to war, and he accepted a commission as a major, second-in-command to the veteran Henri DesRosiers, one of the original group of 65th Regiment officers who had served with the 14th Battalion at Ypres. Asselin spoke to a large crowd at the Monument National in January 1916 explaining his decision to enrol. His description of the importance of France, "whose defeat would condemn us her children of America to drag out henceforth diminished lives," resonated with many in the audience, but phrases such as "we march for British institutions, because by themselves and independently of the half-civilized persons who apply them today in Ontario they are worth fighting for" prompted "shouts and hisses from the gallery." In response Asselin declared he felt sorry for young men who could not distinguish between fighting for a great principle and the local issues that had taken possession of their minds.[127]

DesRosiers returned from France to lead the 163rd with Asselin in charge of recruiting. By April 1916 the battalion was close to full strength, but after Sam Hughes authorized another battalion, the 206th, to recruit in Montreal and share the Guy Street barracks a crisis atmosphere quickly developed. The commander of the 206th, Tancrède Pagneulo, a Conservative politician and militia officer, invited volunteers to join the 206th because it was to be "the last to leave Canada and the first to profit from victory." When Asselin drew attention to Pagneulo's recruiting campaign and the poor discipline in the 206th,[128] Hughes simply ignored the problems and suggested the 163rd replace the 38th Battalion in Bermuda. Desrosiers and Asselin welcomed the opportunity to get away from Montreal and train the 163rd, but when they embarked for Bermuda in May 197 men quit the battalion leaving, just 663 men on strength.[129] In Bermuda, the officer commanding the garrison inspected the battalion. His report, sent to the War Office in London, described the 163rd as "perfect novices," untrained and lacking officers or NCOs capable of giving instruction. The language barrier made the situation especially difficult, but poor discipline and problems due to the availability of cheap rum played into the situation.[130] The 163rd returned to Canada before sailing to England with 38 officers and 822 other ranks.[131]

Asselin tried to save the 163rd from the fate of other battalions broken up for reinforcements. His letter to the prime minister asked for "a draft of 200 to 300 men" to bring the 163rd to full strength, "a favour which I believe our record so far and the fact that only one French Canadian battalion as yet has been allowed to reach the front trenches entitles us to."[132] Neither Borden nor Hughes made any attempt to assist the 163rd, which was disbanded soon after arriving in England.

Hughes continued to authorize the formation of new battalions across Canada, including Quebec.[133] Few of them would succeed in recruiting to full strength, and almost all were disbanded in England, with the men joining the reinforcement stream. Inevitably, hundreds more unilingual French Canadians were sent to English-language battalions to adjust as best they could. While it is impossible to demonstrate what might have happened if a rational system had been in place in Quebec, it is reasonable to suggest that there were sufficient French-speaking volunteers to establish a second and perhaps third full-strength battalion; what was lacking was the will to do this.

According to *Le Canada* another problem that plagued the units recruiting French Canadians was the plight of volunteers who could not meet the height standard. Overall, the newspaper reported, 40 per cent of French Canadian volunteers were rejected by medical officers, mostly because they were too small. *Le Canada* claimed that this was due to the natural physique of men of Latin origin and urged the Militia Department to establish a "bantam battalion" for French Canadians.[134] There was no response from Hughes or his officials.

During 1915 the Militia Department authorized the formation of several "Pioneer" battalions, described as units that would "work with engineers in forward areas consolidating positions captured by infantry."[135] Fitness standards were lower, and the first two units organized in Winnipeg and Guelph recruited to full strength without difficulty. The 5th Battalion, organized in Montreal between March and November 1916, got off to a good start, drawing upon men who had previously joined the Canadian Engineer Militia unit established in Verdun near the Grand Trunk Railway Shops. The recruiting posters declared that the 5th was a "special battalion" that would "build bridges, railroads and highways." Engineering students and artisans were invited to join and promised "you will have money in the bank upon your return."[136] It proved impossible to find enough volunteers to form a complete battalion, but by November there were over 600 men available for embarkation. Most of the volunteers were born in Britain, but less than one-third gave next-of-kin addresses in the United Kingdom.[137] The 5th Pioneer Battalion was absorbed by the 5th Divisional Engineers in England.

The history of another Montreal battalion, the 199th Irish Canadian Rangers, is of special interest as it links the city's Irish communities with the dramatic events associated with the Easter Rebellion in Dublin and its aftermath. The decision to transform the 55th Militia Regiment into an overseas battalion was sparked by the transfer of a full-strength Irish company to the 60th Battalion in the summer of 1915. Lieut.-Colonel Trihey proposed that since large numbers of Irish Canadians were enlisting, it was time to organize an overseas battalion made up exclusively of men of Irish descent. Sam Hughes pledged that the Rangers would be sent to the front as a unit under their own leaders, and it was on this basis that recruiting began. The first 300 men, the vast majority of whom were members of the 55th, attested in March and April 1916 before news of the Easter Rebellion in Dublin reached Montreal. Of those who listed a religious affiliation, 145 were Roman Catholics and 125 Protestants, fulfilling the plan to enrol Irishmen regardless of religion. Most were native-born Montrealers, but 92 were born in England or Scotland and 18 in Ireland.[138]

Two previous studies of the 199th – Robin Burns's 1985 article "The Montreal Irish and the Great War" and Simon Jolivet's book *Le vert et le bleu*, which includes a chapter on the 199th in the context of his study of French Canadians attitudes towards Ireland – are of considerable interest, but neither author had access to the attestation papers now available online at Library and Archives Canada. Their estimates of the religious and national composition of the 199th need to be revised.[139] The attestation papers demonstrate that more than 80 per cent of those who enlisted in the 199th had previously served in the 55th Militia Regiment. Despite one of the most elaborate and well-publicized recruiting campaigns ever undertaken in the city, less than 200 men who were not already Irish Rangers attested in 1916. Apparently hundreds of volunteers did come forward but were rejected on medical grounds.[140] The attestation papers also reveal that the proportion of Canadian-born was less than 50 per cent and that, in addition to large numbers of British-born, the list includes Americans, Russians, and other Europeans. It is also evident that less than 50 per cent of those recording a religious affiliation were Roman Catholics.[141] Irishness was apparently a matter of self-identification.

In November 1916, as the 199th prepared to embark for England, the battalion was inspected by Major-General F.L. Lessard. There was a full complement of officers and 860 men on the roll, but on the day of the inspection over 300 men were away, including 66 absent without leave. Lessard was not pleased; the unit, he reported, "is fit for drafts only and will require a lot of work to make them fit for that." Lieut.-Colonel Trihey was described as "an officer of good standing with little or no military experience, he did not impress me as a capable officer nor fitted to command." The second-in-command, Major F. O'Brien was equally inexperienced and, though a "hard worker," was not fitted for promotion. The adjutant, Captain Thomas Shaughnessy, was "very energetic with little experience or instruction." The sergeants and warrant officers all lacked experience, but they and the men on parade were strong and healthy. Lessard was also impressed by the potential of the company commanders, especially Major Edward Knox-Leet,[142] a Dublin-born Montrealer who had gone overseas with the Irish Ranger company of the 60th Battalion.[143]

Normally the British cabinet and War Office tried to avoid involvement in Canadian military affairs, fearful of rousing another quarrel with Sam Hughes, but the temptation to use the Rangers as a propaganda tool in Ireland was irresistible. On 30 October 1916 Bonar Law, the Canadian-born colonial secretary, wrote to the governor-general proposing the battalion visit Ireland. The idea was warmly embraced by Hughes, Doherty, and the officers of the 199th. When the visit was cancelled, bringing "very great disappointment" to the Canadians, the governor-general, on behalf of the cabinet, sought to persuade the

War Office to make new arrangements, and on 5 January 1917 the colonial secretary was able to announce the visit would begin in late January.[144]

Both British and Canadian military authorities in England supported the tour of Ireland, but they were determined to enforce the policy requiring all formations arriving in England in 1917 to be broken up to join the reinforcement stream. After vigorous protests from Doherty and organizations like the Ancient Order of Hiberians, the 199th was given a reprieve and assigned to 5th Division, but not before both Harry Trihey and his second-in-command had resigned in protest.[145] Lieut.-Colonel G.V. O'Donahoe, one of the 55th Regiment's originals, who won the Distinguished Service Order commanding the Irish company of the 60th Battalion, replaced Trihey and led the Irish Canadian Rangers on their tour of Ireland.[146] Despite an exceptionally cold and sometimes snowy January the Rangers were welcomed by large crowds in Dublin, Armagh, Belfast, Cork, and Limerick. The *Tablet's* correspondent in Dublin, reflecting Irish nationalist sentiment, welcomed "these Irish Canadian volunteers who have no part in our controversies or disagreements … There is no Irishman of any party who will not honour them."[147] John Redmond offered his "enthusiastic support" for the tour, declaring that all of Ireland was "proud of these sons of the Irish race" who shared "Ireland's highest purpose, a speedy and victorious ending to the war."[148] Redmond's influence was diminishing rapidly as negotiations over home rule stalled, but the emergence of Sinn Fein as a clear alternative to Redmond's Irish Party was not yet evident to Irish Canadians, who continued to support Redmond's policy of moderation and conciliation.[149] The 199th was the last full battalion of volunteers to be recruited in Montreal.[150]

Chapter Five

Attrition

The First World War is generally remembered as a time when innocent young men were slaughtered in pointless battles planned by stupid generals.[1] This view has proven difficult to eradicate, despite the best efforts of revisionist historians,[2] because the battles the generals planned almost always turned into chaotic bloodbaths rationalized by declaring that the purpose was to wear down the enemy through attrition. If the generals themselves are to be believed, only one major sustained operation, the German offensive against Verdun in 1916, was in fact planned as an attritional battle where the enemy would destroy itself in attempting to recover lost ground.

A sustained critique of generalship on the Western Front requires an understanding that the war was shaped by the initial German advances into Belgium and northern France as well as success on the eastern front. The small group of men in Berlin who decided to wage war to alter the balance of power had no clear ideas about remaking the map of Europe before August 1914, but the German army's initial victories led them to agree on what became known as the "September Program." This document, accepted as reasonable by moderates including Chancellor Bethmann-Hollweg, outlined war aims that included annexations and indemnities from France, control of Belgium as a "vassal state," an expanded colonial empire, and the creation of a new Poland under German sovereignty. Similar ideas about the necessary conditions for peace dominated German opinion through to the last months of the war.[3] The achievement of such war aims required an overall German victory and were incompatible with the minimum demands of the Allies: the liberation of France, Belgium, Serbia, and Russia with reparations for war damages. In the early months of the war France declared that recovery of the "lost provinces" of Alsace-Lorraine was also a war aim, adding to the difficulty of negotiating a peace.[4]

As the limits of offensive military operations became apparent the German high command adopted a new strategy for 1915, fighting a defensive war on the Western Front and shifting resources to support the campaign against Russia.

They fortified positions on higher ground and protected them with stretches of barbed wire. General Joseph Joffre, the commander-in-chief, recognized this reality and declared in November 1914 that his armies could not begin new operations until reserves had been created, shattered battalions rebuilt, and special equipment, especially heavy artillery, was available. After protests from Russia that it would be left to bear the burden of a one-front war Joffre relented, ordering three major attacks between December 1914 and March 1915. From the end of the Battle of the Marne to the spring of 1915 the French army lost close to one million men, including 268,000 fatal casualties in these attacks.[5]

British leaders agreed on the need to continue fighting but not on how the war could best be waged. Field Marshal Lord Kitchener, the war minister, was among the first to recognize that the war might last for years, and he proposed to raise a volunteer force of more than a million men. There was no difficulty in finding soldiers for his "New Army," but time was needed to equip and train them. Producing the guns and shells necessary to overcome the enemy was an equally challenging task directed by the energetic Welsh politician David Lloyd George, who became minister of munitions in April 1915.

Kitchener was reluctant to see his new divisions rushed into the battles of the Western Front and he therefore accepted a plan pressed by Winston Churchill, first lord of the admiralty, to go to the aid of Russia by attacking Turkey. The Gallipoli campaign cost the Allies more than 20,000 casualties at a time when their armies on the Western Front were also suffering heavy losses. The French army's Artois offensive, including an attack on Vimy Ridge, required British support in the form of a diversionary attack north of Arras near the village of Loos. With the enemy at that location firmly entrenched on high ground and the approaches so swept by machine-gun fire that an advance in the open was impossible, senior British commanders resisted the French demands, arguing for an attack further north.[6] Joffre appealed to Kitchener who, fearing a breach between the two nations, ordered his generals to cooperate with Joffre. We must, he declared, "act with all our energies and do our utmost to help the French even though by doing so we suffer heavy losses."[7]

General Sir Douglas Haig, who commanded the British forces tasked with the operations at Loos, had the opportunity to devise a diversionary attack conserving men's lives; instead he chose to stage a break-through battle aimed at Douai, Vallenciones, and beyond. The first use of chlorine gas by the British would, he argued, facilitate the break-in and then, by using the "utmost energy," the infantry would press on through the German defences. Cavalry reserves were to be available for exploitation. Haig converted an operation designed to assist the French offensive into one of the great disasters of 1915. Some 50,000 British soldiers were lost at Loos, almost half of whom were killed or missing.[8] A small number of these were Canadians who tried to assist the British advance with a simulated gas attack and artillery fire.[9]

Canadians had been introduced to frontal assaults on well-defended positions at Festubert, one of the several attempts to seize the Aubers Ridge, a low-lying fold in the Flanders plain that dominated the British front. Haig had tried a "hurricane barrage" in the first attack, but a week later he employed 433 howitzers and guns to target 5,000 metres of frontage over two and a half days of preparation.[10] One hundred thousand shells sounds like a lot unless you do the math and realize that the enemy position was at least 500,000 square metres. Since most of the guns were 18-pounders firing shrapnel at the wire, the burden on the heavy batteries, compounded by poor observation conditions and dud shells, was enormous. Much of the German position remained untouched, and the gaps in the wire were turned into killing grounds as men struggled forward in broad daylight. This did not stop Haig from ordering repeated infantry attacks that over a ten-day period resulted in close to 16,000 casualties.[11]

The Canadian Division was in reserve when Festubert began, attempting to absorb several thousand replacements. There were not enough men in the first contingent's reserve battalions, so company-size drafts from Montreal's 23rd Battalion were sent to the Patricias as well as the 13th and 14th Battalions. The 23rd had recruited a large number of British army veterans and men who had served in the militia, but less than six weeks had passed since their arrival in England.[12] Haig's decision to employ such men as well as dismounted troopers of the Canadian Cavalry Brigade in a failing operation suggests how determined he was to pursue the dreams of a breakthrough.[13]

The most detailed account of the Canadians at Festubert suggests that in a "featureless terrain devoid of cover … officers at the battalion and company levels either modified or ignored orders" to avoid annihilation.[14] Montreal's 14th Battalion went into the attack in as open a formation as space permitted. The two forward companies advanced in four lines, each separated by fifty yards, limiting the damage from both shell bursts and machine gun fire.[15] When the advance stalled, Lieut.-Colonel William Burland, the newly promoted commanding officer, ordered his men to halt and dig slit trenches, the best protection against shelling. The next morning Burland, on his own initiative, withdrew his men. This early example of agency at the sharp end, finding a middle ground "between mutiny and obedience," left the 16th Battalion, which had continued forward, with an open flank until they too ceased to advance.[16] Both battalions avoided the heavy casualties inflicted on other units, which over a ten-day period involving the capture of the "Canadian Orchard" cost the division 2,468 men.[17]

Coming so soon after the struggle in the salient, Festubert was a shock to many Canadians. Officers complained bitterly about the lack of time to prepare and the inadequate artillery support. Sam Hughes wrote a scathing letter to Lord Kitchener, the British war minister, criticizing Alderson's conduct at

Ypres and condemning the Festubert attack as a "silly attempt to gain a few yards here or there with no preconceived plan or effective drive to smash the enemy." Hughes read part of his letter to friendly journalists and briefed the prime minister, so when the governor-general wanted the "conceited lunatic" court-martialed[18] Borden sided with Hughes; but neither man could actually influence the conduct of operations. Fortunately, the next action fought by the division at Givenchy was called off before another heavy bloodletting began, and for much of the next ten months 1st Division was not required to participate in offensive operations. As lightly wounded officers and men returned to their units and replacements were integrated, the division was maintained at full strength.

On 25 May 1915 the 2nd Canadian Infantry Division became part of the British Expeditionary Force with headquarters at Shorncliffe Army Camp in Kent, England. The men had been recruited during the fall of 1914, but as there were no winter quarters available for an 18,000-man division, the battalions remained scattered across the country attempting to train, without proper equipment, in the Canadian winter. The new division was commanded by Major-General Sam Steele, a sixty-six-year-old Canadian warrior who fought in the North-West Rebellion and led Lord Strathcona's Horse in the Boer War. Steele was selected by Sam Hughes, who wanted a Canadian in command. Kitchener was equally determined to appoint an experienced British officer "to do justice to the troops." Kitchener's offer to allow Canada to choose any British general on the "unemployed active list" enraged Hughes, who believed that British commanders at Ypres had sacrificed Canadian lives; he was in no mood to accept claims of British superiority. An agreement to appoint Brigadier Richard Turner to command 2nd Division while Arthur Currie took over 1st Division satisfied Hughes, but he had to accept the promotion of Lieutant-General Edwin Alderson to command the Canadian Corps.[19]

While in England, 2nd Division was able to draw on officers and NCOs with experience on the Western Front for both leadership and training. Lieut.-Colonel H.D. de Prée, a veteran British officer, returned from France to become senior staff officer, and other staff college graduates provided the administrative skills required to integrate the Canadians into the British way of war.[20] There were also opportunities for junior officers to attend battle schools and take part in battalion, brigade, and even divisional exercises. When it crossed to France, the 2nd Division was, by 1915 standards, well prepared for trench warfare on the Western Front.

Montreal's contribution to the 2nd Division, the 22nd and 24th battalions, were part of the 5th Canadian Infantry Brigade, commanded by J.P. Landry, a Royal Military College graduate and Permanent Force artillery officer. Landry was the son of Senator Phillipe Landry, Speaker of the Senate and a leader in the campaign to repeal Regulation 17. Some thought the decision to replace

Landry with David Watson was influenced by such political considerations, but common sense suggests an experienced battalion commander was a better choice.

The division reached France in September 1915 and was given responsibility for a particularly nasty stretch of ground overlooked by the Messines Ridge. There was no opportunity to learn the routines of static trench warfare from veterans; the men were to learn on the job. As the autumn rains continued the trenches became drainage ditches, requiring constant effort to prevent the sides from collapsing. Battalions were rotated in and out of the line every six days. The 22nd was paired with the 25th Nova Scotia and the 24th with the 26th from New Brunswick. The Nova Scotians had the misfortune of holding a sector that the German had mined, and when the mine exploded "half of one platoon simply disappeared … another twenty men nearby were wounded."[21] The Montreal battalions avoided such singular events, but static trench warfare produced a steady stream of casualties and incapacitating sickness. The division initially failed to deal effectively with the problem of "trench foot," a fungal infection caused by prolonged exposure to cold, wet conditions. Discipline and the threat of cancelling leave for officers helped to curb the problem, though what really mattered was enforcing instructions that "all men before going into the trenches should be stripped, rubbed down and anti-frost grease rubbed-in from the waist down to and including the feet." In addition, every man was to have extra socks and to change them every twenty-four hours.[22]

Extra socks knitted by Red Cross and Croix Rouge volunteers were plentiful. Lieut. Georges Vanier noted that he had twenty pairs or more and asked for some maple syrup instead. Vanier, a romantic Francophile who had no doubts about the purpose of the war, wrote frequent letters home and kept a diary. One letter to a young family friend described life in the front lines in reassuring terms. During their six-day tour the officers of D Company, he wrote, lived in a two-room dugout with a "stove blazing away … dry socks, dry boots, hot coffee, Bovril or cocoa" and enough food to have some left over for "the thousands of mice and rats." His diary recorded a different war. A November entry began: "A dismal morning; low clouds; everything is heavy. You feel oppressed and stiffed; you paddle in a foot of mud and water. These are appropriate conditions for the month of the dead."[23]

Influenza and a number of other common ailments added to the steady toll of losses from German artillery, mortars, and snipers.[24] The field ambulances serving the Canadian Corps dealt with a total of 8,472 men in the winter of 1915–16, 3,159 of whom had to be evacuated to general hospitals.[25] Wastage, the military term for losses from all causes, averaged 700 men a month in both 1st and 2nd Divisions.[26] With four Montreal units at the front, the demand for reinforcements exhausted what was left of the 23rd Reserve Battalion, which was replenished by the special reinforcement drafts of 250 men from each new Quebec battalion.

A fifth Montreal unit, the 42nd Royal Highlanders, was also in France as part of the 7th Brigade, which served as corps troops through the winter, supplying working parties to perform heavy labour behind the front. Throughout November 1915 the 42nd provided a daily quota of 580 men who tried to improve communication and support trenches frequently "working in mud above knees." As winter approached all the Highland battalions traded their kilts for "trews," with "kilts, hose tops and sporrans sent to Paris to be renovated and stored."[27]

By February 1916 the situation confronting the British Empire and France was incredibly bleak. The failure of their 1915 offensives on the Western Front and the crushing defeat of the Russian armies in the east were paralleled by German victories in the Balkans, the failure of the Gallipoli expedition, the defeat of British forces in Iraq, and the bloody stalemate in the war between Italy and Austria-Hungary. Then on February 21, the German 5th Army, with forty full-strength infantry divisions, each of 16,000 men, began the assault on Verdun. The German supreme commander, General Erich von Falkenhayn, decided that the war would be won only if the French army was bled to death in a battle of attrition while a campaign of unrestricted submarine warfare was waged against Britain. Falkenhayn was allowed to begin the attack on the "sacred heart of France" but the Kaiser, fearing war with the United States, refused to authorize the full U-boat offensive. The French responded to the attack with determination, and as the battle continued and losses mounted it became evident that both armies were bleeding to death. By mid-August, when the fighting died down, losses on both sides were roughly even, with more than 700,000 killed, wounded, or missing.[28]

Most of the French army was committed to the defence of Verdun, and there was understandable pressure on the British to draw off German forces by a major attack elsewhere on the front. The British Expeditionary Force, now commanded by General Sir Douglas Haig, had been greatly strengthened by the arrival of Kitchener's new divisions, made up of eager volunteers and troops brought back from the Mediterranean. Initially, Haig had hoped to move slowly and allow more time for training, but on March 27 the British and French prime ministers agreed on the necessity of destroying "the morale of the German army and nation" by military action. There was to be "one policy, one army and one front."[29]

The final decision to launch a major offensive in the Somme Valley was made in late May, and the build-up of supplies for eighteen British and eleven French divisions began immediately. While these events unfolded, the Canadian Corps, now including the 3rd Canadian Division, was spending the summer attempting to train while holding the Ypres salient. The enemy was still able to shell the salient from several directions, making life in the forward lines both miserable and very dangerous. Many Canadian (and British) officers expressed their bitter opposition to orders to hold and attempt to expand the Ypres salient. Sam Hughes, always suspicious of decisions made by British professional soldiers, created a major controversy when he publicly denounced the policy in a letter to Kitchener. Hughes claimed that in discussions with a number of Canadian officers he had learned that the sector the corps was to occupy had "no proper trenches … they will be under fire practically on two sides or in fact three sides much of the time." Hughes suggested that since Ypres was no longer "fit for habitation the line should be straightened."[30] The problem with this apparently sensible proposal was the continued possession of part of the main Ypres Ridge, which overlooked the German rear area. No operational commander could easily surrender such an advantage.

As the German army continued the assault on Verdun, it authorized a series of small-scale diversionary operations in other sectors, including the Ypres salient. One such attack was on an unusual piece of high ground constructed from soil evacuated to build the Ypres-Comines Canal. Known to its British garrison as "The Bluff," it was an obvious German target for a limited local attack that quickly succeeded. But capturing such a position did not mean it could be held, and after several days of bitter fighting and several thousand casualties the British won back control of the battered hill. German attention then shifted to other objectives, but General Sir Herbert Plumer, who commanded British Second Army, including the Canadians, was under pressure from Haig to retaliate with his own local offensive. Plumer was apparently willing to sacrifice yet more men and agreed to attack the enemy in an action that became known as the St. Eloi Craters.[31]

The objective was a six-hundred-metre-wide salient containing a half-acre pile of earth from canal excavation known as the "Mound." The position had been captured by the Germans in March 1915 but left alone because it was overlooked by main Ypres Ridge and would be difficult to hold if captured. By late March 1916 tunnels had been dug from three fifty-foot shafts with the intention of exploding mines under the "Mound" and destroying the German defences. After the mines were exploded, Plumer decided to exploit the situation and occupy the salient. A single brigade from the 3rd British Division carried out the assault but were unable to establish a continuous line in the newly cratered landscape.[32]

After seven days in dubious battle for an inconsequential objective, the British had suffered more than 1,000 casualties and required immediate help. The task of relieving the British was given to Brigadier H.D.B. Ketchen and his 6th Canadian Infantry Brigade. They quickly discovered that the British troops were holding ground that was "more of a line on a map than an actual line of defence." The existing trenches were from two to three feet deep in water, in full view of the enemy, and exposed to artillery fire from the left flank as well as from the front.[33] The Canadians did their best to improve the positions, employing more than 600 men to dig a communication trench and pump out water. At dawn, with the work far from completed, an intense artillery barrage inflicted heavy casualties. "The shelling was, as one soldier noted, "painfully accurate … [they are] using trench torpedoes and shells of all kinds and sizes. Hundreds of shells must be bursting per minute. We must expect heavy losses." Casualties began to flow back to the casualty clearing station, where a medical officer recorded "cases of shattered nerves … [due to] some men being buried by shells" and "a number [of men] …coming in with chilled, sodden feet … [from] standing in water and mud for 48 hours [without relief]."[34]

The Canadians endured thirteen days of misery at St. Eloi, losing 1,373 men, including 619 from 6th Brigade.[35] Both 4th and 5th Brigades provided support to their comrades, sending carrying and working parties forward to help improve the defences. One 300-man strong detachment from the 24th Victoria Rifles suffered 7 fatal casualties and 20 wounded while performing this duty.[36] Battalions from both of these brigades relieved the 6th Brigade in the last phase of the battle, enduring more casualties.[37] After the battle, Turner and his divisional staff officers were severely criticized for their inability to resolve conflicting reports about who was where on a battlefield that resembled a water-saturated lunar landscape. Since it is not at all clear what difference it would have made had the actual positions been known, the real issue was one of responsibility for continuing an operation that again demonstrated you could not hold ground if the enemy concentrated a sufficient quantity of observed artillery fire upon it.[38]

Plumer saw it differently, insisting that the operation had failed because of serious command problems in 2nd Canadian Division. He ordered Alderson to take "severe disciplinary measures" and to fire both Turner and Ketchen. Alderson initially chose to make Ketchen the scapegoat, but when Turner refused to endorse an adverse report on his brigadier, Alderson asked Haig to remove both men for insubordination and incompetence. Alderson soon found himself up against a formidable foe, Sir Max Aitken, later Lord Beaverbrook, who was serving as Canada's special representative, publicist, and historian in France. Aitken had just published *Canada in Flanders*, a best-selling book that portrayed the Canadians in heroic terms. He was part of Winston Churchill's circle as well as a friend of Sam Hughes, and had no intention of allowing Canadians to be made scapegoats for British generals; he orchestrated a campaign to replace Alderson instead of the two Canadians.[39] Haig could not afford to allow a feud between British and Canadian generals to develop, and refused to dismiss Turner or Ketchen. In discussions with Aitken, Haig even agreed to remove Alderson if the Canadians could find a position for him. Alderson was informed that he was to become inspector-general of Canadian troops in England.[40]

The new Canadian Corps commander was Sir Julian Byng, a veteran of the South African war who had commanded the Cavalry Corps in France before earning good reports for his leadership in supervising the withdrawal from Gallipoli. Byng was the grandson of a field marshal and a prominent member of the English aristocracy. Like many other British officers, he retained his schoolboy nickname, "Bungo." His self-confidence and easy manner won him friends throughout the army, and especially within the Canadian Corps. Historians have repeatedly lavished praise on Byng as the single most important figure in transforming the Canadian Corps into a battle-hardened formation. Perhaps so, but upon his arrival in late May the problems confronting the Canadians could not be fixed by a Corps commander, however charismatic.[41]

When Byng took over the Canadians were defending a sector of the Ypres salient that included the only part of the dominant ridge still in Allied hands. Known as Mont Sorrel, the flat knoll included the slightly higher Hill 61 and "Tor Top," or Hill 62. From Tor Top "a broad span of largely farm land aptly named Observatory Ridge thrusts nearly a thousand yards due west between Armagh and Sanctuary Wood."[42] Despite the tactical importance of the position and detailed information about new enemy trenches or "saps" running directly to the front line on either side of Tor Top, neither army nor corps believed an attack was imminent, and on the night of 31 May the normal rotation of brigades brought the 8th Canadian Brigade forward, with two battalions up, to occupy 2,000 yards including Mont Sorrel.[43]

The 8th Brigade had been formed by converting the six regiments of Canadian Mounted Rifles (CMR) into four infantry battalions, known as the 1st, 2nd, 4th, and 5th CMR. Commanded by Brigadier General Victor Williams, a Boer War cavalry officer, the battalions had borrowed infantry instructors and worked hard to adapt to their new role. To the CMR's left the 7th Brigade held another 2,000 yards of front line. The 7th was a composite brigade stitched together to include the Royal Canadian Regiment, the only Permanent Force infantry unit, released from garrison duties in Bermuda; the Princess Patricias, reluctantly transferred from the British army; and two 1915 battalions, the 42nd Royal Highlanders from Montreal and the 49th from Edmonton. The 9th Brigade, in reserve on 2 June when the German offensive began, included the 60th Battalion Victoria Rifles from Montreal and three other units recently arrived on the continent. The divisional artillery was not yet formed, and support was provided by British artillery brigades formerly with the Indian army's Lahore Division.[44]

The divisional commander, Major-General Malcolm Mercer, who had led 1st Brigade at Second Ypres, was understandably nervous about the activity on his front and he decided to go and see for himself. Brig. Williams was with him when the German artillery began an intense bombardment. Mercer was killed and Williams taken prisoner, adding to the confusion created by the unprecedented scale of the German barrage, which turned the 8th Brigade's trenches into "a cloud of dust and dirt, into which timber, weapons and equipment and occasionally human bodies were hurled up."[45] Two battalions of the Canadian Mounted Rifles were reduced to "small, isolated bands of survivors … who could offer little effective resistance." On the Canadian left flank, in Sanctuary Wood, the Princess Patricias fought a delaying action that cost them 400 casualties. The 42nd Battalion was also heavily involved in what the men called "the June show," their first major action. Rushed forward to support the Patricias, who were cut off, they re-established contact and helped to close the gap that the enemy had opened. Their losses were 55 killed and 233 wounded.[46]

The next day, June 3, Lieut.-General Byng compounded the corps' problems by ordering an immediate counterattack. Two brigades from 1st Division were placed under the command of the senior brigadier in 3rd Division, who happened to be the commander of Lahore artillery. It is not clear why Byng thought an Indian army gunner was the best person to coordinate such an attack, particularly when employing battalions from Arthur Currie's division.[47] Presumably Byng thought that elements of 3rd Division would be involved and opted for Edward Hoare Nairne, the division's senior brigadier – seniority was a very serious matter in the British army. The advance was as disastrous as all previous attempts to counterattack without adequate preparation. All eight battalions suffered losses, but Montreal's 14th Battalion was the hardest hit. "Every officer taking part in the advance was killed, wounded, blown up or buried by shells." The next day two officers and fifty volunteers returned to the killing ground to search for wounded and recover the bodies of their comrades. Three of these men were killed, bringing total losses to 372 men, half the rifle strength of the battalion.[48] Few men were now left from those who had enlisted in 1914, and no attempt was made to re-establish the original composite character of the battalion with a French Canadian company.[49]

The 13th Battalion, which had been in reserve enjoying a sports day when the Germans attacked, was now committed to join a night advance in driving rain. Orders required each soldier "to carry 270 rounds of small arms ammunition, one day's rations, one iron ration, full water bottles, two grenades and five sandbags. Every second man will carry a shovel."[50] Byng, apparently sadder and wiser, began to plan an organized attempt to recover the lost ground. The Germans pre-empted him, exploding four large mines under the Canadian position at Hooge, then occupying the craters and rubble that were left. For once common sense prevailed and Byng won Haig's agreement to let the Germans keep Hooge and endure British artillery while everyone concentrated on recovering Mont Sorrel.[51]

Two composite brigades of the 1st Division were to attack, this time under Currie's control. After a ten-hour bombardment by more than 200 guns, followed by an intense concentration of fire to cover the approach and final attack, four Canadian battalions quickly recaptured the lost ground. Canadian casualties in the twelve days of combat totalled 8,340, of whom 1,126 were killed and 2,037 missing presumed dead.[52] This was a startlingly high ratio of killed to wounded, making June 1916 one of the most desperate months of the war for the Canadians.

Inevitably, neuropsychiatric casualties added to the toll, with 11.6 per cent of all admissions to medical units labelled as shell shock. Mark Humphries, who has systematically reviewed the available records of Canadian Army Medical Corps for his book *A Weary Road*, notes that 3rd Division suffered almost half of the corps shell-shock cases as well as hundreds of evacuations for exhaustion. Montreal's 60th Battalion, Victoria Rifles, which was supposed to lead Byng's ill-fated counterattack of 3 June, was shelled as it approached the forward trenches, and when it failed to advance was "hammered into pieces" under a torrent of high explosives. As many as 500 men, including 300 who "self-reported," reached medical units. Along with men from other units they were "kept for at least twenty-four hours, given warm baths, hot food and fresh clothing and after a period of sleep sent back to their units." The senior medical officer of 1st Division described such men "as suffering to a slight extent from shell shock but to a greater extent from exhaustion from the hardships they had undergone."[53]

The June battles, collectively known as Mont Sorrel, led to another clash between Canadian and British officers. The minister of militia gave an interview to an *Ottawa Journal* reporter criticizing the decision to hold the apex of the salient and allowed publication of a letter he had written Kitchener in March 1916 before the Canadians took over the sector. Hughes wrote that he had "met a number of Canadian officers" who stated that as "there are no proper trenches or protections, a complete new defensive line will have to be made." Instead of holding on to a position subject to fire from two or three sides they recommended, since "Ypres is no longer fit for habitation," that the new line should be straightened, taking in Ypres.[54] The prime minister shared Hughes's view of the battle and sent a telegram to Canada's high commissioner in London protesting the defence of a "dangerous and useless salient."[55]

The interview and letter were not the only critical commentaries published in Montreal. The *Gazette* carried a detailed account written by Lieut.-Colonel J.W. Bridges, who had returned to Canada after serving as the senior medical officer in 3rd Division. "The portion of the British front held by 3rd Division" was, he declared, "known as a death trap ... spread out like a fan into the German lines." If the enemy attacked "there was no way out, the retreat being smothered by shell fire while the other guns pound the front trenches."[56] There were of course articles casting the events in traditional terms with an emphasis on valour and worthy sacrifice, but there was no attempt to turn Mont Sorrel into the kind of moral victory that had characterized discourse about Second Ypres. Memorial church services were noticeably low key compared to those of 1915, and the long list of casualties, headed with the names of officers and other ranks from Montreal, must have shocked readers. Stories about individuals and families in mourning appeared for several weeks in late June. The deaths of both Major-General Malcolm Mercer and the Eastern Township's popular member of Parliament Lieut.-Colonel Harry Baker, killed at Sanctuary Wood when his Quebec-recruited Canadian Mounted Rifle battalion was overrun, were widely reported. Casualties to the Princess Patricias, who also suffered heavily at Sanctuary Wood, included men from the university companies sent over to reinforce the battalion after Frezenberg. For McGill University, June 1916 was the costliest single month of the war.[57]

The mood in the city did not augur well for the new battalions recruiting in the summer of 1916. The 244th Battalion, announced as "Kitchener's Own" after the iconic British field marshal drowned when the HMS *Hampshire* sank en route to Russia, was to be a third Victoria Rifles battalion, commanded by Lieut.-Colonel Frederick Mackenzie McRobie, a well-known Montreal sports figure. There was no difficulty in finding officers from the McGill Canadian Officer Training Corps and the militia, but despite a well-financed recruiting campaign across the province just 604 men were enrolled, half of whom listed next of kin in Montreal.[58] The 244th left for England in May 1917 to join the reinforcement stream.[59]

The 245th, Canadian Grenadier Guards, also competed for English-language recruits in the summer of 1916. The Guards persuaded Charles C. Ballantyne, the paint millionaire (Sherwin-Williams) to command the battalion, which had ample funds, $30,000, for a recruiting campaign. A history of the Grenadier Guards describes the results:

> Recruiting efforts were directed chiefly to Montreal and district, although recruiting parties were also sent to Quebec, Sherbrooke and the Eastern Townships. A committee of prominent business men ... was formed to assist recruiting but with the other infantry and specialist units being raised simultaneously in the district great difficulty was experienced in obtaining recruits ... Public meetings were absolute failures ... it was becoming abundantly clear that no further substantial response need be expected under the voluntary system.[60]

The Regiment reported that their officers and NCOs had personally canvased approximately 5,000 apparently fit and able men, persuading 1,200 of them to be examined by a medical officer. Of these, 490 were taken on strength to begin training at the Peel Barracks, the former Montreal High School. When the 245th left for England in April 1917 the unit had lost half its strength, with just 259 other ranks available.[61]

The idea of mounting a major offensive in the Somme River valley was first discussed in December 1915 when Joffre proposed a joint Anglo-French operation astride the river where the two Allied armies were in contact. The German assault on Verdun, which forced the French army to commit most of its strength to the defence of the "sacred ground," reduced the number of French divisions available, ramping up pressure on the British to launch an offensive at the earliest possible date. Kitchener's new volunteer army divisions were to provide most of the manpower.[62] Apart from the proximity of the two Allied armies, there was little to recommend the Somme as a battlefield, especially in the British zone north of the river, where rolling hills offered the Germans defensible reserve slopes and the chalk subsoil permitted the construction of deep dugouts. As one German general noted, "Everything that could be dug-in or placed underground, from spare ammunition to entire field kitchens, disappeared downwards."[63]

General Sir Henry Rawlinson, whose Fourth Army was to carry out the operation, had conducted a careful study of the German defences constructed since the occupation of the area in 1914. There were two main positions, with a third under construction. The first position included two thirty-metre-wide belts of barbed wire protecting an outpost line. Two hundred metres behind, the main defence line included well-built trenches and deep dugouts to protect the troops during bombardments. A support line still further back held local reserves in similar dugouts. The second positions, 3,000 metres to the rear, was on a reverse slope and visible only from the air. Here, three lines of trenches linking fortified villages and strongpoints presented a still more formidable obstacle. Rawlinson and his corps commander planned to wage a limited, step-by-step approach designed to overwhelm and consolidate the first position before continuing the advance.[64]

Haig rejected this plan as too cautious. He believed that German casualties at Verdun and a crisis in enemy morale that must surely follow meant a breakthrough was possible. He ordered Rawlinson to seize both positions on the first day and open up the way for exploitation by the Cavalry Corps. Rawlinson's corps commanders protested, arguing that "everyone was strongly opposed to a wild rush for an objective 4000 yards away"; the plan, they warned, risked "losing the substance by grasping at shadows."[65] Haig, whose decisions seemed to be based on intuition rather than evidence, was unmoved; the objectives and the artillery program targeting both positions remained unchanged, and the slaughter known as the first day of the Somme, when 19,240 British soldiers were killed and 37,000 wounded, began.[66]

Several days passed before the full extent of the losses suffered on 1 July were known in London, but there was no disguising the failure of the opening attack. On 2 July Haig was told that "total casualties are estimated at 40,000 to date." His diary entry for that date reads, "This cannot be considered severe in view of the number engaged and the length of the front attacked."[67] Rawlinson's Fourth Army continued to fight a series of costly engagements to secure the German second position, without much success. Even Haig's most ardent defenders were alarmed. The chief of the Imperial General Staff warned Haig that the cabinet "will persist in asking whether the loss of 300,000 men will lead to great results, because if not we ought to be content with something less than we are doing now."[68] Winston Churchill, who returned to England after serving at the front as a battalion commander, composed a confidential memo sent to the cabinet on 1 August, arguing that since the Verdun crisis was over and there was no question of breaking the line or letting loose the cavalry, what was the point of capturing more ground at such cost?[69] The government ignored Churchill and accepted Haig's recommendation to "maintain a steady pressure ... push my attack strongly" and prepare for another campaign next year. The Somme had been transformed into a purely attritional battle to kill Germans and demonstrate "the fighting power of the British race."[70]

The Australian branch of the British race suffered 23,000 casualties in August in a series of attacks on the Thiepval-Pozières section of the front. Exhausted, they were to be replaced by the Canadians, who began to arrive at the end of the month.[71] The sector was dominated by the ruins of Pozières, "a scrambled mound of red bricks, bristling with timber and torn fragments of homes, the whole half-buried under mud." Beyond the village a series of "sterile, shell-pocked ridges" stretched to the north, "above which floated countless observation balloons roughly paralleling the windings of the battle line. The rumble of gunfire was deep and steady." The 13th (Black Watch) Battalion was the first Canadian unit to be introduced to the Somme when it was tasked to support a last Australian attempt to secure one of the original first-day objectives, Moquet Farm, a heavily fortified strongpoint with deep underground tunnels. As the battalion historian notes, they were "thrown into a fight before they had any real conception of the area"; they fought with their "flanks in the air and under strange command until forced to withdraw." Just two companies were committed, perhaps 400 men, of whom 60 were killed, 16 recorded as missing, and 247 wounded.[72]

During the following week, as the Canadians relieved the Australians, a further 600 casualties were reported. By September 13, without further engagement in any significant action, the Canadian Corps' losses totalled close to 3,000 men,[73] not enough in Haig's view "to justify any anxiety as to our ability to continue the offensive."[74] Haig met with Byng to discuss the role the Canadians would play in the new offensive planned for 15 September. He urged Byng to "encourage his men so as to be fresh when an opportunity is offered to exploit our success." He also noted the "presence of comic posters" in the corps area announcing "the Byng Boys are here,"[75] a play upon the corps commander's name and the 1916 hit London musical that featured songs such as

"If You Were the Only Girl in the World and I Was the Only Boy." As the "Byng Boys," the Canadians were to join in another attempt to break through the German lines. Once again, General Rawlinson had prepared a plan designed to wear down the enemy in a "bite-and-hold" operation. He proposed a night attack with modest objectives, a pause to deal with enemy counter-attacks and advance the artillery, then a further advance as a means of attriting the enemy. Haig rejected this proposal, demanding a daylight advance so that a new and secret weapon, the tank, could be employed to demoralize the enemy. He told Rawlinson that "a success sufficient to repay all our great efforts made during the last 2½ months is now within reach" and urged "bold and vigorous action" preparing the way for a "large mass of cavalry" to exploit success.[76]

The Canadians, part of General Hubert Gough's Reserve Army, were also affected by Haig's optimism. Their original assignment, seizing the German position in front of Courcelette to protect the British flank, was in Haig's view too cautious, and Byng was told to capture Courcelette "on the afternoon of the first day as a prelude to a further advance."[77] Three Canadian brigades supported by six of the forty-nine available tanks were to capture Sugar and Candy trenches plus the fortified Sugar Factory, while 5th Brigade prepared to follow through and clear Courcelette. The 4th and 6th Brigades, advancing behind a creeping barrage, seized the trenches and the Sugar Factory, prized for its deep dugouts and abundant supply of drinking water, in the first hours of 15 September. The tanks played a minor role, all six being put out of action during the advance. The attack on Courcelette could not take place until the 15th Scottish Division captured Martinpunch, a village on the right flank. At 6:15 p.m., dusk in northern France, the 25th (Nova Scotia) and 22nd Battalions with the 26th New Brunswick in close support won the village, taking large numbers of prisoners. Then the really hard part began, as repeated German counter-attacks were launched from the maze of trenches north and east of Courcelette.[78]

For the next three days 5th Brigade held on to the Courcelette perimeter, which formed a salient into a maze of trenches, part of the enemy's original second position. On 17 September the 24th Battalion, in reserve, was ordered to try to improve the situation on the open right flank. Three companies were committed to the attack along with two understrength companies of the 22nd. As the troops formed up, the barrage that was supposed to neutralize the enemy "struck well behind the line," allowing the front-line garrison to pour aimed fire on the Canadians. The brigade's casualties now exceeded 1,200 men, reducing the rifle strength of each battalion by more than a third. The division as a whole had lost 3,589, killed, wounded, and missing, in the three days and was withdrawn for a short rest.[79]

Courcelette became a battle honour for all units involved in the fight for the village and was to become a name engraved on memorials across Canada, but in 1916 Max Aitken and his publicity machine associated the capture of the village with the 22nd Battalion. The 22nd had played a major role in se-curing the objective, but as the historian of the Nova Scotia battalion pointed out, "the 22nd took only half the town and the 25th the other fully equally and difficult half ... the 26th and 24th had an equally dirty job and did it just as well."[80]

The identification of Courcelette with the 22nd was encouraged by the need for French Canadian soldier heroes, who some believed could help to inspire recruiting. Thomas-Louis Tremblay, the battalion's commanding officer, was an obvious choice. Tremblay, just thirty years old in 1916, was a graduate of Royal Military College who served in the militia with the Franc-Tireurs du Sa-guenay while working as an engineer and surveyor in Quebec. He volunteered in 1914, serving as second-in-command of the 22nd until late 1915, when he was promoted. Tremblay, like most of the other officers of the battalion, was fluently bilingual, a necessity in an army that issued all order and instructions in English. He was well aware of the difficulties encountered by the other French Canadian battalions and understood the unique role the 22nd would play in 1916. When rumours of a German attack on the battalion's front were circulated he issued an order reminding his men "that we represent an entire race and that a great deal – even the honour of French Canada – depends on the way we conduct ourselves." After Courcelette all French Canadians, even the Bourassa nationalists, took pride in the achievements of Tremblay and his men, which were given abundant press coverage.[81]

The Battle of Flers-Courcelette was portrayed as a significant victory for Haig's armies, suggesting just how low the bar for success had been set. Un-fortunately, the capture of six square miles of shell-torn terrain, at a cost of 25,000 casualties, seems to have inspired Haig to believe that more such op-erations would break German resistance and allow his cavalry divisions to ad-vance "through mud and blood to the green fields beyond."[82] New attacks were ordered for 26 September to clear Thiepval Ridge. The Canadian objectives included a series of trenches on higher ground, including the ones they had named "Regina" and "Kenora," some of the deepest and strongest defensive positions on the Somme front. After two days of brutal combat the enemy gave up 800 metres of ground but not the crest of the ridge. The 14th Battal-ion, which had reached Kenora trench on the 27th and been pushed back, was told to try again. "The battalion, which after 40 hours of continuous fighting could only muster 75 men, attacked through mud and rain. As they neared the Kenora position the Canadians were brightly illuminated by enemy flares and became easy targets for the German frontal and flanking fire."[83] The Royal Montreal Regiment, which had suffered crippling losses at Mont Sorrel, would have to be rebuilt as part of the process of replacing the 6,000 men lost to 1st Division in September. The Princess Patricias, who had lost so many men at Mont Sorrel, experienced similar losses but there were "no more McGill or other university students" available so they had to make do with "indifferently trained" general reinforcements.[84]

According to Haig, "General Byng was disappointed that the Canadians had failed to hold the trench which they gained." Haig suggested that "the cause was that in the hopes of saving lives they attack in too weak numbers" and were unable to overcome fresh German troops in "hand to hand struggle." The Canadians, he complained "have been very extravagant in expending ammunition! This points to nervousness and low morale." Byng told Haig that he hoped for "good results when 4th Division arrives." The corps, he noted, had "suffered heavily and no sufficient drafts had yet joined them." Byng complained that Hughes wanted "the glory of having a Canadian Army in the field and is forming a 5th Division with the reinforcements."[85] Hughes was in fact refusing to break up battalions he planned to use for new Canadian divisions. He told his representative, Major-General Carson, to "stand firm. Let our divisions rest. We will get all six divisions in shape. Surely Byng cannot repeat June 3rd every month."[86] Haig took a different view; his diary entry for 20 October concluded with the comment that the 19,025 casualties suffered since 25 September "must be considered small by the results gained."[87] With such leaders the armies of the British Empire could only look forward to more blood sacrifices.

One 1 October battalions from the 2nd and 3rd Divisions returned to the attack with Regina Trench as their objective. As the men prepared to advance in a light, cold rain, the crucial barrage fell well short, inflicting friendly-fire casualties and inspiring the German defenders, who had little difficulty in fending off the attack. Yet another attempt was made on 8 October, this time with four brigades from 1st and 3rd Divisions. Some men made it through the uncut wire, but only the dead stayed to occupy the position. As one battalion commander complained, the wire might have been "passable" if the enemy trench had been "well battered in." Since little damage had been done, the "flimsiest wire" became an "impassable barrier."[88]

The arrival of the 4th Division allowed the rest of the corps to leave the Somme for the Arras front. Placing an untried Canadian division under direct British command with generals determined to continue the offensive was bound to produce a large number of casualties, and so it proved. On 21 October after days of continuous rain, the sky cleared and the battle for Regina Trench was resumed. The 11th Brigade, including Montreal's 87th Battalion, leaned into the barrage, seizing a six-hundred-metre section of what had become a faint ditch line, punctuated with water-filled craters. The men established an effective blocking position at the eastern end of the penetration and linked up with British troops on their left.. The Germans were still willing to mount local counter-attacks, and this time the 87th prepared an ambush, evacuating the trench and lying flat in open fields. The enemy suffered severe losses, but so did the 87th, which recorded 114 fatalities in the action.[89]

The rain continued, and it seemed as if general mud would put an end to this folly, but Haig met with his army commanders on 12 November to urge them to make one last effort to end the campaign with a dramatic victory. A success as this stage, Haig argued, would "encourage the Russians and help him to win support for a Flanders offensive in 1917." The next Allied conference was less than a week away, and the "British position will be much stronger (as memories are short) if I could appear there on the top of the capture of Beaumont-Hamel."[90]

Haig got his wish. After another costly attack British troops won control of Beaumont-Hamel; a key objective of 1 July was finally in British hands. On the Canadian front the 10th and 11th Brigades seized another stretch of Regina Trench, and after a pause went on to capture 1,000 metres of moonscape, including Desire Trench.[91] Among the thousands of additional casualties were 27 officers, 20 sergeants, and 467 other ranks of the Canadian Grenadier Guards, who as part of 11th Brigade were involved in two major actions.[92] The 73rd Black Watch Battalion served in an arduous but less dangerous supporting role and emerged from the Somme in much better shape. Their padre, who witnessed the agony of life and death in the landlocked lake of mud and blood, described the "incredibly folly" of the Somme in a letter home:

> How the nations and politicians happened to enter such an abyss is impossible to imagine. It is not the dying that is difficult for the men – it is the enduring – the ground work back of it all. The long interminable lines of haggard men coming out of the trenches, unshaven, covered with mud, staring dully in front of them, plodding through the mud and driving rain – telling the men, only a little less weary, who are trudging in the opposite direction to take their places – that is not so bad.[93]

During their three months on the Somme the Canadians suffered 24,000 casualties, a small part of the 420,000 killed, wounded, and missing under British command. Additional tens of thousands were lost, at least temporally, when evacuated for respiratory and other diseases, including shell shock, which had again reached epidemic proportions.[94] Haig and his supporters justified the costs of the campaign, claiming that they had achieved three important goals in 1916: relieving the pressure on the French army at Verdun, preventing the transfer of enemy divisions to the Russian front, and inflicting "well over 600,000 casualties" on the German army.[95] Any one of those three, he believed, justified the continuation of the Somme campaign.

Haig's critics challenge each of these assertions. Australian historians Robin Prior and Trevor Wilson, Haig's severest critics, note that the Somme was not planned with Verdun in mind, fifteen German divisions were transferred to the Eastern front, and British Empire casualties far exceeded those suffered by the

Germans in the British sector. "Every casualty inflicted on the Germans by the British cost them almost two casualties of their own," they conclude. "Haig was wearing out his own armies at a much higher rate than he was wearing down his opponents."[96]

This loss rate might be explained by the fact that it was British Empire troops who were attacking, but heavy losses such as those suffered on the first day of the Somme were also due to Haig's rejection of bite-and-hold tactics in search of a breakthrough. The same criticism can surely be offered of the repeated attacks on Regina Trench, ordered in circumstances that made success unlikely. Even the British official history, generally supportive of the decisions of the high command, commented on this:

> By the middle of October, conditions behind the battlefront were so bad that mere existence was a severe trial of body and spirit. Little could be seen from the air through the rain and mist, so counter-battery work suffered. Objectives could not always be identified from ground level, so it is no surprise that the British artillery sometimes fired short or placed its barrages too far ahead. The ground was so deep in mud that 10 or 12 horses were often needed to move one 18-pounder gun. The infantry, sometimes wet to the skin and almost exhausted before zero hour, were often condemned to struggle painfully forward through mud, under heavy fire, and against objectives vaguely defined and difficult to recognize.[97]

British historian J.P. Harris begins his "assessment" of Haig's conduct of operations in the Somme by arguing that while "the campaign deserves its reputation as one of the most ghastly episodes in modern British history: four and a half months of slaughter and suffering on an almost unimaginable scale," the Somme "wrested the initiative from the Germans on the western front." Haig, according to Harris, is "open to criticism less for his strategic intentions than for his operational methods." Even the "victory of Flers-Courcelette was marred by unnecessarily heavy casualties, the result of Haig's rejection of Rawlinson's plan for a step by step approach." Haig was "slow to realize the likely impact of climate" and acted as if "by sheer willpower" he could "overcome the frequent blindness of his artillery, the collapse of logistics and the misery of his infantry."[98]

Well before the full horrors of the Somme were realized, the British cabinet was confronted with proposals to consider the purpose of continuing the war. On 31 August 1916 Sir William Robertson, the chief of the Imperial General Staff, presented a memorandum suggesting that British foreign policy was historically based on three principles: the maintenance of the balance of power in Europe, maritime supremacy, and preventing occupation of the low countries by a great power. The first aim required the existence of a strong Germany, the second a check to the development of Germany's naval power, and the third German withdrawal from Belgium. Robertson recognized that French demands for the return of Alsace-Lorraine and German insistence on the return of her colonies would complicate negotiations for an armistice, but concluded that from a British perspective "the withdrawal of all enemy troops inside their pre-war frontiers," the "immediate release of all prisoners of war," and the "tentative surrender of a certain portion of the enemy fleet" were the minimum requirements for an armistice.[99]

The prime minister of France, Aristide Briand, also addressed the idea of an armistice in response to a speech by Pierre Brizon, a socialist member of the National Assembly, who argued for negotiations because France had suffered enough. Briand's emotional reply rejected all compromise: "What peace would you set for France? ... if you wish for the idea of liberty and justice to prevail, ask for victory and not the peace obtainable today, for that peace would be humiliating and dishonouring."[100]

David Lloyd George, who succeeded Kitchener as secretary of state for war, went even further than Briand in a September interview with an American reporter. He opposed any peace initiative at this stage of the war and warned the American president, Woodrow Wilson, against butting in "before we could achieve victory." This statement came to be known as the "knock-out blow," a commitment to total victory. At least one of his colleagues disagreed. On 13 November Lord Lansdowne, a former governor-general of Canada and British foreign secretary from 1900 to 1905, questioned the idea of the knock-out blow, asking the cabinet to consider the human cost of a war in which "our casualties already amount to over 1,100,000 ... We are slowly but surely killing off the best of our male population." We must, Lansdowne declared, be receptive to "any movement no matter where originating ... as to the possibility of a settlement." The foreign secretary, Edward Grey, thought that Lansdowne's proposal was premature but should be considered if it became evident the Allies could not further improve their position.[101]

Neither Lansdowne nor Grey survived the change in government of December 1916 that saw Lloyd George became prime minister and leader of a coalition dominated by Conservative Unionists. A War Cabinet of just five ministers was formed, each committed to an all-out effort to win the war. There was no hesitation in rejecting the proposal of an armistice announced by the German chancellor on 12 December. Bethmann-Hollweg believed that the war was all but won, and he offered "to stem the flood of blood and to bring the horrors of war to an end." No peace terms were included in the offer, though Germany and its allies "feel sure that the propositions they would bring forward ... would be such as to serve as the basis for the restoration of a lasting peace."[102] This transparent piece of propaganda was timed to divert attention away from President Wilson's plan to serve as a mediator. Wilson's note, dated 18 December 1916, with its unfortunate words declaring that the war aims of "the belligerents on both sides" are "virtually the same," was even more firmly rejected in London and Paris, though it did prompt formal statements of Allied war aims demonstrating just how impossible a brokered peace was in 1916.

Canadian reaction to the peace proposals was in lockstep with the opinions expressed in France and Britain. Even Bourasssa, who urged the Allies to "take Germany at its word, consider the terms and reject them if they were not acceptable," acknowledged that the Germans were offering peace because "they were in a stronger position than the beleaguered Allies."[103] The Canadian government was as usual uninformed and not particularly inquisitive. Borden was preoccupied with domestic issues, including a new confrontation with his minister of militia, which led to Hughes's resignation in November. During December Borden was on a fence-mending tour of western Canada, and his diary does not mention the German proposal and makes only passing reference to the American note. All that was about to change because Lloyd George decided to establish what came to be called an Imperial War Cabinet, and on 26 December Borden received an invitation to come to London and participate in "special and continuous meetings of the War Cabinet."[104]

Montreal rooftops. Archives de la Ville de Montréal, BM42-G1043

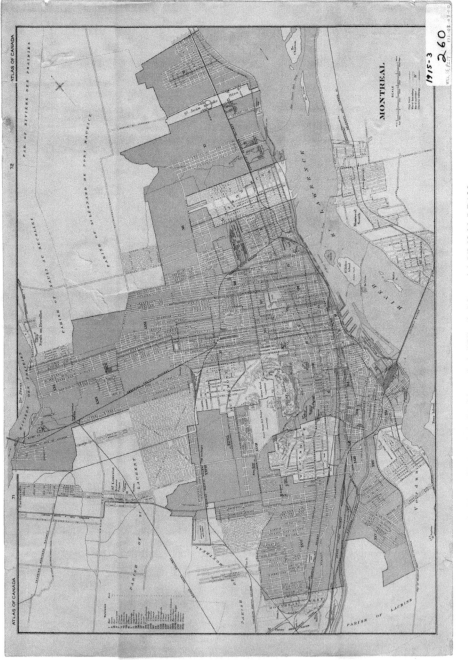

MONTREAL.

Montreal from Mount Royal, 1911. Wm. Notman & Son, McCord Museum,
VIEW-4886

Canadian National Railways tunnel, 1918. Wm. Notman & Son, McCord Museum,
VIEW-6422.1

Windsor Station, 1933. Montreal Gazette Archives

Archbishop Paul Bruchési. Library and Archives Canada, PA-030244

Workers construct tramway lines on Ontario Street, November 1912. Author's collection

Bonsecours Market, 1904. Wm. Notman & Son, McCord Museum VIEW-3729

His Majesty's Theatre. Bibliothèque et Archives nationales du Québec

Old Montreal. Archives de la Ville de Montréal, BM42-G1042

Henri Bourassa, 1917. Library and Archives
Canada, C-009092

Mayor Médéric Martin. Université de Montréal

The 24th Battalion marches through Montreal, winter 1914–15. Library and Archives Canada, PA-004918

The St. Julien Memorial. Gary Maavara

Lord Thomas Shaughnessy

Canadian Patriotic Fund poster. Library and Archives, e010697258

Assembly department, British Munitions Supply Co. Ltd., Verdun. Author's collection

Middle-class Montrealers crowd into the tram. Author's collection

Olivar Asselin

150th Mont Royal Carabiners recruitment poster. Library and Archives Canada, e010697097

ULSTER

CONNAUGHT

ALL IN ONE

LEINSTER

MUNSTER

OVERSEAS IRISH CANADIAN RANGERS 199

WITH THE

IRISH CANADIAN RANGERS

199TH OVERSEAS BATTALION

91 STANLEY STREET ✠ MONTREAL

Lt.-Col. H. J. TRIHEY. O.C.

fight for her

COME WITH THE

IRISH CANADIAN RANGERS

OVERSEAS BATTALION
MONTREAL

Lt.-Col. H.J.TRIHEY - O.C.

RIEL ET CASEMENT

BAPTISTE (tandis qu'on pend Casement) : C'est quasiment comme une autre affaire Riel, cette histoire-là. Riel n'a pourtant pas porté chance à ceux qui l'ont laissé pendre, à ce que je me rappelle.

Le Nationaliste, 6 August 1916

The assembled 199th Irish Canadian Ranger Battalion. Library and Archives Canada, PA-022670

Major Georges Vanier of the 22nd Battalion. Library and Archives Canada, PA-002777

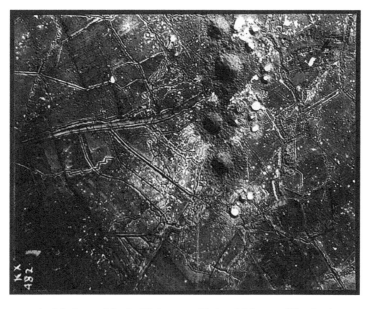

Aerial photo of the St. Eloi craters. National Library of Scotland

Ruins of the Sugar Factory captured by the Canadians during the Battle of Courcelette, September 1916. Library and Archives Canada, PA-001896

Canadian troops prepare to assault Courcelette. Provincial Archives of Alberta

Canadian troops advance through German lines at Vimy, April 1917. Library and Archives Canada, PA-001087

An anti-conscription demonstration, Victoria Square, Montreal, 1917. Library and Archives Canada, C-006859

French children march alongside the 14th Battalion (Royal Montreal Regiment) as it returns from the Battle of Hill 70, 1914. Library and Archives Canada, PA-001983

Canadian stretcher bearers move through the Passchendaele battlefield. Library and Archives Canada, PA-002367

1917 Anti-Liberal election propaganda. Library and Archives Canada, e008748929

Jewish-Canadian recruiting posters printed in English and Yiddish. United States Library of Congress

Allied tanks advance during the Battle of Amiens, August 1918. Library and Archives Canada, PA-002879

The Canadian Motor Machine Gun Brigade east of Arras, September 1918. Library and Archives Canada, PA-003398

The Canadians crossing the Canal du Nord. Library and Archives Canada, PA-003287

Conscription

Throughout the last months of 1916, Canada's prime minister was under pressure from organizations in Ontario and the west to recognize that the limits of the voluntary system had been reached and some type of compulsory military service was needed.[1] The argument in its simplest form was that with four divisions in the field the monthly "wastage rate" was roughly 6,000 men.[2] If less than 6,000 men volunteered each month, and a proportion of them were unfit for front-line service, the Canadian Corps would eventually wither away. When the Canadians moved to the Somme in September 1916 monthly losses doubled, creating a reinforcement crisis that left the infantry battalions severely understrength.

This was the common perception of the problem, but the reality was quite different. The wastage rate included large numbers of men evacuated as sick or wounded who would return to their units. Dr. Andrew MacPhail, who wrote the official medical history, suggested that 88 per cent of the non-fatal casualties eventually returned to duty.[3] It was also evident that large numbers of men, 130,000 at the end of 1916, were training in England and a further 30,000 were still in Canada.[4] The Somme reinforcement crisis had more to do with Sam Hughes's decision to hold back the best-trained troops to create a fifth and if possible a sixth division.[5] The battles of 1917 from Vimy Ridge through Hill 70 and Passchendaele did place considerable strain on the reinforcement system, but more than 84,000 men were sent to France from training camps in England during 1917,[6] none of them conscripts. Maintaining the combat power of four divisions – 67,000 men – was well within the capacity of the voluntary system until the "Hundred Days" offensive began in August 1918.

Borden understood the reality as well as the perception, and although he feared that "registration in the end means conscription and that might mean civil war in Quebec," he decided to create a National Service Board to gather information derived from the voluntary return of cards mailed to two million Canadians. Borden hoped that "an appeal for voluntary service would render unnecessary any resort to compulsion." After the announcement he approached Laurier, asking for his endorsement of the plan with the opportunity to nominate half the members of the board. Laurier declined, refusing further cooperation with the Conservatives. He would, he said, "continue to serve according to his own ways."[7]

The data from national registration would not be available until well into the New Year, but in the meantime Borden gathered his courage and forced the resignation of the minister of militia. With Sam Hughes gone, the reorganization of the department and the overseas army administration could proceed quickly, and although the prospect of employing a fifth division was kept alive, the necessary reinforcements reached France in time to rebuild the Canadian divisions for their part in the 1917 spring offensive.[8]

Next on the agenda was a well-publicized national recruiting campaign, which began in Montreal. Borden met with Archbishop Bruchesi, winning his support for registration by promising that the cards were not intended and would not be used to implement conscription. A public meeting at the Monument National provided the prime minister with a polite hearing, but his cabinet colleague E.L. Patenaude and the director of national registration, the future prime minister R.B. Bennett, were interrupted and heckled, especially by students from the nearby Montreal campus of Laval University.[9]

After a meeting in Quebec City Borden spoke to large audiences in Ontario and the west, winning grudging approval from pro-conscription groups, who accepted registration as a step towards their goal. When pressed by representatives of organized labour, Borden refused to renew his promise to stick to the voluntary system. "I hope," he told Trades and Labour Council officials, "that conscription may not be necessary but if it should prove the only effective method to preserve the existence of the state and of the institutions and liberties which we enjoy I should consider it necessary to act accordingly."[10] Borden did not explain exactly how the "existence of the state" would be protected by finding another 100,000 men to fight in Flanders, but few English-speaking Canadians cared about such details.[11]

The sudden death of Thomas Chase Casgrain,[12] Borden's senior Quebec minister, forced the prime minister to find a replacement from his dwindling French Canadian caucus. Casgrain, whose Conservative credentials dated back to his role in the prosecution of Louis Riel, had used his newspaper *L'Événement* to support the war effort and the Conservative party cause, making him a controversial figure in Quebec. The man selected to replace Casgrain in the cabinet, Albert Sévigny, was one of the most ardent of Bourassa's supporters in 1911, but he quickly abandoned his nationalist politics, endorsing Borden's naval policy and serving as Speaker of the House of Commons. Sévigny's appointment as minister of inland revenue required a by-election, and initially Laurier was inclined to continue the political truce, allowing an acclamation.

Fears that a nationalist candidate might appear and local pressure to nominate the formidable provincial member for the riding, Lucien Cannon, persuaded Laurier to change his mind. After a series of public debates (*assemblées contradictoires*), Sévigny's promise to continue to provide "great material advantages" to the county convinced a majority of voters to stick with the Conservatives.[13] Montreal's newspapers followed the contest closely, with the nationalist and Liberal press attacking Sévigny mercilessly.[14] The Conservative victory was difficult to explain, but it was evident that rural Quebec, or at least Dorchester County, was not yet caught up in the anti-government sentiment prevalent among the urban French Canadian elite.

Borden, reassured by Sévigny's victory and the generally positive reaction to getting rid of Sam Hughes, asked for an adjournment of Parliament while he attended meetings of the Imperial War Cabinet in London. The new British prime minister, David Lloyd George, had established a five-person war cabinet, which together with a permanent secretary was supposed to streamline management of the war. He also decided to invite the Dominion prime ministers and a representative of the twenty-seven "large native states" in India to come to London "to be more formally consulted as to the progress and course of the war" and "the steps that ought to be taken to secure victory."[15] The presence of a "representative" of India and separation of the meetings of the real War Cabinet from the imperial version clearly demonstrated the limitations of the system, but as Craig Brown, Borden's generally sympathetic biographer, notes, the Canadian prime minister had his own agenda. He recognized that Lloyd George was seeking "more troops in return for consultation," but since Borden was already "rock solid" on sending more men he could use the Imperial War Cabinet to pursue his own ideas, including a voice in imperial policy, the direction of the war, and the possible conditions for peace. Borden's other wish list involved enhancing the prospects of Confederation with Newfoundland and Canadian control of the British West Indies.[16] He also wanted to escape from the problems of governing Canada and concentrate on larger questions, assuming the role of an international statesman.

None of these things were of much interest to Montrealers, who were hunkering down to survive another winter. The first three months of 1917 provided them with daily mean temperatures well below freezing. On 3 February the thermometer dropped to 23 below, causing a disruption in train and tramway service.[17] The weather made life especially miserable for the men, women, girls, and boys involved in an ongoing conflict in the city's clothing industry. Gerald Tulchinsky argues that when wages failed to keep pace with the rising cost of living, the ground was prepared for a "new and more radical industrial union" – the Amalgamated Clothing Workers of America.[18] The Amalgamated established locals in Montreal during the 1915 and was able to win union recognition and wage increases with two companies the following year.

A third attempt to unionize the large Semi-Ready Factory, which was producing soldiers' uniforms, met resistance from the owners and the newly formed Montreal Clothing Manufacturers Association (MCMA), created to develop a common front in the growing confrontation with the union. The president of the MCMA, Lyon Cohen, was both a factory owner and a prominent member of the "uptown" or "west-end" Jewish community, an indication of the differences between the experience and values of established Jews and their working-class co-religionists.[19]

The Semi-Ready strike was marked by violence against both picketers and strike-breakers, with the police intervening to support the "scabs" entering the plant. Sidney Hillman, the Amalgamated's president, on a visit from New York described "scenes of uncommon hardship ... in temperatures of twenty below zero." The picket lines, he wrote, "were filled mostly by young girls who came out at six in the morning."[20] These young girls, largely French Canadian, and the skilled Jewish workers were determined to prevail, and by mid-January 4,000 were on strike. The MCMA took out newspaper ads in both French and English charging the union with an attempt to control the work process and diminish production.[21] After repeated attempts at mediation failed and smaller firms began to settle with the union, "the longest, most bitter and probably most violent strike in the history of the Canadian needle trades industry" ended with a compromise that allowed the MCMA to avoid dealing with the Amalgamated while accepting the recommendation of a board of inquiry for "a 48 hour week, a one dollar across the board increase and the recognition of shop committees."[22]

The Semi-Ready strike was the only major labour action of 1917 in Montreal, accounting for most of the days lost in the last three years of the war. The climate of labour relations was shaped by the demands of the war economy. Few employers could afford to allow their operation to be interrupted, and they bought peace with modest wage increases that were quickly wiped out by the rising cost of living. The typical family that could be fed, clothed, and sheltered for $14.15 in 1915 required $21.24 by the end of 1917 – a 50 per cent increase.[23]

The Montreal Trades and Labour Council (MTLC), the local branch of the American Federation of Labour and Trades and Labour Council of Canada (TLC), used its weekly *La Monde Ouvrier/Labour World* to denounce profiteering and the government's inability to check the rise in the cost of living, but the Dominion government lacked the capacity as well as the will to intervene. The MTLC represented about 35,000 workers, largely in the skilled trades, and was consequently a moderating rather than a radicalizing force in the city. The executive did support the idea of independent labour political action, and when the TLC endorsed the Canadian Labour Party Montreal labour leaders agreed.[24] They had long endorsed direct political action, supporting Alphonse

Verville, the member of Parliament for Maisoneuve, who regularly tried to win parliamentary support for an eight-hour day, and Joseph Ainey, a member of the city's Board of Control and Labour candidate for mayor. Both men were essentially Laurier Liberals who marched on Labour Day but stayed clear of the various ethnicity-based socialist groups on May Day.[25]

Escape from the city's conflicts came in the form of familiar seasonal attractions. The movie palaces and vaudeville theatres flourished, as did stage plays, concerts, and hockey leagues. The Montreal Canadiens were playing in what proved to be the last season of the National Hockey Association. The "Flying Frenchmen," as the English-language press insisted on calling the team, led by Newsy Lalonde and Georges Vézina, won the Stanley Cup in 1915–16 and were equally successful in the first half of the new season, playing against the Montreal Wanderers, Quebec Bulldogs, Ottawa Senators, and two Toronto teams, the Blueshirts and the 228th Battalion.[26] Both Toronto teams withdrew from competition before the second half of the season began, and Ottawa dominated the four-team league. All of this provided sportswriters and fans with much to talk about, as did on-ice violence, which seemed to reach a new peak. Penalties for tripping, slashing, and fighting were so common that many games featured a continuous parade to the penalty box. The eastern final, a two-game total-point series between Ottawa and the Canadiens, was especially rough, with Lalonde suspended for game two. The final match, played in Ottawa before 7,000, was described as the most violent and gruelling game of the season. Ottawa won but without scoring enough goals to overcome the deficit from the first game in Montreal. The Canadiens therefore travelled to Seattle to unsuccessfully defend their Stanley Cup title.[27]

Among the other activities that drew attention away from the war was the annual Montreal automobile show, held in January. One-third of all automobiles on the road in the United States were registered in 1916, and the proportion was similar for Canada. Everyone interested in this fascinating new technology was confident that sales in 1917 would exceed the previous record, and there was enormous competition between established brands like Ford and dozens of rival companies. The Montreal show featured the Chalmers, made by Allis-Chalmers, the Marmon, Maxwell, McLaughlin, and the Stanley Steamer as well as many other names that would soon disappear. The excitement all of this caused is evident in the newspaper coverage of the show and the follow-up stories and advertisements.[28]

There was also a great deal of news about the war to report, with information and speculation about the German and American peace notes of December 1916 and the statements of war aims from Britain and France issued in the new year. The German announcement of unrestricted U-boat warfare and the subsequent movement towards a declaration of war by the United States in early April were much discussed, as was the first Russian revolution, the abdication of the czar, and the formation of the Kerensky government in March.[29] What was missing from the news reports was information about the Canadian Corps, which from December 1916 to April 1917 were holding a quiet sector of the front near Arras and preparing to play a major role in the spring offensive with an attack on the formidable defences of Vimy Ridge. Large-scale raids and normal trench warfare losses continued to produce casualty lists, and those with Montreal next-of-kin were regularly highlighted, but the numbers were relatively small.[30] These personal tragedies did not lend themselves to public demonstrations of collective mourning. One issue that did gain attention was the threat to the survival of the city's front-line battalions. One or more of them, the *Star* reported, would "be swallowed up ... if enough recruits do not go forward from this district."[31] The *Gazette* highlighted the problem, noting that as of 30 March 1917 Quebec province had enlisted 44,427 men compared to more than 120,000 for Ontario. Military District 4, encompassing Montreal, contributed 36,282 to the Quebec total, but this figure faded in comparison to Toronto's contribution. Overall, one in three men in the age group had volunteered in Ontario compared to one in seven in Quebec.[32] The figure for Toronto was one in two.[33]

While Montrealers debated national registration, professional hockey, the rising cost of living, and the first signs of a coal shortage, the Canadian Corps was preparing for its part in the 1917 campaign. A young, dynamic, and fluently bilingual French general, Robert Nieville, who had organized innovative operations in the last phase of the fighting at Verdun had replaced Joffre as commander-in-chief of the French armies. His plan for the April offensive required the full support of Haig's army to draw reserves away from the French front.[34] The battle of Arras was to involve fourteen British and Canadian divisions on a frontage of similar length to the Somme battle of 1 July 1916.

The Canadians, now part of Lieut.-General Henry Horne's 1st Army, were to capture Vimy Ridge and hold it against all counter-attacks as a firm defensive flank for the main advance by the 3rd British Army. The four Canadian divisions were each allocated a sector of the 7,000-yard front. To the south 1st Division on 3rd Army's left faced the lower slope of the ridge, while at the north end 4th Division confronted the highest ground, including Hill 145 where Vimy Memorial stands. Giving the least experienced division the most difficult task does not seem to make much sense, nor does the decision to order Major-General Watson to launch the largest Canadian raid of the war a month before the opening of the Arras Offensive. The raid was a disaster. The artillery failed to cut the wire; the barrage fell short, striking the advancing troops; and gas from shells fired at the Germans drifted back on the Canadians.[35]

Montreal's 73rd Royal Highlanders was one of the attacking battalions, despite or perhaps because of plans to break it up for reinforcements. With Sam Hughes gone and a more systematic regime installed at Canadian Military

Headquarters in London, reserves were grouped corresponding to military districts in Canada. It was quickly evident that there were not enough replacements for English-speaking Montreal units, and both the 73rd and 60th were to be used to reinforce their sister battalions from the city.[36]

The Battle of Vimy Ridge began in earnest on 20 March when the artillery began to fire the first of more than one million shells directed at the German defences, creating a "pock-marked wilderness of mud-filled craters." On 2 April the rate of fire was stepped up for what the German soldiers called "the week of suffering."[37] As the men moved into position,

each man carried his rifle and complete equipment less pack, 120 rounds of small arms ammunition, 2 Mills bombs (grenades), 5 sandbags, 48 hours rations, unexpended portion of current ration, waterproof sheet, box respirator (gas mask) worn at the alert, smoke helmet, goggles, 1 ground flare and filled water bottle. In the case of bombers, rifle grenadiers, Lewis gunners and runners small arms ammunition was reduced to 50 rounds to permit the carrying of special equipment or to aid rapid movement. Warrant officers and NCOs were instructed to carry rifles and fixed bayonets and officers were to equip themselves with revolvers and signaling pistols. All ranks were ordered to wear steel helmets and half the battalion was to carry forward 33 picks and 67 shovels.[38]

At 5:30 a.m., 9 April 1917, after a hot meal and a rum ration, the attack began[39] as "a driving north-west wind swept the countryside with snow and sleet."[40] On the 1st Division front the slope of the ridge was barely noticeable; Currie's division advanced with six battalions, following a creeping barrage through acres of mud, seizing the first and most of the second German lines before confronting serious resistance from well-sited machine guns in the undamaged shelter of a German strongpoint. As the reserve brigade passed through, advancing down the eastern slope of the ridge to the final objective, stretcher bearers worked to save the wounded. Victory came with a price; the experience of the Royal Montreal Regiment – 98 killed and 176 wounded[41] – was particularly severe. Overall, the division suffered more than 3,000 casualties in a four-day period.[42]

The 2nd Division, supported by a British brigade, and the eight tanks made available to the corps also met resistance at the intermediate line. Montreal's 24th Battalion, with a company of the 22nd attached as "mopper uppers," lost 250 men in securing its objective.[43] On the 3rd Division front progress was rapid but by mid-day, as the men consolidated their gains, German strongpoints that had survived the barrage as well as snipers exacted a terrible toll. On the left, where the problems encountered by the 4th Division in front of Hill 145 presented 7th Brigade with an open flank, losses were especially severe. In total, the division reported 1,913 casualties.[44]

By the standards of any previous First World War battle the 9 April assault on the south and central portions of Vimy Ridge was a spectacular success, but this was not the case on the northern flank, where the 4th Division suffered heavy losses and failed to reach all its objectives. The 87th Canadian Grenadier Guards were especially hard hit, advancing uphill over broken ground against enemy troops who had survived the bombardment in deep dugouts. The 87th lost 309 officers and men, close to half their strength.[45] Hill 145 was captured the next day, and by 12 April the entire ridge was in Canadian hands. Brave men, supported by the massive application of firepower, had won a significant victory, one that was immediately celebrated as "Canada's Easter gift to France."[46] Eight battalions originally recruited in Montreal were part of that victory.

News about the battle for Vimy Ridge began to appear on 10 April, and for the next week stories about the "Canadian triumph" appeared daily in both the English and French popular press. Most were credited to Stewart Lyon, a Canadian Press correspondent and former managing editor of the *Toronto Globe*. The Canadian success at Vimy was linked to the British advance from Arras, but the seizure of Vimy Ridge was reported as a singular victory, and both British and American newspapers were quoted praising the Canadians. The *Montreal Witness* issue of 17 April carried many of these stories, but the editor's own summary began with an account of the British heavy guns collected in back of the Canadian front "to pound the German trenches of Vimy Ridge into unrecognizable form." Since casualty figures had not yet been released, the article suggested that there were only "slight losses" when the Canadians "charged the hill." Other articles credited to Phillip Gibbs and official British sources emphasized "the outstanding gains" made by the Canadians and their success in "outfighting both the Bavarians and the Prussians."[47]

La Press, *La Patrie*, and *Le Canada* translated the Lyons and Gibbs dispatches, adding their own take on the events. On 14 April a *Le Canada* editorial titled "Courcelette et Vimy" praised the "glorious part" played by French Canadian volunteers in the battle, noting that "our heroes of the 22nd were not alone in overcoming the Germans as many of our French Canadian volunteers were with other units. Canadians of both races fought side by side."[48]

When the casualty lists began to appear in late April the *Star* and *Gazette* printed capsule biographies of Montrealers killed or wounded alongside the lengthy casualty lists. By the end of April, 11,776 were known to be killed, wounded, or missing. According to press reports, 370 men from Montreal were included in the total, but a review of the war diaries of battalions originally raised in the city offers a "rough count" of 1,500, including 305 dead, an indication of how many listed their next of kin in Britain or other parts of Canada.[49]

Casualty lists demonstrating the scale of losses to the Canadian Expeditionary Forces did not lead to talk of conscription. Instead, Montreal newspapers focused attention on a new recruiting campaign launched by Pierre-Edouard Blondin, the postmaster-general, who left his cabinet post to raise the 258th (French Canadian) Battalion. Blondin declared that it was time for him to go to the front "with those of my age and race who to honour the Province of Quebec are offering their blood for the defence of rights and ideals."[50] Together with Major-General F.L. Lessard, the highest-ranking officer of French Canadian heritage, Blondin began a tour of the province seeking recruits. Battalion headquarters was located at the Peel Street barracks in Montreal, and a cadre of officers and NCOs began to take shape. All of the city's daily newspapers except *Le Devoir* actively supported the battalion, which received financial support from Montreal and Toronto businessmen. Blondin suggested that his battalion would become part of a French Canadian brigade, soon to be established, though it is unlikely that he or anyone else believed this to be likely.[51] He was able to announce that the sons of two prominent Liberals, Rodolphe Lemieux and Charles Murphy, were joining the 258th as lieutenants, adding a bipartisan note to recruiting. Leading Liberals joined Conservatives on the platform for a recruiting meeting in Montreal's Monument National, but constant interruptions from young men in the galleries created what *Le Canada* described as "disgraceful and regrettable scenes."[52] The well-publicized visit of General Joffre, "the Hero of the Marne," to Montreal was also linked to the Blondin-Lessard campaign, as was the National Unity Convention,[53] an outgrowth of the Bonne Entente movement. These efforts collapsed after 18 May when Borden rose in the House of Commons to announce his plan to introduce "selective compulsory military service" and conscript 50,000 to 100,000 men.[54]

While in England Borden had repeatedly sought information on the numbers of new recruits, the results of the national registration, and the progress of attempts to release men already in the army for overseas service through the formation of a Home Defence Force.[55] Enlistments in January had totalled 6,690, the best record since the summer of 1916. More than 10,000 more men enlisted before the Vimy battle began, raising the strength of the CEF to 304,585.[56] Nevertheless, the news that National Registration reported close to 300,000 men of military age not engaged in essential occupations was enough for Borden. Upon his return to Canada he told his cabinet and then the House of Commons that he was "responding to a call from the wounded, the men in the trenches and those who have fallen to obtain the necessary reinforcements" to maintain the Canadian army in the field as one of the finest fighting units in the British Empire.[57]

The conscription decision had been the subject of rumours since early May, but it still came as a surprise. Reaction in Montreal split along predictable lines. The English-language press endorsed the government's decision, as did the reliably Conservative *La Patrie*. No one doubted the reaction of the nationalists but both Bourassa and Omer Heroux avoided comment until

28 May, when Heroux's front-page editorial explained that Bourassa was examining the issue with his customary care. The next day Bourassa published the first of nine articles on conscription, offering historical background, reminders of past warnings, and vigorous condemnation of British imperialism both at home and abroad.[58]

Laurier's response to Borden's announcement surprised his friends and foes. His statement that "a good deal of consideration must be given before traditional policy [voluntary service] is set aside"[59] was followed by weeks of discussions with Borden over the prospect of a coalition government. Laurier appears to have strung out the negotiations, buying time to gain support for his own policy – a referendum and, as *Le Canada* reported, "giving public opinion time to be heard."[60] *Le Canada*, the semi-official newspaper of Montreal Liberals, did not wait for Laurier to condemn conscription. The editor challenged the prime minister's belief that there was a reinforcement crisis, declaring that since four divisions required just 60,000 men and the strength of the army was now 300,000, enough men were available to sustain the Canadian Corps.[61]

With both Laurier and Bourassa maintaining silence and Archbishop Bruchesi protesting in private letters to Borden, the leadership vacuum was filled by younger men vying for influence in the streets of the city. The most ambitious of these new leaders, Tancrède Marsil, was a fringe journalist currently publishing *La Liberté*, a nationalist weekly. He was also the principal speaker at large rallies held at Parc Lafontaine and elsewhere in the city and was said to be "at the head of a movement to prevent the enforcement of conscription."[62] A number of Liberals, including members of the provincial legislature and Mayor Méderic Martin, also participated, but their message was to remain peaceful and wait for Laurier. Violence erupted on the night of 24–25 May with surging crowds of young men breaking windows and clashing with the police.

Historian Serge Marc Durflinger has recently examined the "protests and public disturbances" that rocked Montreal throughout the summer of 1917. They were, he writes, "characterized by almost nightly gatherings ... acts of violence against individuals and property, sporadic displays of gunfire (normally using blank ammunition) ... and increasingly inflammatory, seditious and even rebellious public rhetoric."[63] Durflinger argues that after the initial flurry of protest the situation calmed down until the actual introduction of the Military Service Act on 11 June. Tancrède Marsil was soon back in action, claiming the leadership of a new organization, Les Fils de la liberté,[64] but there were now many would-be leaders to rouse demonstrators.

The most sensational account of the anti-conscriptionist movement was published in the *New York Times* on 23 July. The reported quoted Elie la Lumiere, a young activist who claimed "he was ready to form an army and already had 500 men drilling." Military intelligence officers dismissed such claims, and Sir Percy Sherwood, chief commissioner of the Dominion Police, said he had someone in the membership of every radical organization and was confident that there was no sign of any armed uprising. The *New York Times* continued to report all kinds of rumours, including "that cruisers have been dispatched to those waters with considerable forces of marines." The chief censor, Ernest J. Chambers, was outraged, but his notice to Canadian editors to suppress such rumours arrived too late to curb the press. Chambers complained to the American government's Committee on Public Information, condemning "penny-a-line correspondents of US newspapers in Canada of retailing for their papers all sorts of highly coloured and exaggerated stories." He urged the US authorities to "do a good turn for our common cause" by informing American editors that these stories were "grossly exaggerated" and "suspected of being of enemy origin."[65]

Civil disobedience with mass meetings and minor violence continued through the summer, but after Laurier committed the Liberal Party to opposing conscription most French-speaking Montrealers rallied behind the Liberal leader. Both Premier Gouin and Rodolphe Lemieux added their voices, as did a number of English-speaking Quebec Liberals, including Sydney Fisher, the former minister of agriculture, and W.G. Mitchell, the provincial treasurer.[66] This did not mean an end to unrest in the streets, but as the *Montreal Witness* warned, the significance of these activities was subject to interpretation. Under the heading "News Is Not Always What It Seems" a reporter suggested that reports of a crowd of 3,000 at a recent rally were somewhat exaggerated. Less than a thousand were present, he declared and 40 per cent of those appeared to be curious onlookers.[67] Certainly the *Gazette* and the *Star* never missed an opportunity to offer detailed reports on the rhetoric used by the young orators, while *La Presse* and *Le Canada* played down or ignored the demonstrations.

It was difficult to ignore the explosion that rocked suburban Cartierville in the early hours of 9 August. A large bundle of dynamite, stolen from an east-end quarry, blew the corner off the summer residence of Lord Atholstan, who as Sir Hugh Graham had used his newspapers – the *Star*, *Standard*, and *Herald* – to support win-the-war policies, including conscription. Both he and his family escaped injury. *La Presse* carried the story on its front page, as did Atholstan's own newspapers. The pursuit, capture, and subsequent trial of the "dynamitards" was too good a story for any newspaper to resist, and coverage was extensive.[68]

Protests continued throughout August, culminating in a "Lafontaine Park Declaration" "issued on the day before the Military Service Act became law. The signatories claimed that they would use violence to prevent the implementation of conscription and declared that 'if the Conscription Bill is enforced, Borden and his men will have to suffer the death penalty.'"[69] The next day began with the accidental shooting of an eighteen-year-old by one of his friends who was learning to use a revolver and concluded with a riotous march broken up by police with truncheons and revolvers.[70] Durflinger suggests that by September "the spark seemed to have gone out of the demonstrations as arrests, more aggressive police tactics and perhaps the fact conscription had been made into law dampened the ardour of the anti-conscriptionists."[71]

Despite riots, rumours, and organized violence, the Dominion government and the Montreal police acted with restraint throughout the summer of 1917, contributing to the decline in street protest. Of equal importance in restoring peace was the growing consensus on the need to support Laurier as the unchallenged leader of French-speaking Quebec. Bourassa and his nationalist allies were among those who swallowed their pride, put aside their egos, and accepted Laurier's dominant role.[72] Laurier avoided a break with Liberals in Ontario and the west by conceding the legitimacy of their pro-conscription views while insisting that official Liberal candidates accept the policy of holding a referendum.[73]

Laurier was also able to win over a significant number of Montreal's Irish Catholics who had previously supported their cabinet representative, C.J. Doherty, the minister of justice. When Dr. J.J. Guerin, the last English-speaking mayor of Montreal (1910–12) and a former provincial Liberal minister, organized a meeting at St. Ann's Hall in the heart of Griffintown, a large crowd turned out to applaud an anti-conscriptionist message and to endorse Laurier.[74] The audience was said to be composed of young men who were likely influenced by the publication of an interview given by Henry Trihey, former commander of the Irish Canadian Rangers, to the *New York Evening Post*, which was reprinted in most Montreal newspapers.

Trihey began with an account of the recruitment and break-up of his battalion and then offered additional reasons for Irish Canadian discontent:

> The Irish Canadian realizes what he formerly heard but did not appreciate that Ireland is under martial law and is occupied by an English army. He reads in the press that English soldiers are in Dublin and Cork with rifle and machine guns. The Irish Canadian believes Ireland to be a small nation worthy of freedom. He wonders if the conscription of 100,000 Canadians would still be necessary if the 150,000 men comprising the English army in Ireland were sent to fight in France. He wonders where Canadians may best maintain the war purpose vital to Canada – small nations must be free. If conscription becomes law of course Irish Canadians will loyally observe the law for they are Canadians.[75]

The interview created a tempest in Ottawa, requiring Doherty to intervene on behalf of his friend, but in Montreal Trihey's words gave expression to the feelings of many Irish Catholics.

The vote on the second reading of the Military Service Act on 5 July 1917 was a shock to Montreal anti-conscriptionists. Frank Oliver, MP for Edmonton, and Charles Murphy, spokesman for Irish Catholics in Eastern Ontario, were the only prominent English-speaking members to oppose the bill. Twenty-six out of thirty-eight English Canadian Liberals voted with the government. Laurier was not ready to concede defeat. When Ontario Liberals met on 20 July the pro-conscription, pro-coalition forces were overwhelmed by those who supported Laurier and a referendum. A similar grass-roots movement turned a western Liberal convention intended to promote both conscription and coalition into "a bomb that went off in the hands of its makers" as a large majority endorsed Laurier.[76]

Montrealers played no significant role in the protracted negotiations to establish a Union Government. Borden was determined to bring conscriptionist Liberals into a coalition before calling an election, and he did not hesitate to use the Conservative majority to pass two laws designed to persuade reluctant Liberals to join a Union Government. The Military Voters Bill allowed all those serving in the Canadian military to vote in whatever constituency they indicated, for either the government or the opposition. The parliamentary debate considered the possibility of votes being directed strategically, but no one anticipated the level of dishonesty later displayed by Unionist election organizers.[77] The second measure, the Wartime Elections Bill, described by *Le Canada* as even more outrageous, was introduced on 6 September. The wives, mothers, widows, sisters, and daughters of Canadians serving in the military or who had served overseas were to have the vote, while all persons of any enemy alien birth or who spoke an enemy alien tongue, and were naturalized after 1902, were disenfranchised unless they had sons, grandsons, or brothers serving overseas. Arthur Meighen, the solicitor general, defended the legislation, declaring that "the franchise depended on war service," and he relentlessly advanced the case for rigging the election. He told the House:

> If it is true, and apparently it is true, if hon. gentleman opposite are [*sic*] right –
> that the majority of women of this country whose near relatives are overseas,
> those who spend their days in anxiety and their nights in tears will support us and
> those who of our population are likely to favour the enemy, will reject us[,] then
> in the name of the government which has been striving for three years to fight that
> enemy, I accept the compliment.[78]

The War Times Election Act became law after the government invoked closure to break the opposition of a temporarily united Liberal Party. Once it passed, Liberal unity gave way as conscriptionist Liberals recalculated their chances of electoral success under the new franchise. Within days they were competing with each other for positions within a Union Government, where they would be "outnumbered and unranked"[79] but electable. The Laurier Liberals now faced near-certain defeat and began to focus their attention on what could be saved. Liberal candidates still loyal to the leader were told that they could run on a pro-conscription platform so long as they did not endorse Borden or the Union Government.[80]

Women's groups were divided in their response to the government's selective enfranchisement, especially in Montreal. Historian Tarah Brookfield has examined the complexities of the situation, describing the very different responses of the Féderation National St. Jean-Baptiste and the Montreal Council of Women. The Féderation opposed both conscription and the partial franchise while the Council of Women ended up accepting both measures, despite opposition from its president, Dr. Ritchie-England, who endorsed Laurier and actively campaigned for the Liberals. Brookfield describes the controversy stirred by Ritchie-England's role in the election, noting the critical letters to the editor published in the *Star* and *Gazette* as well as the resolution of the Montreal Women's Club calling for her resignation. The controversy did not end with the election, but an attempt to replace Ritchie-England as president failed to secure a majority.[81]

The Montreal Trades and Labour Council was also divided by deeply held positions on conscription. Gustav "Gus" Francq, the editor of *Le Monde Ouvrier/Labour World* and one of the best-known figures in the city's labour movement, was Belgian by birth and firmly committed to "conscription in its most complete form known as the best means to ensure our national safety and future welfare." Francq had considerable support from British-born trade unionists but was "deposed" as secretary of the Montreal Council when his own Typographical Union local "called for a vote of censure and cut him off as their delegate."[82] Francq continued to support conscription, running advertisements in *Le Monde Ouvrier/Labour World* for Union Government.

Overseas, the British Expeditionary Force had embarked on a new offensive in the Ypres sector, which Field Marshal Haig declared was designed to clear the Belgian coast. The chief of the Imperial General Staff, Sir William Robertson, and the British cabinet accepted Haig's plan on the understanding that the purpose of the offensive operations was now

> no longer a question of breaking through the enemy's front and aiming at distant objectives. It is now a question of wearing down and exhausting the enemy resistance ... relentlessly attacking with limited objectives and making the fullest use of our artillery. By this means we hope to gain our ends with the minimum possible loss.

No one addressed the contradiction between Robertson's caution and Haig's ambitious distant objective – the Belgian coast.

The offensive, officially known as Third Ypres but forever associated with the village of Passchendaele, was preceded by a successful attack on Messines

Ridge, which overlooked Ypres and the British lines. Haig interpreted this minor victory as a sign of German exhaustion, arguing that Germany was within six months of total collapse, and on 31 July the main offensive began. German resistance was formidable, with no signs of collapse, so Haig ordered the First British Army to mount diversionary operations in the Arras area to draw German reserves away from Ypres.

As the most powerful corps in the First Army, the Canadians were ordered to attack the coal-mining town of Lens. Arthur Currie, who had succeeded Julian Byng to become the first Canadian to command the corps, planned to secure Hill 70, the high ground north of Lens, using artillery to destroy German attempts to regain the hill. Despite heavy rain that postponed the attack, rehearsals were carried out as in the preparations for Vimy. The first phase of the August battle, capturing and defending Hill 70, was a considerable success: the artillery "smashed the ground and the German counter-attacks to pulp."[83] With both 1st and 2nd Division holding Hill 70, the German army employed a new and terrible weapon introduced at Ypres in July. On 17 August their gunners fired fifteen to twenty thousand shells filled with an oily liquid that turned to a mustard-smelling gas on impact. The gas could burn exposed skin and do serious damage to the eyes and throat. Fortunately, the medics were prepared for mustard gas, and if men could reach a field ambulance, they were stripped of clothing, bathed in soda solution, and carefully treated for swollen eyes, which were washed and covered with gauze. John Singer Sargent's famous painting depicts men who had been treated and were moving to the rear.[84]

Historians Douglas Delaney and Serge Durflinger have edited a book of essays on the capture of Hill 70, inspired by the campaign to create awareness of what is described as an important but forgotten battle. Contributors to the book recognize the very different character of the two phases of the operation: the seizure of Hill 70, in military terms a brilliant victory; and the subsequent attempt to capture Lens, a hastily improvised attack that produced some of the hardest fighting the corps had ever known. Philip Gibbs, the British war correspondent, described Lens as "a charnel house" with "roofless buildings and gaping walls packed with German soldiers fighting from tunnels amid the rubble."[85] The German Sixth Army suffered heavy casualties in the defence of Lens, where "entire city blocks were destroyed" and "shell hole joined shell hole," but they held against the "best English attack troops, the Canadians."[86] Recently a new and impressive memorial was inaugurated near the start line for Hill 70 in Loos. Memorial plaques have also been placed within Lens commemorating a very different experience of war, which historian Geoff Jackson has described as a "bloody setback" that "no amount of rationalization can obscure."[87]

All of Montreal's seven remaining infantry battalions (the 60th and 73rd were disbanded before August) were involved in the fighting at Hill 70 or Lens, sharing in the very heavy casualties experienced by the corps. More than 2,000 men were killed in action during August, with 6,677 wounded or missing. Montreal newspapers carried the usual heroic stories from Canadian Press as well as Gibbs, but also continued to publish the daily list of casualties with a note on the number from Montreal. On 27 August, in "the heaviest list since Vimy," 41 of the 788 losses had next of kin in Montreal; the next day the toll was 35 out of 661; and on the 29th, "the heaviest list on any one day," 1,028 men, 60 from Montreal, were recorded. The *Gazette* was careful to separate the number of those killed in action from the wounded, and as the losses continued to mount it noted that on 30 August, when 55 Montrealers were on a list of 766 men, only one had died and overall fatalities were just 1 per cent.[88]

Despite the scale of losses to the Canadian Corps there were enough reinforcements immediately available in England without taking men from the 5th Division.[89] Neither the newspapers nor the Borden government advertised this, as their eyes remained fixed on the longer term. The war, Borden believed, would last into 1918 and perhaps beyond, so conscripts would surely be required, especially if the Canadian Corps was drawn into Haig's offensive in Flanders. October was the third-worst month of the war for the British army, with losses reaching towards the numbers recorded at the Somme in July 1916.[90] If this was not bad enough, the news from the Eastern Front was bleak and then, on 27 October, the joint German-Austrian offensive at Caporetto crushed the Italian army, creating a crisis situation that forced the British and French to respond.

Haig had opposed sending guns or troops to Italy before Caporetto, and he continued to argue that further action in Flanders would better assist the Italians. He ordered the Canadian Corps to join the offensive, replacing the exhausted Australians for another attempt to seize the higher ground at Passchendaele. Arthur Currie, ordered to submit plans for the capture of the village, developed a step-by-step approach based on a series of 500-yard "bites" with pauses for consolidation and replenishment of the artillery. A great deal of engineering work was required to build roads and one way duck-board routes, raised above the mud- and water-filled shell holes.

The first Canadian advance began on 26 October with battalions of the 3rd and 4th Divisions forming up in countryside that had been "reduced to an unrecognizable waste of ridge and hollow … half the area in front of Passchendaele was covered with water or deep mud."[91] Currie, on first seeing the ground, noted in his diary that "the battlefield looks bad. No salvaging has been done and very few of the dead are buried."[92] Despite the conditions, the assault battalions of both divisions reached their objectives. The second phase began on 30 October with 1st Division joining in. Finally on 6 November the ruins of Passchendaele were in Canadian hands. Reaching the ruins of the village allowed Haig to claim victory and end the offensive without revealing that most of the ridge was still in German hands, leaving the Canadians in a "very bad salient" under "the most severe and violent" artillery fire ever experienced.[93]

The British offensive in Flanders was a major story in Montreal newspapers in the summer, but by October the endless struggle over the same few miles of mud was of less and less interest. The arrival of the Canadians in the bloody salient with place names familiar from 1915 and 1916 revived journalistic interest, but the new Canadian Press war correspondent, Walter Willison, son of the proprietor of the *Toronto News*, offered little beyond the conventional platitudes. After the first Canadian advance readers were told the Canadians had "covered themselves with glory" but there was no analysis of the task before them.[94]

Casualty lists were slow in coming, perhaps because of the number of men missing, lost in the mud, but on 6 November newspapers reported the "Heaviest List of Casualties since Lens," and the public was warned that the list of 357 men, eight from Montreal, was the first of "extensive lists to come." Censors prevented information about the use of mustard gas from reaching the public, but on 9 November the 643 casualties included "a large number who had been wounded or gassed." By late November, the local newspapers had identified more than 400 men from Montreal who had been killed, wounded, or gassed.[95]

The only hint of dissatisfaction with British strategy and generalship at Passchendaele came when Canadian newspapers reported on the controversy in England that followed upon the British prime minister's Paris speech of 11 November. Lloyd George, in arguing for the creation of an Allied Supreme War Council to direct strategy, had indirectly criticized the British army. The Conservative press in England, sensitive to any slighting of its heroes, demanded that Lloyd George "exonerate Haig and Robertson" from all such criticism.[96] Lloyd George agreed to devote a day in Parliament to a debate over the direction of the war and overcame his critics with a memorable speech defending the new Supreme War Council. As usual, no one consulted Canada and no Montreal editors or politicians offered opinions on the dispute.[97]

The Military Service Act, which established "classes" of men who could be called up by order-in-council, was implemented on 13 October 1917, when Class I men, single or widowers without children ages twenty to thirty-four, were ordered to appear before medical boards and exemption tribunals. It soon became apparent that those who supported conscription did not intend to allow themselves or their children to become soldiers. Nationally, 93.7 per cent sought exemption, with the Quebec total at 98 percent.[98] Borden and his colleagues began to panic. Would men from the English-speaking provinces who were determined to avoid military service vote for the Unionists in the December general election? Action was required and, as historian John English has written:

> Borden adopted what Richard Hofstader in another context has called the "paranoid style"; the opposition is conceived of as an evil conspiracy acting to

undermine the nation, hence unusual measures are acceptable. The interests of the nation were ever more closely linked with the interests of Unionism. Thus [review] tribunals were instructed to be exacting when applying the guidelines for exemption in Quebec where Unionists had little chance, and to be flexible in the Unionist stronghold of Ontario.[99]

A more flexible exemption policy in Ontario failed to stem anxiety in rural areas, and the minister of militia, General S.W. Mewburn, "tried to quell the storm of protest" by promising to exempt farmers' sons, a commitment that was then embodied by an order-in-council two weeks before the election. Taking no chances, Borden authorized an aggressive Unionist campaign portraying Bourassa and Laurier linked together as "traitors."[100] There was little point in extending such a campaign to Quebec, where few ridings were in play, but both the *Gazette* and *Star* echoed this theme. Unionists hoped to re-elect H.B. Ames and C.J. Doherty and win a seat for a Liberal-Unionist, minister of marine C.C. Ballantyne, in the three ridings with reliable Anglo-Celtic majorities. Albert Séveigny and Pierre-Edouard Blondin had abandoned hope of winning their rural Quebec constituencies, so they also sought election in Westmount-St. Henri and Outremont-Laurier respectively. Few observers gave them much chance.

French-speaking Montrealers were uniting behind Laurier and the Liberal Party, accepting his decision to support the war effort while insisting on a referendum before further proceeding with conscription. When Laurier announced a wide-ranging platform that addressed railway nationalization and other issues, his words on the war and conscription were closely monitored. His declaration that he would appoint "the ablest men in the country to his cabinet" so that "Canada could find the men, money and resources to ensure the fullest support for our heroic soldiers at the front"[101] was coupled with a promise to accept the results of a referendum on conscription whatever the outcome. Bourassa's two-part commentary on "le programme de M. Laurier" tried to identify the nationalists with parts of the manifesto but noted that Laurier still "glorified the war" and failed to understand the dangers of more voluntary enlistment.[102]

Patrice Dutil and David Mackenzie, who have published the most detailed account of the 1917 election, note that the Liberals were anxious to distance themselves from Bourassa because of the "negative effect on Laurier's campaign in English Canada." The *Toronto Globe*, once the party's stalwart supporter in Ontario, speculated that Bourassa would be named to the cabinet if Laurier won and did not hesitate to use the slogan "A vote for Laurier is a vote for Bourassa is a vote for the Kaiser." Laurier responded with an attempt to persuade *Le Devoir* to attack the Liberals more vigorously, but both Bourassa and Heroux continued to offer qualified support to Liberal candidates.[103]

Rodolphe Lemieux, Laurier's faithful lieutenant who was running in Maisonneuve as well as his home riding of Gaspé, orchestrated the campaign in Montreal marginalizing both the Bourassa nationalists and the young activist groups. Lemieux, with a son serving in the 258th Battalion, made sure the Liberals avoided the bitter anti-British, anti-war discourse of the nationalists. Premier Gouin was also determined to distinguish the Liberals from the nationalists, emphasizing Quebec's support for Victory Loans, the Red Cross, and the Patriotic Fund.[104] Newspaper coverage of the election followed predictable lines: the *Star*, *Gazette*, *Herald*, and *Standard* supported the Unionist "Win the War" cause while *La Presse*, *Le Canada* and, in a sense *Le Devoir* supported Laurier. *La Patrie* largely ignored the election, though it carried ads for Blondin and Séveigny. *Le Canada* was transformed into the Liberal party's campaign newspaper, with added columns in English since all the English-language newspapers backed Borden and the Unionist candidates.

Reviewing the daily and weekly newspapers, one is struck that, with the exception of *Le Canada*, relatively little space was devoted to the election, presumably because the results were a foregone conclusion. The war in France, Italy, and the Middle East dominated the front pages, with particular attention to Palestine and the British entry into Jerusalem. Inside the newspapers readers could enjoy the local news, several pages of sports stories, and extensive entertainment coverage. The Halifax Explosion, 6 December 1917, was on the front page for several days, with follow-up stories as the scale of a disaster that took two thousand lives became apparent.[105]

The "Lansdowne Letter," published in the London *Daily Telegraph* on 29 November, made public the views that Lord Lansdowne had presented to the British cabinet in 1916. He now urged the British and French to coordinate their war aims with the policies of the American president and explore ways of ending the war through negotiation.[106] Unionist supporters in Canada, like their counterparts in Britain, were outraged by Lansdowne's views, but the French-language dailies provided supportive coverage. Bourassa insisted that the letter, written by an Ulster Protestant, was a paraphrase in political language of the most recent papal peace proposal.[107] The most thoughtful account was written by Eve Circé-Coté in *Le Pays*. Writing under several pen names, Circé-Coté was a regular contributor to *Le Pays* and after 1916 *Le Monde Ouvrier*. As a progressive-liberal and Francophile, she initially supported Canada's participation in a just war fought in defence of Belgium and France, but as the war continued her views gradually changed. By 1917 Circé-Coté, writing as "Fantasio," was questioning the costs of the war and joining her compatriots in opposition to conscription. For her, Lansdowne's letter held out hope of ending a war that seemed to threaten humanity.[108]

There were few surprises on election day. A Unionist majority based on an almost solid Ontario vote and equally one-sided result in the west gave Borden and his colleagues a mandate without needing the soldiers' vote. In Montreal Ames, Doherty, and Ballantyne won their ridings, with all other urban and rural seats in Quebec going to Laurier. Doherty's victory in St. Anns raised questions about Irish Canadians, but since they were small minority of voters in a constituency that included the British immigrant community in Verdun, historians dispute the meaning of the result. *Le Canada* insisted that the Irish polling stations gave a majority to the Liberals, and Matthew Barlow in his study of Griffintown, "The House of the Irish," agrees.[109] Perhaps so, but without a more rigorous study based on polling stations and the street directories we will never know.

A similar problem exists in analysing the Jewish vote in Montreal, which was split between several ridings. Did the large majority of voters in Geroges-Etienne Cartier vote for S.W. Jacobs, KC because he was a Laurier Liberal opposed to conscription or because he was Sam Jacobs the lawyer who had won the Plamondon libel case in 1914? The pages of the *Canadian Jewish Chronicle*, published weekly in Montreal, allow us to follow the events in the community. From the earliest days of the war through the agonies of the following years the newspaper endorsed Britain's war policy and Canada's involvement. Women's organizations from the Council of Jewish Women to the Young Women's Hebrew Association raised money for the Patriotic Fund and created committees to encourage knitting and sewing circles.[110] The *Chronicle* echoed the reservations all Jews shared about Britain's alliance with Czarist Russia, providing regular news about the fate of Jews in Eastern Europe and helping to raise funds for the relief of Jewish "war sufferers." One debate that divided the community was whether to encourage enlistment in existing battalions or to establish Jewish units. The *Chronicle* favoured integration, but when in 1916 a "Jewish Reinforcing Company" was established there was broad support. Captain Isidore Freedman, an officer in the 6th Duke of Connaughts' Hussars, was asked to recruit "five officers and 250 men from among Montreal Jews who were British subjects."[111] Since the vast majority of the city's Jews were not yet British subjects and many of those who were had already volunteered, Freedman faced a difficult task. When the draft sailed for England in March 1917, the company numbered three officers and eighty-three other ranks.[112]

Recruiting for the Reinforcing Company may also have been influenced by competition from the Jewish Legion, an international military unit that would serve with the British army in the campaign to free Palestine from Turkish rule. One of the four Royal Fusiliers battalions that served in the Middle East, the 39th, was made up of North American volunteers including as many as 350 to 400 Canadian Jews.[113]

During 1917 the focus of the *Chronicle* shifted to the prospects of fulfilling the Zionist dream after the British liberation of Palestine. Well before the Balfour Declaration of November 1917 Montreal's Jews were rallying to the

Zionist cause, promoted by Clarence de Sola and other community leaders.[114] When the British foreign secretary visited Ottawa in the spring of 1917 his invitation to de Sola to discuss the future of Palestine was major news.[115] Preparations for the 1917 Canadian Zionist Federation convention included attempts to broaden representation and encourage as many as possible to travel to Winnipeg and participate in what was seen as a significant moment in the struggle to establish a Jewish homeland.[116]

The *Chronicle* generally ignored the issues raised by the introduction of conscription. A brief editorial argued that terms like "conscription" and "compulsion" were too negative and disruptive and suggested instead the use of the American term "draft." A second comment, printed after the Military Service Act became law, declared that "Canada will now be able to fulfil its promise to the mother country of securing half a million men" and noted that "we will be called upon to demonstrate our loyalty in still greater numbers – we are ready."[117] Apart from a mild rebuke to French Canadian street activists who had chanted "conscript the foreigners," the *Chronicle* ignored the election, certain that Sam Jacobs would be victorious. A portrait of Jacobs with the title "First Canadian Jew elected to the Federal Parliament" was the only election news published by the *Chronicle*.[118]

Election day in Montreal was remarkably calm; the police, out in force, reported no significant incidents at the polls or in muted victory celebrations. Laurier, at age seventy-six, was still on a train, returning from an exhausting ten-day tour of western Canada where large crowds had gathered to hear him speak. As the results came in and the extent of the Unionist victory became clear Laurier remarked, without rancour, that westerners had "cheered for me but they didn't vote for me."[119] Neither had the once-reliable back concessions in south-western Ontario. The large Unionist majority demonstrated the determination of British, Protestant Canada to support a win-the-war government that would impose its will upon all dissenters.[120]

The Unionist majority of 45 in a Parliament of 235 members meant that the much-disputed soldier's vote would have a marginal effect on the results. In the end fourteen additional ridings, including Frank Oliver's seat, Edmonton West, were added to the Unionist total. Desmond Morton, who has provided the most balanced account of the voting overseas, agrees that "massive organized vote switching" did occur but adds that most of these ballots were not counted. He concludes that the soldiers "voted with grim cynicism and without much thought for Canadian unity or French Canadian disaffection."[121]

Chapter Seven

1918

For Montreal, as for much of Canada, 1918 proved to be a difficult year marked by political crises, rampant inflation, coal shortages, and a deadly flu epidemic. For many French Canadians the imposition of conscription, after what most saw as a rigged election, was a special source of bitterness. Isolated, without representation in the federal government or allies in the other provinces, they saw their mood crystalized three days after the election when a member of the provincial assembly, J.N. Francoeur, gave notice of a motion to be introduced in January that read:

> That this house is of the opinion that the Province of Quebec would be disposed to accept the breaking of the Confederation Pact of 1867 if in the opinion of the other provinces it is believed she is an obstacle to the union, progress and development of Canada.

The Francoeur motion was debated in both the legislature and the newspapers, but apart from *La Croix*, which had been advocating separation for some months, the consensus was that Francoeur was providing an opportunity to express the anger and frustration felt by many French Canadians. Premier Gouin brought the debate to a close in a widely reported speech on the advantages of Confederation to Quebec. He declared that if he had been present in 1864, when the negotiations over Confederation began, he would have argued for the same protection for the French Canadians of Ontario that was obtained for the English minority in Quebec. If, however, "I did not succeed I would have still voted for the Federation pact." Gouin went on to describe the benefits of Confederation, especially for Montreal, and the necessity of Quebec supporting the 500,000 French Canadians in other provinces. After the war ends, he argued, the language question in Ontario as elsewhere will settle itself:

> We complain of insults, of appeals to prejudice, but our fathers always suffered from those things. For sixty years they have been constantly used for party ends.

These appeals pander to the appetite for power and the lust for patronage ... We have been insulted, it is true, but I persist in believing that it is not by the majority but by a small number. I believe the majority of people in this country are good people ... I am proud of my name of Canadian, proud of my country Canada.[1]

At the conclusion of Gouin's two-hour speech, Francoeur withdrew his motion, bringing the debate – though not the conflict – to an end.

One reason for the moderate tone of the debate was the growing awareness that very few men were being conscripted. Ninety-seven per cent of the 115,602 men from Quebec required to register in late 1917 sought exemptions and, as the newspapers regularly reported, both the local and appeal tribunals were accepting the vast majority of exemption requests. Setting aside the 1,888 men who joined the army voluntarily after registering, just 3,681 requests were rejected by the local tribunals.[2] Eventually, after Central appeal judge Lyman Duff intervened, 10,691 men from Quebec were refused exemption, but this process was strung out over many months.[3] As Laurier told a correspondent who had voted for Borden because of the need for "speedy reinforcement of the army":

The conscription measure was introduced in the first week of June. We are now in the third week of January and not ten thousand men, if indeed half that many, have been brought into the ranks by this measure. By next June you will not have one conscripted man across the ocean.[4]

Laurier exaggerated. The first Quebec conscripts, drawn from the men who had voluntarily reported, were part of a draft sent to England in February 1918. *Le Canada*, in reporting their departure, complained that the conscripts were denied the opportunity to even say goodbye to their parents.[5]

If newspaper coverage is an appropriate gauge of public interest, it is necessary to remind ourselves that the Francoeur debate and reports on the progress of exemption tribunals competed for space with other events. The church sponsored La ligue antialcoolique and the Montreal branch of the Dominion Alliance had long fought to bring prohibition to Quebec, and in early 1918 it appeared as if victory was in sight.[6] Most rural municipalities and small towns had adopted prohibition by local option, as had Quebec City, but Montreal remained stubbornly "wet." The Gouin government's decision to impose prohibition on Montreal through provincial legislation provoked a considerable backlash from citizens as well as organizations such as the Brewers Association and the Montreal Trades and Labour Council.[7] On 12 February 1918 the provincial treasurer, Walter Mitchell, introduced a bill tightening existing regulations and announcing that total prohibition would be enforced from 1 May 1919 after existing stocks of liquor were exhausted. In his remarks Mitchell said the bill was required as the Dominion government had outlawed the production of alcoholic beverages as a war measure. The legislation sparked an intense campaign to allow beer, wine, and cider to be sold, an issue finally resolved in 1919 by allowing a referendum on the question.[8] (The beer, wine, and cider side won.)

Montrealers also focused on an even bigger automobile show and their winter passion for hockey. The 1917–18 season was the first year of the new National Hockey League, but the war and a disastrous fire threatened its survival. Quebec City's team had disbanded before the season began, and on 2 January the Montreal Arena burnt down, destroying the equipment of both the city's teams. The Wanderers gave up, their players joining the three remaining clubs. The Club de Hockey Canadien was now everyone's team, with a roster of both French- and English-speaking players.[9]

Fires were frequent occurrences in Montreal, especially in winter, but no one was prepared for the tragedy that overwhelmed the city on 14 February 1918. The Soeurs Grises or Grey Nuns had been active in caring for citizens since the eighteenth century, and their building in the west end was one of the largest in the city. In 1918 the sisters were providing accommodation and care for wounded veterans as well as seniors and a large number of illegitimate and abandoned children. The fire, later determined to have been deliberately set by a deranged worker,[10] drew all available fire engines and thousands of spectators alerted by the wail of sirens heard throughout the city. Both the seniors and veterans were escorted to the nearby Montefiore Club that served as a temporary evacuation centre. The fire was concentrated on the ward where the babies were sleeping, and while some were rescued at least fifty-three died of smoke inhalation or burns.[11]

Newspaper coverage included pictures of the ward with its long row of cots, prompting various responses. Archbishop Bruchesi organized a diocesan-wide fundraising campaign for the sisters to rebuild, prompting *Le Pays* to suggest that an investigation of the conditions was required before money was raised.[12] The *Montreal Herald* drew attention to an article published in the popular American magazine *Literary Digest* titled "The Cradle Is More Fatal than the Trenches." The author calculated that babies born in the United States were seven times more likely to die in their first year than a British soldier in trenches of the Western Front, and 50 per cent of these deaths were easily preventable.[13]

The *Herald* noted that public interest in the loss of fifty-three babies in a fire was not matched by concern over the city's notorious infant mortality rate, with one in every five newborns dead before their first birthday.[14] Edouard Montpetit, an economist and nationalist intellectual, elaborated on this theme in an address to L'Assocation des femmes d'affaires. Montpetit titled his talk "La Veillée des berceaux" (the watch over the cradle), a reference to a recent article by Louis Lalande SJ, who used the phrase "La Revanche des berceaux" (revenge of the cradle) to describe the need to maintain a high birth rate, promote colonization, and avoid distractions such as feminism.[15] Montpetit, one of the more data-oriented nationalists, agreed with Lalande about the necessity of maintaining French Canada's high birth rate but argued that it is "not the babies born but the babies saved that will ensure our survival." He calculated that despite the decline in infant mortality in the past decade, a Montreal newborn was nine times more likely to die than a soldier in the army.[16] The Municipal Board of Health Report for 1918 emphasized the declining rate of infant deaths, noting that "in 1918 there were 20,373 live births and the number of children saved was 1,379 compared to 1908," but the deaths of some 3,488 babies, most of them in their first year of life, was still too easily accepted.[17] It took until the mid-1920s to enforce the pasteurization and inspection of all milk sold in the city. This, together with new methods in the treatment of gastroenteritis in children, finally brought the infant mortality rate down to closer to the Canadian average.[18]

Throughout the winter of 1917–18 the daily newspapers printed dispatches from the Associated Press and other agencies that offered readers a remarkably detailed and reasonably accurate picture of events in the wider world. Woodrow Wilson's "Fourteen Points" speech of 8 January was well received, with the *Gazette* reporting that Canadians were reassured "the United States will stand with the Allies to the end."[19] The protracted negotiations between Germany and the new Russian government were linked to the prospect of the transfer of German divisions to the Western Front and the likelihood of a major spring offensive. Trotsky's February declaration that Russia was no longer at war – no war, no peace – and the German attempt to underwrite an independent Ukraine were detailed, as were the terms of the Treaty of Brest-Litovsk. Editorial writers insisted that the harsh terms of the treaty ended any prospect of a negotiated peace in the West and informed readers of the likelihood of a new and powerful German offensive in the west employing divisions transferred from the Eastern Front.

The prospect of more costly battles forced both the British and Canadian governments to re-examine their manpower policies.[20] British divisions were reduced in size by removing one battalion from each brigade and using the men to bring the remaining nine battalions to full strength. The War Office wanted the Canadians to adopt the new order of battle and send two additional, small divisions to France.[21] The corps commander, Currie, was totally opposed to the proposal even though it would lead to the establishment of a Canadian army of two corps that Currie would command. His counterproposal was to use the men from 5th Division, still training in England, to increase the combat strength of the front-line battalions and create additional engineer and machine gun units.[22] Borden refused to disband the division before the election, avoiding opposition from the troops and from Sam Hughes, whose son commanded the formation. With the election won, Borden was content to follow Currie's advice.

The newly strengthened Canadian Corps was holding the Vimy sector when on 21 March the long-anticipated German offensive began. With an additional 500,000 men transferred from the Eastern Front and specially trained and equipped divisions, the German army struck at the British Fifth Army. Outnumbered eight to one, the British yielded ground and thousands of prisoners. Survival depended on the arrival of Allied reserves.

The French provided Haig with nine divisions while additional men in Britain, training or on leave, were rushed to France.[23] By 27 March, with the Germans approaching Amiens, the possibility of separating the British and French armies galvanized Allied resistance. Haig agreed to the appointment of Foch as commander-in-chief of the Allied armies. Fortunately the German offensive was bogging down, and Germany's supreme war lord, Erich Ludendorff, decided on a new attack south of Arras. Infiltration tactics and surprise won early tactical success, leading Haig to issue a dramatic order of the day:

> Every position must be held to the last man: There will be no retirement. With our backs to the wall and believing in the justice of our cause, each one of us must fight on to the end ... Many amongst us are tired. To those I would say that victory will belong to the side that holds out the longest.[24]

The Canadian Cavalry regiments and elements of the Motor Machine Gun Brigade were involved in the defence of Amiens, but the Canadian Corps played a modest role in this period, extending its line and temporarily providing divisions to assist the British. According to Haig, Currie's attempt to retain all four divisions under his command created serious problems for the British. Currie, he noted in his diary, "wishes to fight only as a Canadian Corps ... As a result the Canadians are together holding a wide front near Arras but they have not yet been in battle." Two weeks later, after a meeting with Edward Kemp, Canada's overseas minister of militia, he wrote, "I could not help feeling that some people in Canada regard themselves as 'allies' rather than fellow citizens of the Empire."[25]

Newspaper coverage of the German offensive was on the front pages of most Montreal newspapers from 22 March on, though other issues competed for public attention. The death of John Redmond, the leader of Ireland's home rule movement, was deeply felt in the city's Irish community, leading to the decision to cancel the St. Patrick's Day parade, scheduled for the week after his funeral.[26] Lloyd George's proposal to extend conscription to Ireland and stories about the reaction in Ireland were widely reported, with inevitable comparisons to the situation in Quebec.[27] The introduction of legislation to establish daylight savings time produced a major controversy in Quebec as well as the rest of Canada. Montrealers, like most urban dwellers, generally favoured the measure, which became law despite opposition from farmers and their elected representatives.[28]

On 22 March the prime minister introduced a bill to enfranchise women who were twenty-one years of age and British subjects who possessed the same qualifications as male voters, words that excluded Indigenous and Asian women. Five provinces had already extended the vote to women and a sixth, Nova Scotia, was preparing legislation, so Borden's announcement was expected and widely supported in most of Canada. A *Montreal Gazette* editorial noted that there was little controversy: "Canadians will generally accept such legislation as something foreordained."[29]

Women's organizations in the Anglo-Celtic city were less restrained in their support for the law, but with so much happening that spring, neither the Montreal Suffrage Association nor the Montreal Local Council of Women marked the occasion with public celebration. The Féderation nationale St. Jean Baptiste was divided over the issue, with its president, Marie Lacoste Gerin Lajoie, ready to endorse the law while other leading members were opposed. It was decided to ask Madeleine Huguenin to write the "Entre nous" editorial in *La Bonne Parole*, as her views more closely reflected those of the majority. Huguenin opposed enfranchisement for its "negative effects on women" and declared that she "dreaded" the consequences.[30] The majority of French Canadians women appear to have agreed, and did not obtain voting rights in provincial elections until the 1940s. The most intense reaction came in the pages of *Le Devoir*, with Bourassa expressing his opposition in a series of front-page editorials. The legislation, as well as other aspects of "feminism," were, he believed, linked to war fever and would have terrible consequences for marriage, the family, the education of children, and the moral welfare of women.[31] French Canadians in the federal Liberal caucus offered pro forma opposition but allowed the bill to pass without division.[32]

Montrealers were also caught up in the 1918 mayoralty campaign, in which Joseph Ainey, the long-term labour representative on the Board of Control, was running against Méderic Martin. Montreal's financial problems, aggravated by the forced annexation of the bankrupt "Promoters City," Maisonneuve, led the provincial government to assume control of Montreal, replacing the elected Board of Control with an appointed Administrative Council.[33] Since the mayor and elected alderman would have no significant power, the election was largely a popularity contest. This did not stop business leaders, the daily newspapers, and various good-government groups from waging an aggressive campaign to elect Ainey.[34]

Martin was easily returned for his third term, winning broad support among French Canadian voters. His margin of victory may have been enhanced by reaction to the events unfolding in Quebec City over the weekend preceding the vote. The outbreak of violence soon to be known as the "Easter Riots" began when two locally notorious Dominion Police constables entered a pool hall in working-class Lower Town seeking men evading conscription. One young man, Joseph Mercier, who had left his exemption papers at home was taken into custody until friends brought his certificate to a police station used as a detention centre. A large crowd attacked the building and assaulted the police constables. Mayor Henri-Edgar Lavigueur[35] declined to send municipal police to assist, and shortly after midnight the riot ended. The next day, Good Friday, was quiet but "stories of all kinds were carried throughout the entire city," with rumours spreading about a mass rally in Upper Town that night.[36]

C.J. "Chubby" Power, a veteran and recently elected Liberal MP for Quebec South, watched the crowd gather in front of the offices of the Military Service Branch, which was protected by a thin screen of city police. Children began to throw snowballs; then a cry of "Let's burn the military papers" roused a group to action, breaking through the police line and setting fires in the MSA offices. The mayor, with about three hundred soldiers, arrived to quell the demonstration, but once again Lavigueur declined to read the Riot Act.[37] The night ended without arrests or serious injury. In Ottawa the prime minister called an emergency cabinet meeting to discuss the situation. His diary entry reads:

Saturday March 30 Severe rioting in Quebec City last night which was only quelled when troops called in … Debated question for two hours, decided to send immediately 1000 men to reinforce garrison, to order [Major-General François] Lessard to proceed immediately to Quebec and to bring 200 troops from the West. [Lieut.-Colonel H.A.C.] Machin reported by telephone that the situation is very serious … wants martial law proclaimed. Further rioting expected this evening.[38]

The streets were quiet throughout the day, but rumours of a planned attack on the Drill Hall, where draft evaders were incarcerated, were widespread. Power recalled:

Again thousands of onlookers congregated at the spot, the principal residential street of Quebec City, and again in the evening crowds appeared as if from nowhere, having climbed the steep hills from the Lower Town. They began shouting and marching in the vicinity of the small square fronting the Drill Hall … suddenly we saw emerging from among the crowd mounted soldiers galloping down the breadth of the street scattering the population in all directions. The soldiers were armed with axe handles which they waved about but to the best of my knowledge did not wield on the heads of spectators.[39]

The crowd disbursed, but not until the offices of the two pro-government newspapers, the *Quebec Chronicle* and *L'Evénement*, were attacked. The next day Borden was told that all was quiet in Quebec City and there were no reports of trouble in Montreal or elsewhere in the province. However, no new instructions were issued to General Landry, who deployed additional troops from the Central Ontario Regiment throughout the city. General Lessard and "trainloads of English-speaking troops, horses and military supplies from Ontario arrived at Quebec City" in the late afternoon, adding to the numbers already patrolling the streets. After several failed attempts to secure guns by breaking into hardware stores, the core of activists and thousands of onlookers gathered to listen to Armand Lavergne, who claimed to have made a deal with the military that troops would stay in their barracks if the crowds went home. Lessard denied making any such commitment, and soldiers continued to protect key sites like the Ross Rifle factory as well as conducting street patrols.[40]

The next morning, Monday, 1 April, was cool with rain and fog. Lessard, who had established military authority over the city, placarded the streets with a notice forbidding unlawful assemblies and warning citizens to stay home. The military, he declared, "would use every means at their disposal to maintain peace and order."[41] Martin Auger, who has examined the available evidence, summarized what happened that evening when Lessard ordered Quebec-based regiments to stay in their barracks and sent 1,200 soldiers from Ontario into the streets. Crowds soon assembled in Lower Town and could not be disbursed; "as soon as they cleared an area the angry mob reassembled and hurled stones, snowballs, ice and bricks at the soldiers." Shots were fired by armed protestors, and after several soldiers were wounded "the troops were ordered to open fire on the crowd."[42] A fourteen-year-old, Georges Demeule, and three young men who also appeared to be onlookers were killed along with an estimated thirty-eight wounded.

The shooting deaths of four civilians in the streets of a Canadian city evoked no sympathy from the prime minister, who gave the House of Commons a version of events based on dubious information:

> From house tops, side streets, snow banks and other places of concealment, the rioters opened point-blank fire on the troops who, as one the previous night, displayed great steadiness and forbearance under severe provocation. But at length after several soldiers had received bullet wounds, it became absolutely necessary for the troops to return the fire in self-defence, for the protection of the public, and to prevent the situation passing entirely beyond control. Five soldiers were wounded and of the crowd four were killed, many injured and 58 arrested.[43]

Borden also introduced orders-in-council retroactively authorizing military intervention without the reading of the Riot Act and cancelling the exemption of anyone resisting the enforcement of the Military Service Act.[44] Many of his colleagues pressed for the suppression of *Le Devoir* and the arrest of Bourassa, but Borden "told them a man behind bars some times has more influence than outside the bars." Instead he proposed tightening censorship regulations.[45] This encouraged the Dominion Police to seize a printing plant "circulating Ukrainian socialist and I.W.W. literature" as well as the offices of *"Le Bulletin,"* a weekly that had "recently published a burlesque on military and government action."[46]

Montreal newspapers carried detailed reports on the riots and their suppression, deploring the violence while raising questions about the behaviour of the Dominion Police. Mayor Lavigueur's cable to Borden, which blamed "the lack of discretion, tact and discrimination on the part of officers responsible for the enforcement of the Military Service Act," was widely cited,[47] as were statements about the failure of the civic authorities to intervene early. *Le Devoir* initially provided sympathetic coverage of the rioting and of Armand Lavergne's intervention, but on 5 April Bourassa's front-page editorial insisted that public order must be maintained. The editors of *Le Pays* responded, blasting Bourassa for his hypocrisy.[48]

On the surface life in Quebec City returned to normal, though there were minor clashes in April and June.[49] The Dominion Police commissioner's report of 12 April stated that "while things appear quiet, indications are that when active enforcement of the Military Service Act starts, there will be resistance in the city of Quebec and elsewhere in the province."[50] An Ontario battalion was to be permanently stationed in Quebec City. Martin Auger has described the precautions taken in Montreal, where local regiments "remained on high alert until 7 April":

A small detachment of soldiers also guarded the office of the local MSA registrar, while larger contingents of up to two hundred soldiers were assigned to the Montreal Port to protect the Imperial Munitions Board hangars. Military officials also monitored telegraph correspondence passing through Montreal's cable station to uncover information about possible future riots.[51]

Large contingents of Ontario and western Canadian troops were maintained in the province until the end of the war, including several hundred from Manitoba who were stationed at Saint-Jean close to Montreal.

While attention was focused on the riots, the news of German victories on the Western Front could not be ignored. Haig's "backs to the wall" order of the day and other signs of a possible Allied collapse challenged newspaper editors, who tried to cloak stories of enemy advances in optimistic language, emphasizing heavy German casualties. The *Montreal Standard* criticized this approach, declaring that the crisis meant the war was now less about "saving the world for democracy" and more about "making it possible for democracies to exist."[52] In Ottawa, where the cabinet had little more information than newspaper readers, Borden noted on 7 April that the "enemy is evidently preparing for another heavy attack" and recorded his view that "British generals and staffs were not equal to the Germans or French."[53]

Borden must have believed that others might reach a similar conclusion, for on 16 April his government tightened censorship. Order-in-council PC 915 prohibited the press from expressing "any adverse statement, report or opinion concerning the actions of the Allied nations in the prosecution of the war." Montreal's newspapers found the new rules difficult to understand. *La Patrie*, which rarely questioned the wisdom of the government, was asked if this meant that no one could question the actions of the government if they related to the war? Why, the editor wondered, after four years of war during which such censorship was non-existent, was it implemented now? *Le Canada*, *La Presse*, and *Le Devoir* had similar questions, while the *Star* and *Gazette* accepted the regulation as necessary.[54]

After a "secret telegram" arrived offering new details, Borden decided to call for a closed session of Parliament to explain the scale of the crisis and announce the government's intention to cancel exemptions for military service. On 18 April the public learned the details. All men in Class I, nineteen to thirty-four years of age who were single or widowers without children, were now liable for service and no claims of exemption were to be allowed. Initially men from twenty to twenty-two inclusive were to be called up. The prime minister admitted that the Military Service Act had failed, blaming the exemption tribunals, which "were attended with great inequality and sometimes with marked injustice," especially in "some parts of the country." He dismissed the argument, pressed by the Liberals, that the United States already had more available men than could be transported, insisting that he had "assurances" that shipping for the Canadians would be found. He then undercut his argument and the claims of urgency by adding, "if they cannot be transported in the immediate future they can be trained here in Canada and sent forward when ships can be provided."[55] Borden's determination to proceed with universal conscription was further evident when nineteen-year-old men were ordered to register, facilitating a future draft, and when he faced a massive farmers' protest in Ottawa. Quebec was well represented in the crowd, but the protest was led by men from Ontario and the west who had voted Unionist after promises that farmers would be exempt. Borden offered no apologies, telling the demonstrators that in this crisis nothing mattered more than the military. "If a scattered and broken remnant, overwhelmed because not reinforced should return to Canada it would profit little to tell them that while they were being decimated our production had been largely increased."[56] The prime minister's determination to pursue a total war policy was also evident when the government enacted PC

1241, which "forbade any individual from persuading or inducing any person to resist or impede the Military Service Act."[57] This order-in-council, passed under the authority of the War Measures Act, led to further self-censorship by newspaper editors.

It took some time to organize a call-up, but nationally by mid-June close to 72,000 of the 95,000 required to report had done so. The figures for Military District 4 (Montreal) and 5 (Quebec City) were somewhat different. Montreal registrars had notified 11,470 men to appear but 4,189 of them, more than a third, ignored the order. Quebec City reported that 1,702 of 4,126 failed to register.[58] Was the glass half full or half empty? Pro-government newspapers *La Patrie* and *L'Evénement* and the English-language dallies insisted that the attitude of French Canadians towards military service had changed, and military officials were said to be elated over the results in Quebec. Laurier, Gouin, and other prominent Quebecers renewed the proposal to establish a French Canadian brigade with Brigadier Thomas-Louis Tremblay brought back from France to command. The idea was greeted with enthusiasm in much of the press.[59] The minister of militia vetoed the idea in early June, promising that French-speaking conscripts would be kept together while in Canada and "as far as possible overseas but an entire brigade of fresh and untrained troops, wholly by themselves in the trenches would ... incur great risk.[60] Keeping French Canadian conscripts together overseas was not possible because the unilingual Canadian army was determined to "spread about" French Canadian reinforcements and avoid establishing additional French-language companies, never mind battalions.[61]

Both pro- and anti-government newspapers publicized the efforts of French Canada's Roman Catholic clergy to encourage men to report. Since the bishops and the parish priests were opposed to conscription, support took the form of sermons and pastoral letters urging the faithful to obey the law. The words of Monseigneur Emard, the bishop of Valleyfield, in what *La Presse* described as a touching farewell to conscripts in his diocese, were typical:

> The law commands you and duty calls you. You respond, if not with joyous heart at least with courage and generosity ... Since it is the final decision there is no turning back, go ahead and never forget while you are with the colours that you have with you the honour of the race and your creed.[62]

This was less than a clarion call to wage war for civilization and democracy, but it was in tune with the mood of French Canada.

The government's decision to amend the Military Service Act by order-in-council rather than legislation led to court challenges that further slowed the enlistment process in Montreal. The crucial case was heard in the Alberta Supreme Court with R.B. Bennett acting for a conscript whom Bennett argued was held in custody illegally by the army. The court ordered his release and declared that the order-in-council was illegal. This decision encouraged many draftees to seek release from service through writs of habeas corpus. In Quebec the courts embraced this ruling, ordering the release of men exempted by the regular tribunals.[63] Very few conscripts could hire a lawyer to pursue court action, but the Alberta decision had broader consequences. Officials at Military District 4 headquarters admitted that up to 10 July "no legal proceedings had been taken against those who fail to report." Less than half of the 400 men required to appear on 9 July were taken on strength, and no one could say when further action to deal with them would be taken.[64]

Legal uncertainty was not the only problem in Montreal, where a bitter dispute between the Dominion Police and the military led to open conflict. The situation arose after influential members of Borden's cabinet complained that the MSA would never be properly enforced as long as C.J. Doherty, the minister of justice, was in charge.[65] Borden agreed to transfer authority to the military, who were to supervise the Dominion Police. The change went smoothly in Toronto, but in Montreal language and culture stood in the way of cooperation.[66] District registrar Eugene Godin, Dominion Police chief inspector J.A. Belanger, and their deputies and staff were French Canadians carrying out a very unpopular task. To be subordinate to the unilingual English Canadian authority of Major-General E.W. Wilson and his assistant provost, Marshal Major P. Mackenzie, was too much to ask. Resignations, "desmission en bloc," as *La Presse* described it,[67] followed and for some weeks there were few serious attempts to round up deserters or those evading the call up.

The challenges confronting the military police, many of whom did not speak French, were evident during an attempt to arrest an alleged evader in the village of Saint-Lazare, west of Montreal. Ten armed men confronted the officers and one of them accidentally discharged his weapon, wounding himself while striking a police driver. Hit in the leg, he bled to death in the confusion. The police returned to the village with one hundred soldiers from the Montreal garrison and arrested six men, including one who had deserted in 1914. The others were not charged.[68]

On 19 July, the Supreme Court of Canada reversed the Alberta court decision, holding that the order-in-council was within the powers of the government under the War Measures Act. Mr. Justice Anglin, who wrote the majority opinion, emphasized "that we are living in extraordinary times which necessitate extraordinary measures."[69] The next such measure adopted by the government was to offer an amnesty "to all deserters and defaulters" who reported voluntarily "on or before 24 August 1918." Three-quarters of the 5,477 Canadians who reported under the terms of the amnesty were from Quebec, most from Montreal.[70] The amnesty was part of an overall plan to increase the share of conscripts from Quebec, so instructions were issued to registrars in other provinces "to temporarily stop the call up of men in order that Quebec might catch up."[71] Shortly after this order was issued, pressure from farm groups persuaded the government to grant "harvest leave" of six weeks to all conscripts who were previously resident on farms.[72]

Despite the amnesty and harvest leave, the military police in Quebec appear to have stepped up their pursuit of draft dodgers. On 12 August, with almost two weeks left in the amnesty period, the *Gazette* and *Star* reported the shooting of a "defaulter" in the Eastern Townships and the dispatch of police to St. Therese, north of the city, where "forty young men" were said to be living in the woods. The *Star* sent a reporter to interview the men, reporting that they "are not holding back in order to work on farms ... but instead are enjoying wild day and night orgies." The reporter, well trained in the journalism characteristic of the *Star*, added, "They do not limit themselves to the company of the one sex but neighbouring farmers' families join in the 'doings' at the camp."[73] No arrests were made. By October, when it was believed that as a result of the amnesty and better cooperation with the authorities, Quebec "had reached parity with the other provinces ... the epidemic of influenza had broken out in practically every district ... Registrars were asked to call no more men."[74]

Measures to enforce conscription on a population that was actively or passively opposed to serving in a unilingual, British-Canadian army were justified in English-speaking Canada by news from the Western Front. The series of German victories that began in March 1918 continued well into the summer, suggesting that at a minimum the war would continue into 1919. This was certainly the government's view; conscripting 100,000 men would keep the army up to strength through the balance of 1918 and into the next year, and if more men were needed the nineteen-year-olds would be called up. It did not matter that one and a half million American troops had reached Europe; conscription was about Canada's army and Canada's place in the world. These priorities were evident when the prime minister and three of his most important cabinet ministers travelled to London to participate in a new series of meetings of the Imperial War Cabinet. They left Ottawa on 24 May, and on arrival in London Borden heard from Lloyd George the depressing details about the state of the Allied armies. He then sent for Sir Arthur Currie to obtain a Canadian perspective. Currie was harshly critical of British strategy, especially with regard to Passchendaele, which had cost the Canadians 16,000 casualties to no purpose as "the British army immediately went on the defensive ... no advantage in position was gained and the effort was simply wasted." He was later to claim that he had tried to keep the Canadian Corps out of Passchendaele, but there is no contemporary evidence supporting his recollections. Once the corps was committed to action, he insisted on pressing the attack to secure Passchendaele village and arguing for a continuation of the offensive.[75] Both his army commander, Plumer, and Haig were opposed to further action but Currie believed his army should keep fighting to secure the rest of the ridge. He was also critical of British preparations to meet the German's March offensive, comparing the extensive preparations of his own corps – 375,000 yards of barbed wire entanglements – which he claimed were ten times as much as installed by neighbouring British corps.[76] Borden presented Currie's views to the Imperial War Cabinet to the evident delight of Lloyd George, whose disdain for General Haig and staff was as strong as ever. According to Borden, Lloyd George "exploded with regard to the high command" during a walk in the countryside; he told Borden that he had been "boiling with impotent rage" against them.

> He explained at great length their constant mistakes, their failure to fulfil expectations and the unnecessary losses which their lack of foresight had occasioned. I asked him why he had not dismissed those responsible during the previous autumn, and he replied that he had endeavoured to do so but did not succeed in carrying the cabinet; the high command had their affiliations and roots everywhere and it was for the purpose of strengthening his hand in dealing with the situation that he had summoned the Dominion Ministers to the Imperial War Cabinet.[77]

During his time in England Borden was confronted with an issue that challenged his long-held belief in imperial unity. At the 1917 Imperial War Conference Border had co-authored Resolution IX calling for the "right of the Dominions and India to an adequate voice in foreign policy" secured through a method of "continuous consultation" such as the Imperial War Cabinet. When news of this reached Canada through a statement by the British prime minister, Liberals, especially in Quebec, denounced it as a backward step.[78] Borden was still determined to pursue his dream, but when the British Admiralty proposed a scheme involving Dominion participation in a unified imperial navy Border refused to consider it. He agreed that from "the point of view of efficiency it was probably the best that could be devised but in the Dominions it was politically impossible as it would offend the newly awakened sense of nationhood which pervaded the people of Canada."[79] Borden did not explain how this new sense of nationhood could be made compatible with an imperial Commonwealth and a common foreign policy.

The German attempt to break the French army north of Paris was initially successful, but French reserves and German exhaustion forced a halt. The French army, with the support of American divisions, then seized the initiative in what was to be called the Second Battle of the Marne. This counteroffensive of 18 July marked the beginning of the end for the German army in the west, but German leaders still believed they could control events and negotiate a peace that secured their new empire in the east while retaining Alsace-Lorraine and control of Belgium.[80] Ludendorff advocated a policy of "strategic defence" to wear down the Allies by inflicting enough casualties to force them to negotiate. Such fantasies could be entertained in Berlin, but at the sharp end, weary troops who had to defend one hundred kilometres of new front line in hastily prepared positions lacking depth were unconvinced. To make matters worse, the German army was the first to be affected by the 1918 influenza epidemic – the so-called Spanish flu. This initial phase of the viral infection killed few men, but tens of thousands of German soldiers were out of action, sick or in recovery, further weakening front-line units and reserves.[81]

The Allies planned to follow up their success at the Marne with a major offensive in the Somme. Their operational plan was influenced by the Australian attack at Le Hamel, a village near Amiens. Sir John Monash, the Australian Corps commander, attacked without preliminary bombardment, using tanks to support the infantry. The position was captured in just forty minutes.[82] General Rawlinson, the Fourth Army commander, planned a larger version of Le Hamel with the Australians and the Canadian Corps leading the attack. Both corps had resisted the British move to reduce the number of battalions per division from twelve to nine and were at full strength. The Canadians, who had not fought in a major battle since Passchendaele, eight months before, were as fresh as any formation on the Western Front could be. Divisional war diaries document extensive training exercises that fully integrated reinforcements, including conscripts. The first conscripts to join units in France were undoubtedly drawn from the men who had "voluntarily reported" in 1917, but by August those "ordered to report" in the first months of 1918 were completing their fourteen-week infantry training program in England, and entering the reinforcement stream.[83] Patrick Dennis's 2017 book *Reluctant Warriors* tells the stories of individual conscripts who fought and were killed or wounded during the Hundred Days Campaign. Dennis presents the conscripts as reluctant but effective soldiers who overcame prejudice and integrated successfully into Canada's army. Richard Holt examined the fatalities listed by the Commonwealth war graves and concluded that 1,032 (12.5 per cent) of the 8,227 men killed from August to November 1918 were MSA conscripts.[84]

Secrecy was vital to the success of the Battle of Amiens, and only a select number of senior Canadian officers knew the plan for the offensive. All four Canadian divisions were transported to the Somme at the last possible moment under tight security, so there was no time to recce the battlefield. The battle was fought on the *plaine du Santerre* south of the River Somme, an area of wheat fields, orchards, and brick-walled villages that offered ideal ground for tank-infantry cooperation. The Germans had not attempted to build a continuous defensive line on recently conquered ground, relying on fortified positions to provide interlocking fire with artillery in support. Intelligence reports accurately identified ten German divisions in the area but noted that many enemy battalions were understrength.

Rawlinson's plan called for close cooperation between the Australians and Canadians as well as with the flanking formations, British on the left and French on the right. Brigadier Raymond Brutinel's "Canadian Independent Force," composed of the 1st and 2nd Motor Machine Gun Brigades, was to secure the Amiens-Roye road, which served as the boundary between the Canadian and French forces. Amiens is remembered as a tank battle, and each Canadian division was supported by a battalion of 36 Mark V heavy tanks plus supply tanks for infantry and engineers.[85] As with all battles on the Western Front, artillery played a principal role. Over 2,000 guns supported the attack, 646 for the 8.5-kilometre-front attacked by the Canadians. The attempt to achieve surprise meant no preliminary bombardment and no opportunity to register guns for counter-battery. At 4:20 a.m. on 8 August the Australians and Canadians moved forward against a startled enemy beaten down by a hurricane of high explosive. Early morning mist helped to add tactical to operational surprise.

The 13th Battalion war diary described the scene: "The stillness of the night ... grim, stern men with bayonet fixed ... the artillery barrage laid down 200 yards in advance of the jumping off point ... the seven tanks ... were all knocked out before reaching our objective but showed great resolution."[86]

The Second Canadian Division's first major obstacle was the fortified village of Marcelcave. The 4th Brigade, which was to lead the attack, had been under artillery fire for more than an hour when the Allied barrage began. The 28 Mark V tanks available assisted the infantry advance, but Marcelcave could only be entered after "a punishing forty-five minute artillery bombardment reduced much of the village to rubble." The remaining German soldiers forced the Canadians into a battle for the ruins before the advance could continue. Good cooperation between 7th Australian Brigade and the Canadians assisted both brigades in the rapid penetration of the "Green Line," which was secure by 7:45 a.m., less than four hours after the advance began. The 5th Brigade then took over the Canadian advance, reaching the "Red Line" by early afternoon. Montreal's 24th Battalion, Victoria Rifles, moved quickly forward, reaching Guillaucourt where "house-to-house and hand-to-hand combat cleared the village." To this point casualties had been light, but advancing well beyond the barrage had its cost. German troops, holding a small quarry and a nearby woods, caught the battalion in crossfire. Four lieutenants leading their platoons were killed. The toll for the day was 35 dead and 152 wounded. The battalion history notes that after their objective was secured,

> cavalry which came up from the rear to exploit the infantry's success could make little progress. The horsemen rode through the 24th Battalion lines and attempted to gallop "out into the blue" but machine gun fire was intense and the effort was checked abruptly, the survivors forced to dismount.[87]

The next morning the 22nd and 25th battalions took the lead, fighting their way forward with tank support. The village of Méharicourt was reached, and once again British cavalry with "flashing swords" charged gallantly forward to be "caught in a concentration of enemy machine gun fire."[88] The 22nd reported losses of 6 killed and 14 wounded on the day that Lieut. Jean Brillant won the Victoria Cross for his courage and leadership in successive and successful attacks on enemy machine-gun positions.[89] Twice wounded, he continued to lead his men forward until struck a third time. Brillant died of wounds the next day.

In the centre, 1st Canadian Division had run into strong resistance at Hangard Woods, where enemy machine guns well protected by barbed wire required extraordinary efforts by small groups of men. Two Victoria crosses were awarded in this action, to Private John Croak and Corporal H. Good, both of the 13th (Black Watch) Battalion. Both men were from the Maritime provinces, an indication of the changing composition of Montreal battalions. Once through the crust, 1st Division reached the "Blue Line" by early evening.[90]

Major-General L.J. Lipsett's 3rd Division faced the most challenging tasks. The lead brigade was to advance along the main Amiens-Roye road, which was naturally well defended. The French Corps on their right flank employed an hour-long artillery barrage before attacking, and this obviously could not begin until the Canadian advance was underway. Fortunately, Brutinel's force acted swiftly, protecting the exposed flank. The division's left flank straddled the River Luce, which was bordered by marshes, making much of it impassable. Canadian engineers played a crucial role in maintaining momentum, repairing bridges and building pontooned cork footbridges across the marshy Luce valley. Despite gas shells and cratered ground the infantry reached their objective, dug in, and watched in amazement as the 3rd Cavalry Division with the Canadian Brigade in the lead came forward to test the long-promised chances of deep pursuit. The "Whippet" tanks, in support, proved too slow for the cavalry and German machine guns cut down horses and riders. The Canadian brigade lost 245 men in a series of "gallant but futile charges." Elsewhere, the cavalry enjoyed some success, one regiment intercepting a trainload of reinforcements and taking 600 prisoners.[91]

Haig and Rawlinson now believed that the Amiens-Roye road was the best axis of advance. The Germans were equally committed to defending the sector, and despite the commitment of fresh Canadians troops the enemy held a key Canadian objective, Le Quesnel (where the Canadian Memorial for the Amiens battle is now located), against repeated attacks. Le Quesnel fell to the 4th Division the next morning, but the strength of the German defence pointed to a significant change in the rhythm of the battle. The Canadians had advanced thirteen kilometres, a distance unprecedented on the Western Front, but there was no breakthrough. Despite a further advance of up to three kilometres on 9 August it was becoming evident that German reinforcements, nine additional divisions by 10 August, were closing off the chances of reaching Péronne or Roye. Just thirty-eight tanks were available across the entire Fourth Army front, and the Allied soldiers were exhausted. Currie and other commanders sought to persuade Haig to call off the offensive. Currie was not just a highly successful commander; he was also the head of Canada's national army, and his written protest persuaded Haig to end the Amiens offensive. Sir Julian Byng's Third Army was to stage the next attack while the Canadians returned to First Army and the Arras sector to prepare for a major assault on the Hindenburg Line.

News of the Canadian Corps' leading role in the Amiens offensive did not reach Canada for some days, and the various press services provided little detail. J.F.B. Livesay, the Canadian Press correspondent "with the Canadian forces," provided a brief report on 10 August noting that it was the first time the Canadian infantry and cavalry had fought on the same battlefield.[92] The next day Sir Edward Kemp issued an official statement proclaiming that "the achievements of the Canadians in the present offensive were the greatest in the corps' history" while casualties "were the smallest by a long way of any previous major operation."[93] The French-language press in Montreal, with the exception of Le Devoir, carried Livesay's stories and Kemp's statement, but other issues attracted greater attention. The prime minister's decision to send 4,000 Canadian soldiers to support the Allied intervention in Siberia was welcomed by the Gazette, condemned by Le Canada, and mocked by Le Devoir. Le Canada's editorial suggested that the decision was evidence of the influence of militarism on Canada and noted that because of censorship that was all they were permitted to say.[94]

With the German army reeling, Sir Julian Byng's Third Army began an advance north of the Somme towards Bapaume. Known as the "Battle of Albert," this success, coming on the heels of Amiens and Tenth French Army's five-mile advance on the British flank, led Haig to send a new message to his army commanders. The enemy, he insisted, "has not the means to deliver counterattacks on an extended scale nor has he the numbers to hold a position against the very extended advance which is now be directed upon him" by all the Allied armies. "Risks which a month ago would have been criminal ought now to be incurred as duty." It was, Haig believed, the return of open warfare where a division would act "independently of its neighbour advancing to distance objectives."

The initial task assigned to the Canadian Corps at Arras was to overcome the German defences based on a series of hills. The official historian described the scene, which included the previously bloodied heights of Monchy-le-Preux:

The enemy's main defence positions, supplemented by various subsidiary switches and strong points, were amongst the strongest on the Western Front. The ground was pocked with scars of 1917 and early 1918, and in the litter of old trenches and fortifications German engineers had found ready-made positions which they had considerably strengthened. Furthermore, topography was on the side of the Germans. The battle area spread over the north-eastern slopes of the Artois Hills, whose summits about Monchy were over three hundred feet above the valley-bottoms of the Scarpe and the Sensée. The latter river, flowing generally eastward, together with its tributaries had dissected the hills into numerous deep valleys. The intervening ridges and high points, often mutually supporting, the enemy had fortified with a skill that demonstrated his mastery in military engineering.[95]

Known as the Battle of the Scarpe, the operation began at 3 a.m. on 26 August 1918 with fourteen brigades of field artillery and nine heavy artillery brigades. There were few tanks available after the losses east of Amiens, and just nine were allotted to each of the two divisions leading the attack.

North of the Arras-Cambrai road, the centre-line of the corps advance, 3rd Canadian Division seized their first objectives in less than five hours. The division, commanded by Major-General L.J. Lipsett, a British officer of exceptional ability who had previously commanded 8th Battalion at Ypres and 2nd Brigade at Mont Sorrel, was confident enough to stage a complex night attack. The 8th Brigade with three battalions of the (dismounted) Canadian Mounted Rifles in the lead overcame the German defences at Orange Hill and the heights of Monchy-Le-Preux by outflanking the enemy and attacking from two directions. The 2nd Division also made good initial progress, but orders to shift their weight to the south-east, capturing the Wancourt Ridge, to assist Third Army slowed the advance to the division's objectives.

Among the many casualties suffered in the last days of August were the men killed and wounded near the village of Chérisy in 2nd Canadian Division's sector. Chérisy has, along with Courcelette, become identified with the 22nd Battalion, which suffered 105 killed and 206 wounded on 27 and 28 August.[96] The 22nd was one of three 5th Brigade battalions ordered to attack through Chérisy and across the River Sensée as part of the corps' attempt to break the Fresnes-Rouvray line. From the first moments of the advance, on the morning of 27 August, it was evident that the German defences had survived the Allied artillery barrage. "A hail of machine gun fire and heavy gas shelling"[97] broke battalion formation, and it was up to small groups of men to work their way forward across a small stream flowing with water after heavy rains. The slope beyond the Sensée was an obvious defensive position.[98] Rows of uncut barbed wire, concealed from air observation by long grass that had grown up around them, stopped the brigade advance, as "the leading sections of the forward three battalions were hung up by this wire."[99] Committing the reserve battalion, the 25th (Nova Scotia), did not restore momentum, and the survivors dug in on the lower part of the slope. Neither the 4th nor 5th Brigade was in any condition to continue the advance, but those were the orders, leading to yet more losses.

The official history summary reads:

> Casualties for the day were very heavy and brought the total reported by the 2nd and 3rd Divisions in the three days fighting to 254 officers and 5547 other ranks. The 22nd Battalion lost all its officers and the 24th Battalion was also grievously stricken. Major Georges Vanier [a future governor-general of Canada] who had taken command of the decimated 22nd Battalion on the previous day lost his right leg in the action. Lt-Col. W.H. Clark-Kennedy, the 24th C.O., amalgamated the remnants of both battalions and in spite of a serious wound continued to direct his focus against the German lines. His heroic and distinguished leadership in this and the previous day's fighting brought him the Victoria Cross.[100]

After the relief of 2nd Division, fresh troops from 1st Division were able to roll up the defences, attacking from the south where a breach had been made.

Casualties to British and Dominion troops were now causing grave concern in Britain, where the War Cabinet decided to send a telegram to Haig (29 August) warning against incurring heavy losses in the next weeks, as infantry reinforcements for the British Expeditionary Force were simply not available. Due to the breakup of 5th Canadian Division and the arrival of conscripts, the Canadians were the only one of Haig's Corps able to restore formations to full strength. This inevitably meant that they would be asked to take the lead in the next series of costly assaults. The situation was worsened when 4th British Division, which had fought under Currie in the second phase of the late-August advance, reported that only one brigade was fit enough for action against the Drocourt-Quéant Line, forcing the Canadians to take an even larger share of the assault.

Breaking through the Drocourt-Quéant Line required detailed planning and lots of artillery. There was little opportunity for any kind of "open warfare." Five brigades following a rolling barrage would have to overcome three defensive lines before reaching the ground overlooking the Canal du Nord. Currie decided to attack at dawn, hoping that Mark V tanks could move forward with the infantry at zero hour. By the end of the day, seven Canadians had won the Victoria Cross and the Drocourt-Quéant Switch, as it was also known, had been breached on a 7,000-metre front. The next morning the enemy was gone, retreating behind the Canal du Nord. Over 6,000 German soldiers were in corps prisoner-of-war cages, and many more were killed or wounded, at a cost of some 5,600 Canadian casualties.

Montreal's 87th Battalion, Canadian Grenadier Guards, went into the battle for the Drocourt-Quéant Line with a strength of 35 officers and 725 men. Most were reinforcements from the disbanded 60th Battalion, but drafts had also arrived from French Canadian units. An entry into the March war diary records the arrival of 98 men from the 150th Battalion and notes that they are "a good looking lot, apparently well trained."[101] The 87th's part in the assault on the Drocourt-Quéant Line at Dury, where the Canadian memorial is located, was to cost the battalion 98 men killed and 209 wounded, half their rifle strength. Private John Francis Young, an English-born Montrealer from St. Henri who was employed as a "tobacco packer" before enlisting, was awarded the Victoria Cross for actions as a medic and stretcher-bearer who worked through the day dressing wounds and then organizing stretcher parties to bring in the wounded.[102]

The British press was lavish in its praise of the Canadian success in breaking the Drocourt-Quéant Line. The *Times* reported that "the Canadians won imperishable fame" and the *Daily Telegraph* wrote of the "bewildering success" of the battle. The *Daily Sketch* described "those splendid threatening troops, the Canadians" as having "accomplished one of the most brilliant feats of the war." The *Montreal Gazette*'s London correspondent and local editors managed to confuse the late August battles with the fight for the Drocourt-Quéant Line, lauding the efforts of a famous Quebec battalion whose achievement "will outrank its glorious record at Hill 70 and Courcelette."[103]

The successful assault on the Drocourt-Quéant Line was supported by a parallel British-Australian advance to Bapaume, forcing a German retreat all along the front. Third British Army resumed the offensive on 12 September, and Fourth Army joined in six days later. On 26 September a large-scale Franco-American offensive began on a forty-four-mile front. The next day First Army was ordered to cross the Canal du Nord and seize Bourlon Wood. General Sir Henry Horne, who commanded First Army and has been described as "a rather shadowy figure for historians," seemed content to leave the planning and conduct of operations to Currie, which meant the Canadians, again at full strength, would lead.[104]

Currie decided to advance on a narrow front, less than 2,500 metres, where the Canal du Nord was under construction and still largely dry. The enemy had strengthened defences in the area with dense belts of barbed wire, but there was little protection from the kind of bombardment the corps and army artillery could apply. Beyond the canal, a second defensive position, the Marquion Line, crossed the front. The main objective, the high ground at Bourlon Wood, was to be attacked after the reserve brigades of 4th Canadian Division had crossed the canal to add weight to the advance.

A massive creeping barrage mixing smoke, shrapnel, and high explosive led the way. Although the German armies had been depleted, machine guns situated in concrete pillboxes along high railway embankments and dense woods still did their damage. Despite losses, the Canadians overwhelmed the defenders, and in less than five hours Bourlon Wood was brought under attack. This heavily wooded hill above Bourlon village could well have been the scene of protracted battle, since the high ground and an open flank to the south combined to challenge the determination of David Watson's 4th Canadian Division. One need only visit the quiet, hauntingly beautiful Bourlon Wood Cemetery, tucked away just past the Canadian hilltop memorial, to find evidence of the cost. Fortunately, with darkness the enemy withdrew, and Bourlon Wood was in Canadian hands by midnight on 28 September. Elsewhere air support and superb work by the engineers who bridged the canal helped to maintain the momentum, and by nightfall leading elements were probing the last fortified positions in front of Cambrai. Unfortunately, the Germans were determined to hold the city as long as possible. The battle for Cambrai turned into a bitter, attritional struggle.

Currie ordered the corps to stage a set-piece attack on 1 October. After initial progress enemy resistance stiffened, and then a series of German counter-attacks forced a withdrawal. For the moment, the enemy had stabilized the front. Cambrai, badly damaged by shelling and arson, was finally cleared on 9 October after Third Army succeeded in crossing the canal south of the city, threatening a double envelopment. The Canadians fought their way into Cambrai, overcoming rear guards and dealing with mines and booby traps. On 11 October, the corps was sent into reserve. The summary offered by the official historian states:

> Its casualties were many, but by First World War standards not excessive in light of their task. The total officially reported killed, wounded, and missing between 22 August and 11 October numbered 1,544 officers and 29,262 other ranks. In achieving its victory the Corps had captured 18,585 prisoners, together with 371 guns and nearly 2,000 machine guns. Besides depriving the enemy of the great distributing centre of Cambrai, the Canadians had liberated 54 towns and villages standing on more than 116 square miles of French soil.[105]

From Cambrai the corps advanced to Valenciennes and Mons in the last month of the war. The story of the final advance needs to be understood in the context of the German effort to achieve an armistice that would preserve the Kaiser's regime, the prestige of the German army, and as many territorial conquests as possible. As the Western Front disintegrated and the Allied armies advanced east, similar breakthroughs were being achieved on other long-stalled fronts. In Macedonia, a multinational force of French, British, Serbs, Italians and Greeks, totalling over 700,000 men, burst through the Central Powers defences. Their drive continued northward to liberate Serbia and threaten Bulgaria and Constantinople. On the Italian front, Austro-Hungarian summer offensives had been blunted and the Italian army was preparing a counter-offensive. The Battle of Vittorio Veneto would begin on 24 October, and would effectively knock the Austro-Hungarian Empire out of the war.

On 10 September, the German High Command agreed to permit an approach to the Allies through the Queen of the Netherlands. This gambit was abandoned when on 14 September the Austrian emperor, fearing the complete disintegration of his armies, issued a public appeal for a peace conference in a neutral state. This transparent attempt to preserve a collapsing empire was followed by a public declaration of German war aims that called for preserving the Treaty of Brest-Litovsk, the return of all German colonies, and effective control of Belgium.

President Wilson's reply to the Austrian peace note included his enunciation of five essential conditions for peace, an elaboration of the famous "Fourteen Points." Wilson declared, "There can be no peace obtained by any bargain or compromise with the Governments of the Central Empires." The next day Bulgaria, one of the four Central Powers, surrendered. Ludendorff subsequently wrote that 28 September was the day he knew "the war was now lost ... If we had the strength to reverse the situation in the West, then of course nothing would yet have been lost. But we have not the means ... We had to count on being beaten back again and again."[106] Insisting that "Every [delay] of 24 hours could worsen the situation," Ludendorff led an effort to reconstitute the German government and issue an immediate call for an end to the fighting.[107] A new chancellor, Prince Max of Baden, was appointed on 4 October, and "with a view to avoiding further bloodshed" he signed a letter to President Wilson requesting an immediate armistice. Wilson's reply, on 8 October, demanded immediate "withdrawal of their forces everywhere from invaded territory" – not the response the German government was hoping for.[108] On 12 October the Germans agreed to evacuate occupied territory but with an international commission supervising the process. Any chance of a conciliatory response from Wilson or other Allied leaders was diminished by the sinking of the Irish mailboat RMS *Leinster* on 10 October. Over 500 men, women, and children, including soldiers returning from leave, were drowned in the pointless U-boat attack. Wilson echoed the public outcry, insisting on 14 October that peace could not be brokered while Germany's "submarines are engaged in sinking passenger ships at sea."[109] The small coterie of decision-makers in Germany remained divided and uncertain. Ludendorff wanted to avoid any responsibility for a military surrender, while Crown Prince Rupprecht warned that "we must obtain peace before the enemy breaks through into Germany."[110]

Prince Max crafted a new note on 20 October accepting the need to have military advisers determine the details of the armistice as long as no demands were made "that would be irreconcilable with the honour of the German people and with paving the way to a peace of justice." He did promise to end the sinking of passenger ships. Wilson then announced that the Allied forces would neither negotiate with nor accept terms from the kaiser, who would have to abdicate if discussions were to lead to an armistice. This led to Ludendorff's resignation, while the kaiser fled into exile in Holland: there was nothing the German army could do to dictate terms or stabilize the line. The war was effectively over.

The collapse of the German army and the imperial state was remarkably swift. The German people had been starved of both food and reliable information for four years. The previous winter had been known as the turnip winter, when most supplies of grain, meat, and fat had disappeared. German newspapers had convinced a highly literate and patriotic population that the war could still be won as long as the spring offensives went as planned, and so they persevered. News of the defeats that summer and fall had been kept secret, and so the collapse of the German army seemed inexplicable. Rioting and socialist uprisings inspired by the Bolshevik Revolution the previous year in Russia quickly swept across the country, feeding off the hunger and anger of the people. As Ludendorff left his post, he also attempted to deflect blame from himself and the German generals: the German army had not actually been defeated in the field, he argued, it had been stabbed in the back by the socialist politicians and revolutionaries at home who agreed to form a provisional government in the kaiser's absence. This laid the groundwork for the *Dolchstoss* myth that would be so effectively exploited and expanded by Adolf Hitler and the Nazi Party in the post-war period.

Neither the British nor French government had finalized a decision on the exact terms of an armistice, and soon events made such discussion irrelevant. The Turkish government sent envoys to sign a separate peace on 26 October, and Austria soon followed. On 5 November Marshal Ferdinand Foch was authorized to "receive representatives of the German Government and communicate to them the terms of the Armistice." The terms were presented on 8 November in a railway carriage in the Forêt de Compiègne, north of Paris. The German delegates were given seventy-two hours, until 11 a.m. on 11 November, to sign the armistice.

The prolonged armistice negotiations had little impact on Allied military operations, raising the age-old question of the legitimacy or wisdom of continuing combat when the war was all but won. This issue became particularly important to Canadians after Sir Arthur Currie was criticized for the unnecessary deaths of Canadian soldiers in the final hours of the war. Rumours, innuendo, and attacks on his reputation by Sam Hughes, during and after the war, culminated in the famous trial in Port Hope where Currie defended his reputation and won a form of vindication in 1928.[111] He consistently argued that the Canadian Corps had been following explicit orders as it advanced towards Mons in the last week of the war. Certainly the last large set-piece attack of the war for Canadians, the Battle of Valenciennes, was the result of a directive from Haig to General Horne to capture the city. This attack was to be carried out simultaneously with attacks by Third and Fourth Armies. The 51st Highland Division, part of 17th British Corps, began the attack with an assault on 28 October but were unable to hold the ground gained.

The Canadian Corps took over, employing the heaviest artillery bombardment in support of a single brigade ever tried during the war. The 10th Brigade swept over Mont Houy, capturing stunned prisoners and reaching the edge of the city. Brigadier Andrew McNaughton, then serving as the senior Corps artillery officer, described the artillery program: "The barrage and bombardment had left scarcely a yard of ground untouched ... the Canadian Corps had paid the price of victory ... in shells and not in life." Casualties were less than 400 with 80 killed in action. The next day the enemy abandoned Valenciennes.

The 2nd Canadian Division led the advance to Mons with orders to capture it if it could be done "without many casualties." Was the decision to maintain pressure based on the symbolism of Mons, where the war, for the British Expeditionary Force, had begun more than four years before? Currie was to say that "it would be befitting that the capture of Mons should close the fighting records of the Canadian Troops," but the reality was that all the leading divisions continued operations through to 11 a.m. on 11 November. No Allied commander was willing to allow the enemy time to regroup and delay an armistice, including American commander John J. Pershing, who was subjected to similar attacks after the war. On the 11th hour of the 11th day of the 11th month, the war ended.

Canadians who read daily newspapers were well informed about these events through regular updates from Associated Press correspondents and official statements from London, Paris, and Washington. The Canadian Press correspondent J.F.B. Livesay, who was later to write one of the first triumphantly patriotic accounts of Canada's Hundred Days, provided stories about the achievements of the corps.[112] Once again casualty lists, with the numbers and names of Montrealers heading the story, were printed along with capsule biographies of local soldiers killed, wounded, and missing. There was, however, relatively little detail about Montreal's battalions, as attention focused on the larger picture and the growing possibility that victory was in reach.

By late September, a different story of misery and death related to the war began to dominate the news. The Spanish flu reached the city when cases were reported in the barracks of the Depot Battalion. Mark Humphries's article "The Horror at Home: The Canadian Military and the Great Influenza Pandemic of 1918" uncovers the origins of the epidemic in Canada and traces its spread across the country.[113] Humphries also provided a description of the situation in Montreal in his book *The Last Plague: Spanish Influenza and the Politics of Public Health in Canada*,[114] noting that

> the number of cases then began to increase slowly over almost three weeks before peaking around 15 October. Mortality from the pandemic followed a similar pattern, although delayed by about a week ... deaths per day from influenza peaked at 201 on 21 October 1918. At its height, flu killed a Montrealer every seven minutes.[115]

As the flu spread, measures to close schools, theatres, and other public places were introduced but churches, stores, and places of work remained open. A four o'clock closing time was imposed on department and general merchandise stores, a deadline designed to limit crowding on the tramways. On 12 October, as the number of cases and deaths continued to rise, churches were required to close on Sunday and no more than fifty people at a time were to attend services during the week. This was followed, on 18 October, by an order closing all churches in the city. The next day provincial health authorities extended the rule to churches throughout the province. This was a controversial and contested measure, and all churches were re-opened on 5 November.[116] The remaining restrictions were lifted before 11 November.

Between 23 September and 11 November 18,483 cases of influenza were reported to the city health department, a figure that does not include suburban municipalities. The official death toll, 3,155, significantly understates the total but suggests the scale of the epidemic. From 10 November to the end of January 1919 a further 916 cases were reported with 484 deaths, largely from pulmonary complications following infection with influenza.[117]

It is evident that Montreal failed to introduce and enforce timely measures to quarantine those infected or to impose restrictions necessary to limit infection. A recent study comparing the experience of Winnipeg with that of Montreal notes that the western city quarantined soldiers suspected of having the flu on 30 September and "moved rapidly to introduce a broad series of measures to promote social distancing: quarantine was placed on army bases following the ban on public gatherings. The ban remained in place for six weeks until 27 November."[118] As a consequence Winnipeg had a lower transmissibility rate and a lower mortality rate than Montreal. Military officers in Montreal added to the city's problems by continuing to search for deserters and evaders throughout the flu epidemic. Protests from health officials and expressions of outrage from the French-language daily press were ignored by Assistant Provost Marshal, who confirmed the existing procedures for the apprehension of men in an order dated 11 October. Despite the danger of transmitting the virus and despite the collapse of the German army on the Western Front, military authorities continued to pursue defaulters well into November.[119]

Throughout October and the first days of November the influenza epidemic had to share the front page with the news from Europe. The series of defeats inflicted on the German army and the capitulation of the Ottoman and Austro-Hungarian empires were covered in detail. The other major story was the 1918 Victory Loan campaign, which was carried out in the middle of the flu epidemic. Montreal's leading businessmen were involved, and Edward Beatty, the new president of the CPR, arranged to borrow the elaborate decorations used in a Liberty Bonds campaign in New York City. St. Catherine Street was transformed into Avenue of the Allies with flags and decorations on buildings from Guy to Papineau streets. A Victory Arch was constructed at Phillips Square and a Victory Loan parade organized.

By the happiest of coincidences, the guns of Europe fell silent on 11 November, the date already scheduled for Montreal's Victory Loan Parade.

With the ban on crowds temporarily lifted, at 6 a.m. a CPR engine left Windsor Station, its whistle shrieking, and then the whole city exploded with the sounds of whistles, bells, and automobile horns. Windows opened all over Montreal and hundreds, perhaps thousands, of Union Jacks and Allied flags were thrust out into the November wind, in a city already festooned with bunting for the Victory Loan parade. Sherbrooke Street from Atwater Avenue to Lafontaine Park was filled with hundreds of thousands of spectators, and the procession began. Hundreds of veterans and soldiers led the parade.[120]

Victory seemed to heal all wounds – at least for the day.

Conclusion

This book began as an attempt to understand the experience of the city's civilians and soldiers without benefit of hindsight and presentist preoccupation with what the war meant to future generations. This approach often resulted in revisions to accepted views of the past – challenges to both everyone's memory and historical convention. A classic example of this is the Papineau-Bourassa correspondence of 1916, which writers, filmmakers, and historians have used as "an arresting metaphor for Canada during the war years."[1]

Papineau's letter appeared during a week when other news dominated, especially the outbreak of the deadliest forest fire in Canadian history, which swept through northern Ontario, killing more than 200 people.[2] On the international scene the Somme offensive and the later stages of the Brusilov offensive on the Eastern Front dominated the front pages. The human-interest story of the week was the execution of Roger Casement for his role in attempting to recruit an Irish brigade from prisoners of war in Germany and his trip to Ireland in a German U-boat on the eve of the Easter Rebellion. The Montreal press, French and English, had long followed Irish news closely, and the Casement execution was a dramatic climax to coverage of the Easter Rebellion.

As if this were not enough to divert attention from a letter full of platitudes about the war, Bourassa's reply was published on 5 August, when the news included the commemoration of the second anniversary of the declaration of war and a police raid on what today would be called a gay club in Montreal. The city was notorious for its extensive red-light district; brothels were tolerated and only raided if specific complaints were made. The same rule had been applied to what was called the Club Carreau, which had operated for several years before it moved uptown to a residential area. Complaints about the presence of young men forced the police to act, and six adults were arrested, including the organizer, J.L. Carreau. Bail was set at $50.00, following payment of which Carreau promptly fled to the United States, provoking further controversy and questions in the legislature. The Papineau-Bourassa exchange could not compete with Casement or Carreau and was quickly forgotten.[3]

Contextual research also allows us to better understand a number of more consequential issues. It is apparent that in 1914 and early 1915 the large majority of those with the time and energy to focus on a distant crisis believed that Britain and France were engaged in a just, defensive war, and favoured Canada's participation. French-speaking Montrealers focused on France and to a lesser extent Belgium, while English-speakers emphasized their connection to Britain and the Empire, but the result, a modest commitment of volunteers and some charitable fundraising, was the common response.

Henri Bourassa and his colleagues at *Le Devoir* did not directly oppose the consensus but did work to undermine it. Historians, who have long had access to microfilm copies of *Le Devoir* and the weekly *Le Nationaliste*, have allowed this limited perspective on French-speaking Quebec to dominate accounts of the war years. Now that the Bibliothèque et Archives National du Québec has made many more newspapers available online, *Le Devoir* and its editor may be seen in context. When *La Presse*, with a circulation ten times greater than that of *Le Devoir*, is also considered, Bourassa becomes a more marginal figure, a provocateur rather than the leader of public opinion.

Examining press coverage of events also challenges long-standing interpretations of the importance of the Ontario school question in shaping attitudes towards the war. The future of the French language in the Catholic schools of Ontario was a major issue for *Le Devoir* until obedience to the papal encyclical of September 1916 curbed further criticism. The popular press was much less involved except on two occasions: December 1914, in the aftermath of the Ontario Supreme Court's decision to uphold Regulation 17, and January 1916, during the occupation of the Guignes school in Ottawa. Neither event can be correlated with French Canadian enlistments. In the first months of 1916 Olivar Asselin, who had led the attack on Regulation 17, was successfully recruiting the 163rd Battalion. When voluntary enlistments declined in the summer of 1916 the pattern was similar across Canada and in no way peculiar to Montreal.

The city's Anglo-Celtic population offered near-unanimous support for Canada's participation, and numerous volunteers anxious to serve as officers in well-established or new regiments came forward throughout the fall of 1914. This response helped to create what Herbert Ames was to describe as "a British army raised in Canada" because, officers aside, "two thirds to three quarters of those who were able to enlist in the first and second contingents were British-born."[4] Montrealers thought of the young men, born in Britain but living with their families in the city, as part of their community, but that does not alter the reality that there were few Canadian-born volunteers before the summer of 1915.

The events of the spring of 1915 – the German use of poison gas at Second Ypres and the sinking of the *Lusitania* – had particular resonance in Montreal and quickly transformed perceptions of the war. Between June 1915 and May 1916 large numbers of Canadian-born, French- and English-speaking, sought to enlist. The rejection rates for failure to meet minimum height standards, dental and visual problems, and other medical issues meant that roughly one-third of all volunteers were denied the opportunity to serve. Adrian Gregory's description of the British working class can easily be applied to Montreal:

> Ironically the very poverty of the working class (which can be compared to con-ditions in a contemporary third world slum) was for many a salvation. Childhood malnutrition had rendered a staggeringly high proportion unfit for military service.[5]

A post-war study of the effect of socio-economic status on the health of chil-dren in Montreal reported that those from lower-income families were three to five inches shorter than their higher-income counterparts due to nutritional de-ficiencies. The sample group was drawn from English-speaking communities, but the authors were confident that a similar pattern existed in French Canadian neighbourhoods.[6]

Despite the number rejected, thousands were able to join Montreal-based units in the period of active voluntary enlistment. French Canadians were well represented in the surge of volunteers despite the Militia Department's and senior army officers' opposition to allowing a second French Canadian battal-ion to serve in the Canadian Corps. French Canadian leaders repeatedly argued for the formation of a French-language brigade to galvanize recruiting.[7] This may have been overly ambitious, but the decision to disband the 41st, 57th, 69th, 150th, and 163rd battalions meant that more than 4,000 French Canadian officers and men were used as replacements for English-language units as well as the 22nd Battalion. The other option for French Canadians was service in or in association with the French army. The work of two French Canadian hos-pitals established in the Paris suburbs to provide care for the wounded of the French army suggests that such ventures would have succeeded.[8]

The period of active voluntary enlistment ended in the spring of 1916 when the remaining eligible men aged eighteen to forty-five began to show a dis-inclination to risk death or dismemberment in a war that now seemed end-less. The number of enlistments declined sharply before the casualty lists for St. Eloi, Mont Sorrel, and Courcelette appeared, but news from the front may have influenced further declines in enlistment rates. During the months preceding 31 March 1918 Military District 4, centred on Montreal, contributed 32,463 men to the 364,750 then on the strength of the Canadian Expeditionary Force overseas. By way of comparison, in the same period Military District 3, Eastern Ontario, sent 39,393 men overseas.[9]

At least 60 per cent of the District 4 volunteers were born in the United Kingdom, suggesting that around 12,000 Canadian-born volunteered, roughly 5 per cent of the men of eligible age. An examination of the nominal rolls of the infantry battalions raised in the city indicates that 4,000 of the 6,000 French Canadians who joined were from the city, while 3,000 of the 12,000 enlisting in the English-language battalions were Canadian-born residents of Montreal. Another 3,000 were British-born who lived with their families in the city.

Losses – killed, wounded, and missing – appear to be proportionate to service in infantry battalions, so it seems likely that 2,000 families in Montreal lost a son, husband, or brother in the period to 31 March 1918.[10] This is not a large number in a city where infant mortality, tuberculosis, and other infectious diseases, not to mention the 1918 influenza epidemic, killed that many each year. Adrian Gregory noted that contrary to popular and literary tradition in Britain, less than 10 per cent of the population was directly affected by the loss of a close relative. He recognized that such calculations "will strike some as distasteful, demographic hair splitting" but argued it was necessary to escape from the myth that "everyone lost someone."[11]

Gregory was trying to understand the difference between grief, which was personal, and commemoration, a societal attempt to give meaning to the "sacrifice" of young lives. Jonathan Vance in his book *Death So Noble* has described the various kinds of commemoration of the inter-war period as "a mythic version of the events of 1914–1918," but has relatively little to say about the war itself.[12] In Montreal commemoration began in 1915 with ceremonies marking the first anniversary of the outbreak of war, an occasion used to restate a commitment to victory in a just cause against an enemy now seen as the embodiment of evil.

The city continued to mark the August anniversary, but the civic ritual that really took hold was Ypres Day. When the Canadian Parliament unanimously declared that 22, 23, and 24 April 1916 would be days in which everyone should fly the Union Jack, "the emblem of justice, liberty and tolerance," to honour the heroic defenders of Ypres, Montrealers embraced the idea. A parade of some 9,000 troops, returned veterans, militia, and cadets was organized, taking place before large crowds. Various religious leaders provided patriotic addresses on the theme of Christian sacrifice, with Protestants gathering at the Montreal Arena and Catholics at the cathedral.[13]

The second anniversary of the battle fell just a week after news of the Canadian victory at Vimy Ridge reached the city. All daily newspapers recognized the singular nature of the Canadian achievement and quoted from British and American sources praising the Canadians, but in Montreal attention quickly shifted to Ypres Day. The parade, remembrance services, and official opening of a new building to house the Khaki Club for returned veterans were all dedicated to the heroes of 1915.[14] It could be argued that the commitment to memorializing Second Ypres was the result of the publication of Max Aitkin's *Canada in Flanders* or "propaganda" about German atrocities and Canadian valour. It is, however, more plausible to maintain that neither propaganda nor censorship played a significant role in shaping public opinion. The popular press in Montreal was certainly patriotic, and newspaper stories were highly coloured, uncritical, and eternally optimistic, but the basic facts were reported. There were German atrocities and a good deal of Canadian valour to record alongside extensive casualty lists, graphic letters from soldiers, and human-interest biographies of men from Montreal who were killed or wounded.

By April 1918, when the third Ypres Day was observed, fewer French Canadians were willing to participate and the parade was confined to the west-end, English-speaking section of the city.[15] The methods used to suppress the Quebec riots, the transfer of troops from Ontario and the west to garrison sites in Montreal, and general anti-conscription sentiment were reason enough, but cold weather, which forced a postponement to 28 April, meant that the cancelation of exemptions was on everyone's mind. There was little room left for Ypres or Vimy in French Canada's view of the war.

For the Anglo-Celtic community Ypres remained a dominant memory until Vimy was chosen as the site for Walter Allward's memorial, which came to symbolize the achievements and sacrifices of the Canadian Corps. The argument that Canada became a nation on the slopes of Vimy Ridge would have seemed strange to people in 1917, though not as odd as we find the idea that "Vimyism" as a "virulent form of patriotism" is prevalent in twenty-first-century Canada.[16] What mattered in Montreal in 1917 was conscription. Before the announcement of the Military Service Act there was broad support for a voluntary war effort across the city. After May 1917 opposition to conscription and the cancellation of exemptions inspired a defensive, isolationist nationalism that was to dominate Quebec attitudes for generations.

There are many other examples of the difference between history as an enquiry into ideas expressed as actions and history as a search for a useable past. The traditional interpretation of the significance of the Imperial War Cabinet and Canada's role at Versailles, seen as steps towards full Canadian autonomy, is one such example.[17] In 1917 Laurier described Borden's claim that the Dominions would become "autonomous nations of an Imperial Commonwealth" with an "adequate voice" in British foreign policy as absurd, since "foreign policy cannot be divorced from British domestic politics."[18] *Le Canada* declared that Borden's policy was a step back from the quest for autonomy and the negation of a responsible government.[19] When Canada signed the Treaty of Versailles, the famous acquisition of signatory status, Canada along with other dominions and India were listed, indented, below Lloyd George's signature. The decision to allow each of the dominions a vote in the League of Nations allowed American opponents of the treaty to claim that Britain and her possessions had received six times the voting power of the United States because everyone thought that Britain and the dominions were forging a united empire. This was the framework Mackenzie King inherited in 1921 before he ignored Borden's plan and returned to Laurier's step-by-step approach to securing full autonomy.

Perhaps the most important contribution of the approach adopted in these pages is to document the multicultural character of Montreal in the early years of the twentieth century. The experiences of French Canadians, Italian Canadians, the uptown and downtown Jewish communities, the families of Irish descent clinging to their identity, and the large Anglo-Celtic population, which included working-class men and women as well as managers and millionaires, are part of the city's history.

Notes

Introduction

1 All circulation figures are from A. McKim, *The Canadian Newspaper Directory 1914–1919* (1892).
2 Vennat, *Les "poilus" québécois*, vol. 1.
3 The quoted words are from Cook, "Bourassa to Bissonnette," 132.
4 Kerby, *Sir Philip Gibbs.*

1 Metropolis

1 Lewis, *Manufacturing Montreal*, 144.

	Population of Montreal and suburbs, 1891–1931				
Place	Year of annexation	1891	1901	1911	1921	1931
Island of Montreal		277,525	360,838	544,761	724,205	1,003,868
Montreal and suburbs		271,285	352,557	549,190	721,184	1,000,661
Montreal at the census date		216,650	267,730	470,480	618,506	818,577
Montreal at its 1881 limits		182,695	203,078	225,132	230,978	242,984
Suburbs outside 1881 limits		88,590	149,479	324,058	490,206	757,677
Longueuil		2,757	2,835	3,972	4,682	5,407
Saint-Lambert		906	1,392	3,344	3,890	6,075
Verdun		296	1,898	11,629	25,001	60,745
Lachine		3,761	5,561	10,699	15,404	18,630

(*Continued*)

	Year of					
Place	annexation	1891	1901	1911	1921	1931
Ville Saint-Pierre			505	2,201	3,535	4,185
Saint-Gabriel	1887	9,986*	15,959*	18,961*		
Saint-Henri	1905	13,413	21,192	30,335*		
Sainte-Cunégonde	1905	9,291	10,912	11,174*		
Nôtre Dame de Grace	1910	2,305	2,225	5,217*		
Emard	1910	842	1,496	6,179*		
Outremont		408	1,148	4,820	13,249	28,641
Westmount		3,076	8,856	14,579	17,593	24,235
Saint-Laurent		1,184	1,390	1,860	3,232	5,348
Saint-Jean Baptiste	1886	15,423*	26,754*	34,561*		
Côte Saint-Louis	1893	2,972	9,025*	45,670*		
Saint-Louis de Mile End	1910	3,537	10,933	37,000*		
Hochelaga	1883	8,540*	12,914*	28,597*		
Longue Pointe	1910	2,445	2,519	5,531*		
Maisonneuve	1918	1,226	3,958	18,684		

Population of Montreal and suburbs, 1891–1931 (continued)

Source: Lewis, *Manufacturing Montreal*, 144. Data originally drawn from Canada, *Census of Canada*, various years.
* Population after the suburb was annexed to Montreal. The census up to and including 1911 provided the population of annexed suburban municipalities, but this was discontinued after 1911. The suburbs included here are those with a population of more than five thousand at any of the census dates.

2 Lewis, *Manufacturing Montreal*, 215.
3 See Berman, *All That Is Solid*, for an especially challenging study of "the experience of modernity."
4 Gilland, "Redimensioning Montreal," 75.
5 *The Canadian Engineer*, 30 April 1914, 676.
6 Senecal, "No. 5 Terminal Grain Elevator."
7 *The Canadian Engineer*, 7 May 1914, 711.
8 Gournay and Vanlaethem, *Montreal Metropolis*, 49.
9 Lewis, *Manufacturing Montreal*, 193–4.
10 Lewis, *Manufacturing Montreal*, 50–2.
11 Kilbourn, *The Elements Combined*, 31–2, 70–1.
12 Dales, *Hydroelectricity and Industrial Development*.
13 Fong, *J.W. McConnell*, 150.

14 Lewis, *Manufacturing Montreal*, 232.
15 Lewis, *Manufacturing Montreal*, 232.
16 Linteau, "Factors," 28.
17 MacLeod and Poutanen, *A Meeting of the People*, 93–4.
18 *L'Ecole Canadienne* (Montreal: 1946), 77–81.
19 Ryan, *The Clergy and Economic Growth*, 210.
20 Barlow, "House of the Irish."
21 My family was fairly typical. My maternal grandfather, James Wilson, left Brighton, England, for Verdun, Quebec, in 1907 after being recruited by the Grand Trunk Railway to work as a cabinet maker. My uncle Cecil Percy Copp arrived in Canada in 1910, obtaining work as a clerk. He enlisted in the Canadian army in 1915, becoming a sergeant in the service corps. My father, born 1908, joined his brother in Montreal in 1924. After night school he became a draftsman employed by Bell Telephone.
22 Nuhuet, "Une experience canadiene la Taylorism."
23 *Montreal Star*, 25 March 1914, 6.
24 Van Nus, "A Community of Communities," 59–70.
25 Bryce, "Making of Westmount."
26 Marshall, *Secularizing the Faith*.
27 Richard Virr, "Symonds, Herbert," in *Dictionary of Canadian Biography*, vol. 15 (University of Toronto/Université Laval, 2003), http://www.biographi.ca/en/bio/symonds_herbert_15E.html.
28 Hanaway, Cruess, and Darragh, *McGill Medicine,* 2.46.
29 Fong, *Sir William C. Macdonald*, 55.
30 Fong, *Sir William C. Macdonald*, 27–8.
31 Fong, *Sir William C. Macdonald*, 231–3.
32 Marelene Rayner-Canham and Geoff Rayner-Canham, "Brooks, Harriet (Pitcher)," in *Dictionary of Canadian Biography*, vol. 16 (University of Toronto/Université Laval, 2003), http://www.biographi.ca/en/bio/brooks_harriet_16E.html. See also Miller, "Big Ladies Hotel."
33 W.H. Atherton, *Montreal under British Rule* (Montreal, 1914), 2.331–2.
34 Linteau, *The Promoters' City*.
35 Prince, ed., *Montreal*; Fournier, *Un pionnier*.
36 *Le Canada Ecclesiastique, 1913* (Montreal, 1914). See also Voisine and Hamelin, *Histoire du catholicisme quebecois*.
37 MacDonald, "Who Counts?" 369–91. See also Danylewycz, *Taking the Veil*.
38 Atherton, *Montreal, 1535–1914* (Montreal: S.J. Clarke, 1914), 2.347–8.
39 McKeagan, "First Fifty Years," 14.
40 Primeau, "Le libéralisme," 241–77.
41 Laperrière, "Le Congrès eucharistique de Montréal," 21–39.
42 Dutil, *Devil's Advocate*. See also Patrice A. Dutil, "Langlois, Godfroy," in *Dictionary of Canadian Biography*, vol. 15 (University of Toronto/Université Laval, 2003), http://www.biographi.ca/en/bio/langlois_godfroy_15E.html.

43 Gagnon, *Histoire de la Commission des Écoles Catholiques*, 100. Amalgamation was deferred until 1917.

44 Dutil, "Adieu, demeure chaste et pure," 247.

45 Langlois, *Still Paddling*.

46 Brown, *Jew or Juif?*, 134–7.

47 Tulchinsky, *Canada's Jews*, 134–40. See also Anctil, *Eyes of the Eagle*.

48 See, for example, "Redivivus, Un Article d'Edouard Drumont," *Le Devoir*, 23 March 1912, 6; "Henri Bourassa et Edouard Drumont," *Le Pays*, 23 June 1917, 9.

49 Brown, *Jew or Juif?*, 136. See also Rome, *Early Anti-Semitism*.

50 D'Agostino, *Rome in America*, 84.

51 The protest meeting was reported by all the daily newspapers. See *La Patrie*, 17 and 18 October 1910; *Montreal Gazette*, 17 October 1910. When Nathan's appointment as Italy's commissioner for the International Panama-Pacific Exhibition in San Francisco was announced *L'Action Sociale*, the unofficial voice of Cardinal Bégin, joined other Catholic journals to protest his arrival in North America. *The Montreal Witness* reported this incident, but it was quickly forgotten. See *Montreal Witness*, 31 March 1911.

52 Figler, *Sam Jacobs*, 23–7; MacFadyen, "Nip the Noxious Growth," 73–96.

53 Figler, *Sam Jacobs*, 22–3.

54 MacLeod and Poutanen, "Little Fists," 61–99.

55 Copp, *Anatomy of Poverty*, 67.

56 Gagnon, *Histoire de la Commission*, 130–1.

57 *Souvenir Handbook, Child Welfare Exhibit 1912*, 32. Cited in Copp, *Anatomy of Poverty*, 33.

58 Copp, *Anatomy of Poverty*, 34.

59 See Bradbury, *Working Families*, for a discussion of the family economy in nineteenth-century Montreal.

60 Lévesque, *Making and Breaking the Rules*, 11.

61 MacDonald, "Who Counts?" 371.

62 Copp, *The Anatomy of Poverty*, 56.

63 Copp, *The Anatomy of Poverty*, 45.

64 *The Montreal Star*, 17 January 1914, 17.

65 *The Montreal Star*, 21 January 1914, 3. See also Campbell, *Rose Henderson*. Rose Henderson was the English-speaking Protestant probation officer for the Montreal juvenile court from 1912 to 1919. An active proponent of children's rights and the movement for "Mother's Pensions," Henderson often referred to such pensions, which were proposed for widows with children, in broader terms. She was an important source of information leading to the passage of "An Act to Prohibit the Improper Use of Opium and Other Drugs," claiming that the young children in Montreal were developing a "cocaine habit." See Campbell, *Rose Henderson*, 19.

66 Calculations of gross national product per capita and savings per capita have been used to track the impact of economic growth over time. See, for example, Byron Lew and Marvin McInnis, "Guns and Butter: World War I and the Canadian Economy," https://citeseerx.ist.psu.edu/viewdoc/download?doi=10.1.1.1072.2930&rep=rep1&type=pdf; and McCalla, "Economic Impact of the Great War," 138–53. This reality, together with evidence on the paucity of savings deposits, $93.79 per capita in 1914 (*Montreal Star*, 10 January 1914, 10), needs to be considered in any discussion of income redistribution.

67 The summary is based on a review of strikes and lockouts in Montreal 1901–14 originally prepared by Michael Piva for my book *The Anatomy of Poverty*. See chap. 8, "Labour Unrest and Industrial Conflict." Since then a number of studies have examined the issue using a similar source base. See, for example, Johal, "Responses to Change." The most detailed account of the history of organized labour in Montreal is Ewen, "International Unions."

68 Canada, *Royal Commission on the Cotton Textile Industry in Quebec* (Ottawa: J.O. Patenaude, King's Printer, 1938.)

69 Copp, *Anatomy of Poverty*, 97.

70 For a comprehensive study of this topic, see Baillargeon, *Babies for the Nation*.

71 Atherton, *Montreal, 1535–1914*, 2.447.

72 Province of Quebec, *Report of the Royal Commission on Tuberculosis, 1909–1910*, (Quebec: 1911), 2.

73 See *Quebec Statistical Yearbook 1915* for mortality and morbidity rates in 1914.

74 Canada, *Board of Inquiry into the Cost of Living* (Ottawa: 1913), 483.

75 Legault, "Architecture et Forme Urbaine," 1–10.

76 *Montreal Star*, 7 April 1914.

77 *Annual Report Quebec Board of Public Health 1908–1909*, 10. Cited in Copp, *Anatomy of Poverty*, 75.

78 Copp, *Anatomy of Poverty*, 85.

79 Vaughan, *Life and Work*, 345.

80 Croteau, "La financement des Écoles Publiques." See also Gagnon, *Histoire de la Commission*, 42; and Copp, *Anatomy of Poverty*, 63.

81 Protestant School Board of Greater Montreal, *Annual Report* 1907–08, 8, cited in Copp, *Anatomy of Poverty*, 66–7.

82 Copp, *Anatomy of Poverty*, 67.

83 Copp, *Anatomy of Poverty*, 63.

84 Lamonde and Montpetit, *Le Parc Sohmer*.

85 Metcalfe, *Canada Learns to Play*, 97–8.

86 This account is based on Pearson, "Decline of Professional Baseball." The quotation from *La Presse*, 23 April 1910, is cited in Pearson's thesis, 14. See also Pearson, "Montreal's Delorimier Downs Baseball Stadium." I thank Robert Pearson for sending me a copy of his honours BA thesis.

87 Gopnik, "How Montreal Perfected Hockey."

88 Vigneault, "La naissance d'un sport organisé." See also Vigneault, "Cultural Diffusion of Hockey in Montreal."

89 MacKenzie, *Screening Québec*, 72–83.

90 Barrière, "Montréal, microcosme du theatre lyrique," 373.

91 Germain, Johanne, and Bethsabée, *Le diable en ville*, 128–31.

92 Hawthorn, "Sarah Bernhardt and the Bishops," 97–120.

93 See *Montreal Star*, 5 January 1914, 5, 7; 8 January 1914, 5; 9 January 1914, 4; 10 January 1914, 1; 12 January 1914, 1.

94 Lévesque, "Éteindre le Red Light," 191.

95 Taschereau, *The Social Evil*.

96 Pineault, "Les clubs de 'Manches de Ligne,'" chap. 3.

97 *Le Canada Francais*, 30 October 1908, 3. See also Domeier, *Eulenburg Affair*.

98 *Montreal Standard*, 8 May 1914.

99 Prince, *Montreal Old and New*, 109.

100 Le Moine, "Deux loges Montréalaises," 526–7.

101 Meteorological data were drawn from climate.weather.gc.ca. The *Montreal Standard* describes preparation for St. Patrick's Day, which "will be the greatest in history in view of the possibility of early Home Rule"; *Montreal Standard*, 14 March 1914. All newspapers reported on the snow and work for the unemployed at $2.00/day.

102 *Labour Gazette*, 15 January 1914, 804. In 1913, 418,838 immigrants reached Canada.

103 R.S. Gourlay, "Presidential Address," *Industrial Canada*, November 1913, 465.

104 Quoted in the *Montreal Standard*, 2 May 1914, 10.

105 Sir Wilfrid Laurier used this figure in the House of Commons, basing it on reports from the *Labour Gazette* and other sources. See Canada, *Debates of the House of Commons*, 12th Parliament, 3rd Session, vol. 1 (19 January 1914), 18.

106 *Labour Gazette*, 15 January 1914, 804.

107 Gauvin, "Municipal Reform Movement." See also *The Canadian Engineer*, January to March 1914, which provides a detailed account of the water issue.

108 The articles appeared in *Le Devoir* on 11, 12, 13, and 14 March 1914.

109 Lew and Cater, "Canadian Emigration to the U.S.," table 1. See also Roby, *Les Franco-Americains*.

110 Barber, "Ontario Bilingual Schools Issues," 227–48.

111 Gaffield, *Language, Schooling, and Cultural Conflict*.

112 Choquette, *Language and Religion*, 261–4.

113 Barber, "Ontario Bilingual Schools Issues," 243.

114 Walker, *Catholic Education and Politics*, 2.229.

115 Bélanger, *Henri Bourassa*, 323–8.

116 Walker, *Catholic Education and Politics*, 2.281–2.

117 *Le Devoir*, 14 March 1914.

118 *Montreal Star*, 24 March 1914; *Montreal Star*, 29 March 1914.

119 All newspapers provided coverage of the campaign. The quote is from *Montreal Gazette*, 25 March 1914.
120 *Montreal Star*, 3 April 1914 and 11 April 1914.
121 The Martin quotations are from *Montreal Gazette*, 3 April 1914.
122 *La Patrie*, 4 March 1914. The estimate of 13,000 is from *Montreal Star*, 6 April 1914.
123 Brisebois, "La Fédération Nationale Saint-Jean-Baptiste," 105–24. See also Lacombe, "Marie Gerin-Lajoie's Hidden Crucifixes."
124 Linteau, *Histoire de Montréal*, 466–7.
125 Bacchi, *Liberation Deferred*. The minutes of the MSA are available online at Archives de Montréal, https://archivesdemontreal.ica-atom.org/fonds-de-la-montreal-suffrage-association-1913-1919.
126 *Montreal Gazette*, 8 April 1914.
127 All newspapers reported the results of the election on 7–8 April 1914.
128 *Le Devoir*, 8 April 1914.
129 Even the *New York Times*, 28 June 1914, carried the story. *Montreal Standard*, 2 May 1914, 7, ran a feature article on the redesigned park.
130 The quotations from the newspapers – *Montreal Gazette*, 26 March 1913; *Montreal Herald*, 26 November 1913; *Montreal Star*, 29 November 1913 – are available online as part of the database created by the Canadian Women Artists History Initiative–Concordia University, CWAHI.concordia.ca. See also Huston, "1913 Spring Exhibition," 13–55; and Dorais, *Morrice and Lyman*. Lyman's paintings can be viewed online, though few of those reproduced are pre-1913.
131 *Montreal Gazette* 27 March 1914; *La Presse* 26 March 1914.
132 *Labour Gazette*, May 1914, 1383–4; June 1914, 20.
133 The most recent account of the *Komagata Maru* is Johnston, *Voyage of the Komagata Maru*.
134 Symonds's sermon was reported in *Montreal Star*, 6 July 1914, 2.
135 *The Montreal Witness*, 24 July 1914, 2.

2 War

1 Borden diary, 23–31 July 1914, Sir Robert Borden Fonds, Manuscript Group 26, vol. 450, Library and Archives Canada (hereafter cited as LAC).
2 Nicholson, *Canadian Expeditionary Force*, 9–24.
3 *Secretary of State for the Colonies to the Governor-General*, 3 August 1914, in Duguid, *Official History*, 2.16.
4 Duguid, *Official History*, vol. 2, appendix 29, 47.
5 *Montreal Star*, 24 and 25 July 1914, 1.
6 *Montreal Witness*, 27 July 1914, 1.
7 *Christian Guardian*, 5 August 1914, 1; *Presbyterian Record*, 5 August 1914, 1.

8 Wilson, *Decisions for War*, devotes a chapter to the actions of each belligerent. Among the hundreds of books examining the outbreak of war, see Fischer, *Germany's Aims*; MacMillan, *The War That Ended Peace*; and Chickering, *Imperial Germany*.

9 Gregory, *The Last Great War*, 13.

10 *Montreal Star*, 4 August 1914, 4.

11 *Montreal Star*, 3 August 1914, 6.

12 *Montreal Star*, 3 August 1914, 7.

13 Finnan, *John Redmond and Irish Unity*. See also Howie and Howie, "Irish Recruiting."

14 *Montreal Star*, 3 August 1913, 16.

15 *Montreal Witness*, 4 August 1914, 1.

16 There is extensive coverage of the nature of the war in Belgium in all newspapers. The burning of Louvain was widely reported, but the deliberate massacres of Belgian civilians were not yet known. See Horne and Kramer, *German Atrocities*; and Kramer, *Dynamic of Destruction*, chap. 1, "Burning of Louvain."

17 *Montreal Standard*, 10 October 1914, 1.

18 *Le Devoir*, 5 August 1914, 1.

19 *Le Devoir*, 22 August 1914, 1.

20 The full text of the editorial, translated into English, is reproduced in Anctil, *"Do What You Must."*

21 *Le Devoir*, 12–14 September 1914; *Le Canada*, 14–18 September 1914. Bourassa was wrong about Grey's policy but could not know this at the time. Brenton McNab, the former editor of the *Montreal Star*, also criticized Bourassa's article in a letter to the *Winnipeg Tribune* that was translated and published in *La Patrie*, 2 January 1915, 11.

22 For a more detailed and sympathetic discussion of Bourassa's position in 1914, see Keelan, *Duty to Dissent*, 55–67.

23 Lachiver, "Le soutien humanitaire Canadien-Français," 147–73.

24 One member of the delegation spoke briefly in English; otherwise the language of the evening was entirely French. *La Presse*, 25 September 1914.

25 *Quebec Chronicle*, 14 September 1914, 1.

26 On 31 July 1914, the *Canadian Jewish Chronicle* carried one of many stories on events in Russia, reporting the "dangers of bloody pogroms." On 7 August the newspaper reported on the "vehement protest" of the *London* (England) *Jewish Chronicle* "against England associating with Russia of all nations."

27 The debate, which was resolved in favour of assimilation, was discussed at public meetings and reported in the *Canadian Jewish Chronicle* 7, 14 August 1914, and *Montreal Star*, 14 August 1914, 8.

28 *Le Devoir*, 15 September 1914, cited in Durocher, "Henri Bourassa, Les évêques," 253. See also *Le Canada*, 15 September 1914.

29 The pastoral letter was published in the provincial newspapers on 12 October 1914. See Pollard, *The Unknown Pope*.

30 Melnycky, "Badly Treated." See also Otter, *Internment Operations.*
31 Melnycky, "Badly Treated," note 41. By November 1916, the release of internees reduced the Spirit Lake Camp population to 275 men.
32 *La Presse,* 3 August 1914; 5 August 1914, cited in Vennat, *Les "poilus" québécois,* 1.19–20.
33 Morton, "French Canada and the Canadian Militia."
34 The story of the dispute over the Corpus Christi procession was widely discussed in the newspapers.
35 A further example of Hughes's failure to respect the traditions of the Quebec militia occurred at the Trois Riviérés summer militia exercises when the 85th honour guard for an open-air mass was ordered to return their rifles to the tents before the mass would proceed. See "Encore une affaire à la Sam Hughes," *Le Devoir,* 30 June 1914.
36 Militia regiments, as distinct from the numbered battalion authorized by the militia department for overseas service.
37 Williams, *First in the Field,* 64.
38 *Montreal Star,* 5 August 1914, 2.
39 Duguid, *Official History,* 36, appendix 45.
40 Fetherstonhaugh, *The Royal Montreal Regiment.*
41 Alexander Maavara and Brendan O'Driscoll have developed a database tracking those Montrealers listed in Sandwell, *The Call to Arms: Montreal's Roll of Honour, European War, 1914* (Montreal: Southam, 1914) by checking names on the attestation papers and the sailing list for First Contingent. All statistics are from that database.
42 Duguid, *Official History,* vol. 2, appendix 94, 62. See also Clarke, *Unwanted Warriors.*
43 Williams, *First in the Field,* 69.
44 *L'Action,* 26 September 1914, 6.
45 Vennat, *Les "poilus" québécois,* 2.29–41.
46 *Labour Gazette,* August 1914, 343–4.
47 War diary, Royal Montreal Regiment, 25 January 1915.
48 *Le Canada,* 26 October 1914, 4.
49 Gagnon, *Le 22e Battalion,* 56–61.
50 Speaight, *Vanier,* 35.
51 Fetherstonhaugh, *The 24th Battalion,* 8.
52 *Montreal Star,* 30 October 1914.
53 *Montreal Star,* 22 January 1915.
54 Based upon a review of the attestation papers of the 23rd Battalion. Just 201 of the 1078 recruits listed Montreal as the address for next of kin. 23rd Battalion CEF Nominal Roll, LAC. My thanks to Mike Kelly for creating the database on the 23rd Battalion.
55 *Montreal Star,* 22 September 1914, 6.

56 Burns, "Montreal Irish," 67–81. Proposals to establish both a Jewish and a Welsh battalion were announced, but common sense prevailed as community leaders urged enlistment in existing units.
57 Fetherstonhaugh, *McGill University at War*, 5–7.
58 Fetherstonhaugh, *No. 3 Canada General Hospital*, 4–6.
59 Litalien, "Un projet trop ambitieux?" 75–97.
60 Litalien, *Dans la tourmente*, 38–46.

3 Ypres

1 Nicholson, *Canadian Expeditionary Force*, 34–5.
2 War diaries of all the Canadian Expeditionary Force units are available online through Library and Archives Canada.
3 The newspaper accounts cited are from the website of the Royal Montreal Regiment Association, which, as part of an anniversary project developed by Hamilton Slessor, reproduces the daily war diary entry with additional material from newspapers. *Montreal Daily Mail*, 19 November 1914, 2; and the Toronto *Globe*, 16 November 1914, may also be found online at Google Newspaper Archives.
4 Fetherstonhaugh, *The 13th Battalion*, 22.
5 Iarocci, *Shoestring Soldiers*, 25. Iarocci notes that training continued despite the weather and argues that the Canadian division was well trained when it sailed for France.
6 Haycock, *Sam Hughes*, 232–4.
7 Duguid, *Canadian Grenadier Guards*, 55.
8 Morton, *Peculiar Kind of Politics*, 35–7.
9 Carr, *Canadian Red Cross Information Bureau*.
10 Williams, *First in the Field*, 75.
11 Williams, *First in the Field*, 81–3.
12 Vennat, *Les "poilus" québécois*, 1.60.
13 Fetherstonhaugh, *The 13th Battalion*, 35.
14 Vennat, *Les "poilus" québécois*, 1.64.
15 Fetherstonhaugh, *The 13th Battalion*, 35.
16 Philpott, "Britain, France and the Belgian Army," 121–36.
17 Edmonds, *Military Operations, France and Belgium, 1915*, 1.162.
18 The 14th Battalion stationed the French-Canadian company beside the Algerians; Fetherstonhaugh, *Royal Montreal Regiment*, 35.
19 Nicholson, *Canadian Expeditionary Force*, 57. The British referred to this position as the GHQ Line. See "Report on condition of the trenches 21 April 1915," *Official History of the Canadian Forces in the Great War 1914–1919*, vol. 1 (Ottawa: Ministry of National Defence, 1938), appendix 334.
20 Nicholson, *Canadian Expeditionary Force*, 55.

21 Fetherstonhaugh, *Royal Montreal Regiment*, 36. A parapet is on the forward side of a trench; the parado is on the rear side. A traverse was dug at an angle to the trench, ideally connecting with a second position.

22 Jaramowycz, "Montreal and the Battle of Ypres."

23 R. Jaramowycz, *The Black Watch: A History* (unpublished manuscript), 332. The late Lieut.-Colonel (retired) Roman Johann Jaramowycz, a friend and former student, allowed me to read and cite from a draft of this manuscript that is currently in my collection.

24 Duguid, *Official History*, 1.220.

25 Van der Kloot, "April 1915," 149–60.

26 August Jaeger's identity as the deserter was made public in a French newspaper in 1931. He was arrested and tried for treason and received a ten-year sentence. See Reference Online: http://www.greatwar.co.uk/battles/second-ypres-1915 /prelude/deserter-jaeger.htm.

27 War diary, Assistant Director of Medical Services, 1st Canadian Division, 15 April 1915.

28 Duguid, *Official History*, 2.227.

29 Cook, *At the Sharp End*, 116.

30 Jaramowycz, *The Black Watch*, 347.

31 See "The gallantry of Lance Corporal Fred Fisher V.C.," www.greatwar.co.uk, a segment of a detailed account of combat in the Ypres salient 1915.

32 Duguid, *Official History*, vol. 2, appendix 352, 240. Captain F.A.C. Scrimger was also to receive the Empire's highest award for valour for rescuing wounded men under fire. Dr. Scrimger, the original medical officer of the 14th Battalion, was a well-known Montreal doctor who became chief of surgery at Royal Victoria Hospital after the war.

33 Jaramowycz, *The Black Watch*, 348.

34 Humphries, "First Use of Poison Gas."

35 Fetherstonhaugh, *Royal Montreal Regiment*, 39.

36 Nicholson, *Canadian Expeditionary Force*, 69–70.

37 Duguid, *Official History*, 1.279.

38 Iarocci, *Shoestring Soldiers*, 154–5.

39 Iarocci, *Shoestring Soldiers*, 288.

40 Helmer, the son of Lieut.-Colonel R.A. Helmer of Ottawa, was born in 1892. A graduate of McGill (1914), he joined the 1st Canadian Field Artillery on 27 August 1914.

41 Edmonds, *Military Operations, France and Belgium, 1915*, 1.312.

42 Williams, *First in the Field*, 90–1.

43 War diary, Princess Patricia's Canadian Light Infantry, May 1915.

44 Edmonds, *Military Operations, France and Belgium, 1915*, 1.357.

45 Edmonds, *Military Operations, France and Belgium, 1915*, 1.356.

46 Crofton, *Massacre of the Innocents*, 264.

47 *Montreal Star*, 24 April 1915, 1.
48 *Montreal Star*, 27 April 1915, 3.
49 *Montreal Star*, 28 April 1915, 4.
50 *Montreal Star*, 28 April 1915, 4.
51 Database, Montreal casualties as reported in the *Montreal Star*. The database was prepared by Alexander Maavara.
52 *Montreal Gazette*, 26 April 1915, 4.
53 *Montreal Star*, 26 April 1915, 6.
54 *Montreal Witness*, 27 April 1915, 1.
55 *The Standard*, 1 May 1915, 1.
56 Davidson, "Private Sorrow Becomes Public Property."
57 *Montreal Star*, 30 April 1915, 3.
58 *Montreal Star*, 30 April 1915, 3.
59 Personnel file, Joseph Adolphe Dansereau, LAC.
60 Vennat, *Les "poilus" québécois*, 1.120–3.
61 *Montreal Star*, 1 May 1915, 1.
62 O'Keefe, *A Thousand Deadlines*, 89–103.
63 *The Standard*, 10 May 1915, 11.
64 The website www.rmslusitania.info offers detailed information about the fate of the passengers aboard the *Lusitania*.
65 *Montreal Gazette*, 4 June 1915, 6.
66 This account of Aubers Ridge and Festubert is based on Harris, *Douglas Haig*, 132–52.
67 Iarocci, *Shoestring Soldiers*, 202–24; and Fetherstonaugh, *Royal Montreal Regiment*, 52–7. For the phrase "between mutiny and obedience" and the most detailed account of agency by front-line soldiers, see Smith, *Between Mutiny and Obedience*.
68 Fowler, "Death Is Not the Worst Thing," 29.
69 *Montreal Standard*, 5 June 1915, 28.
70 *Le Devoir*, 26 April–15 May 1915; *Le Nationaliste*, 9 May 1915, 1.
71 Rumilly, *Henri Bourassa*, 531–3.
72 *La Patrie*, 3 April 1915, 10.

4 Mobilizing

1 *Canadian Annual Review*, 1915, 200.
2 Canada, *Debates of the House of Commons*, 12th Parliament, 5th Session, vol. 3 (10 April 1915), 2367–70.
3 Gagnon, *Le 22e Battalion*, 151. The problems facing the 41st Battalion in Quebec City are alluded to in the pages of the *Quebec Chronicle*. See, for example, "Amusement was Ill-Concealed at City Council" (after a request for money from Archambault), *Quebec Chronicle*, 10 April 1915, 1.

4 One of the mounted regiments, the 5th CMR, was based at Sherbrooke in Quebec's Eastern Townships, and it attracted some officers and NCOs from the city's Hussar regiments as well as 250 men from Montreal, most of them British born with military experience. Nominal Role, 5th Canadian Mounted Rifles, CEF, LAC.

5 *Labour Gazette*, vol. 15, 770.

6 *Montreal Standard*, 15 July 1916, 22. The *Montreal Star* reported in September 1916, 4, that 50 per cent of volunteers were rejected because of vision problems. *Le Canada*, 28 July 1916, 4, suggested that 40 per cent of French Canadian volunteers were rejected and asked for the creation of Bantam battalions to accommodate the smaller Latin race.

7 *Le Nationaliste*, 29 November 1914, 6.

8 *Le Canada*, 22 December 1914, 8.

9 *Le Canada*, 22 December 1914, 8.

10 *Le Nationaliste*, 27 December 1914, 6. The article provided a count of the columns devoted to the meeting in the city's dailies: *Le Devoir*, 17; *Le Canada*, 9; *La Presse*, 3; *La Patrie*, 2. The English-language dailies provided minimal coverage.

11 *Le Canada*, 9 January 1915, 7, printed the full text of the letter.

12 *Canadian Annual Review*, 1915, 564–5. A *Montreal Star* editorial argued that Ontario had "a technical but not a moral right to limit the use of French." *Montreal Star*, 13 January 1915.

13 *Canadian Annual Review 1915*, 562.

14 *Le Pays*, 20–23 April 1915.

15 See, for example, *La Patrie*, 3 April 1915, 10.

16 The Saint Lin event was widely reported, especially in *Le Canada* and *La Presse*. Both *La Patrie* and *Le Devoir* provided detailed coverage on 9 August 1915.

17 Cited in Dutil, "Against Isolationism," 116–17.

18 J.D. Perkins, "Canadian-Built British H-Boats" (unpublished article, 1999), http://www.gwpda.org/naval/cdnhboat.htm. The *Labour Gazette* (vol. 15, 1150) reported that 1,780 men were employed by Canadian Vickers in early 1915.

19 *Montreal Star*, 4 June 1915, 4. The *Labour Gazette* (vol. 16, 25) reported that 80 per cent of the applicants were natives of Great Britain, 10 per cent French Canadians, and 10 per cent citizens of France.

20 *Montreal Star*, 9 June 1915, 3.

21 *Labour Gazette*, vol. 15, 259, 1378.

22 *Montreal Gazette*, 5 May 1915. Ames's words were featured in *Le Nationaliste* under the heading "Une armée anglaise," 16 May 1915, 1.

23 Gervais, *The Silent Sixtieth*, 21.

24 *Montreal Standard*, 10 July 1915, 10.

25 Nominal Roll, 60th Battalion CEF, LAC.

26 Gervais, *The Silent Sixtieth*, 11.

27 *Montreal Star*, 3 June 1915, 17.
28 *Montreal Star*, 5 June 1915.
29 *Canadian Annual Review 1915*, 313.
30 See Kirkland, "Mothering Citizens.
31 *Montreal Standard*, 8 May 1915, 22.
32 Glassford, "Marching as to War." Glassford argues that "the strong patriotic and imperial overtones to its work with the Canadian Red Cross Society were not designed to appeal to French Canadians" (137). The Croix Rouge, however, with its focus on Belgium and France, attracted both rural and urban French Canadian women.
33 Marti, "For Kin and Country," 344–5.
34 Quiney, "'Bravely and Loyally."
35 *Montreal Standard*, 15 May 1915, 10; 22 May 1915, 20. See Haas, "Purple Cross," 37–9.
36 Morris, *The Canadian Patriotic Fund*, 245–56.
37 Morton, "Entente cordiale?" 231.
38 Obituary of H.R.Y. (Helen) Reid, *Montreal Gazette*, 9 January 1941, 21.
39 Morton, *Fight or Pay*, 243–5.
40 *Souvenir Handbook, Child Welfare Exhibit* (Montreal 1912), 32. Cited in Copp, *Anatomy of Poverty*, 33.
41 Morton, *Fight or Pay*, 112.
42 *La Bonne Parole*, publication of Le Féderation nationale Saint-Jean Baptiste, September 1915, 2.
43 Boivin and Landry, "Françoise et Madeleine," 233–43.
44 Le Naour, "Les narraines de guerre."
45 *La Patrie*, 15 September 1915, 19. I thank Anastasia Pivinicki, who examined the weekly women's page of *La Patrie* 1914–18 and the monthly *La Bonne Parole* 1914–18 for me.
46 Lowe, "Britain and Italian Intervention," 533–48.
47 Ventresco, "Italian Reservists," 95.
48 "L'Intervention de L'Italie et al presse de Montréal," *Le Devoir*, 26 May 1915, 1.
49 Salvatore, *Ancient Memories*, 57–9.
50 "Le Sac du Devoir," *Le Devoir*, 29 May 1915, 1.
51 *La Croix*, 29 May 1915, 1.
52 *Montreal Witness*, 1 June 1915, 1.
53 The officer commanding the Canadian Dental Corps was to claim credit for making 50,000 men "who could not otherwise have gone to the front fit for service." *Montreal Star*, 16 September 1916, 4.
54 *Canadian Annual Review* 1915, 226.
55 *Le Canada*, 1 July 1915, 1, reported that the accepting of men shorter than five feet, three inches would make a big difference in Montreal.
56 Morton, *Fight or Pay*, 89–90.

57 The battalion set five feet, four inches as the minimum height, but the changes in dental and vision requirements may have been significant.

58 Nominal Roll, 73rd Battalion CEF, LAC.

59 Hutchison, *73rd Battalion Royal Highlanders*, 40.

60 Nominal Roll, 41st Battalion CEF, LAC.

61 Gagnon, *Le 22e Battalion*, 149–50.

62 Morton, "Short Unhappy Life."

63 Radley, *We Lead, Others Follow*, 81.

64 Gagnon, *Le 22e Battalion*, 153. Mobilizing the 57th was authorized on 20 April 1915; recruiting began in May. Nominal Roll, 57th Battalion CEF, LAC.

65 Gilles Janson, "Scott, Henri-Thomas (baptized Thomas-Henri)," in *Dictionary of Canadian Biography*, vol. 15 (University of Toronto/Université Laval, 2003), http://www.biographi.ca/en/bio.php?id_nbr=7861.

66 Gagnon, *Le 22e Battalion*, 154–5.

67 When the 41st sailed, a full company was made up of Russians who had first enlisted in the 57th. Gagnon, *Le 22e Battalion*, 151.

68 Major-General Sam Steele, diary entry, 22 December 1915, 30 December 1915. Thanks to Rod Macleod, professor emeritus, University of Alberta, for providing access to his manuscript on the diary of Major-General Sam Steele.

69 Gagnon, *Le 22e Battalion*, 148.

70 *Le Canada*, 23 July 1915, 8; *Montreal Gazette*, 23 July 1915, 4.

71 Morton, *Peculiar Kind of Politics*, 44.

72 Nominal Roll, 57th Battalion CEF, LAC.

73 Gagnon, *Le 22e Battalion*, 157–9, reports that Dansereau's parents lost all their savings supporting their son's battalion. At the end of the war other debts contracted by the battalion commander were still on the books. See also Vennat, *Les "poilus" québécois*, 1.207–20.

74 Major-General Sam Steele, diary entry for 29 July 1916.

75 Gagnon, *Le 22e Battalion*, 158.

76 The 117th Battalion included 255 French Canadians, but the language of command was English, as there were 327 Canadian-born and 280 British-born recruits who spoke English as well as 82 others. The 117th was disbanded in England. Men were sent to the 148th and 150th battalions before they too were disbanded. The remaining men were absorbed by the 23rd Reserve Battalion. Nominal Roll, 117th Battalion CEF, LAC. See also Duguid, *Canadian Grenadier Guards*, 91–3; Nominal Roll, 87th Battalion CEF, LAC.

77 Haycock, *Sam Hughes*, 266.

78 *Canadian Annual Review*, 1915, 226.

79 *Montreal Witness*, 4 January 1916, 5.

80 Pickles, *Transnational Outrage*. For a contemporary account see "English Nurse Shot by Germans Despite Appeals for Mercy Made by American Ambassador," *Montreal Witness*, 26 October 1915, 20.

81　Stewart, "Frustrated Belligerence," 32.

82　*Montreal Witness*, 9 January 1916, 1.

83　Borden diary, 30 December 1915, Sir Robert Borden Fonds, Manuscript Group 26, vol. 450, LAC. The entry for 30 December reads: "White, Hughes and Reid came and I propounded the proposed force should be increased on 1 January to 500,000. They agreed."

84　Nicholson, *Canadian Expeditionary Force*, 546.

85　The quotations are from the *Montreal Gazette* in March 1916, 4. An order-in-council restraining Hughes from creating new units was passed in July 1916. Borden diary, 9 July 1916, Sir Robert Borden Fonds, Manuscript Group 26, vol. 450, LAC.

86　Haycock, *Hughes*, 209; Borden diary, 10 March 1916, Sir Robert Borden Fonds, Manuscript Group 26, vol. 450, LAC. The Shell Scandal involved the relationship of Hughes with Wesley Allison, a close friend who served as a middleman in arranging contracts for the manufacture of shells. Hopkins, *Canadian Annual Review*, 1916, 269–70; and Haycock, *Hughes*, chap. 13.

87　*Labour Gazette*, "Montreal Reports," December 1915–March 1916.

88　*Labour Gazette*, "Montreal Reports," June 1915, 1271.

89　Price, *Industrial Occupations of Women*, 21, table 1.

90　Carnegie, *Munitions Supply in Canada*, 136.

91　All quotations are from the *Montreal Gazette*, 10 March 1916, 4.

92　*Le Devoir*, 5 January 1916, 1. Bourassa was in Ottawa speaking about "barbarism versus civilization" the night of the action.

93　The Lapointe Resolution was introduced on 9 May 1916.

94　Cited in Piovesana, "Laurier and the Liberal Party."

95　Dutil, "Against Isolationism," 115. See also Stagni, *The View from Rome*.

96　Keelan, *Duty to Dissent*, 123.

97　Cameron, "Bonne Entente Movement." See also Talbot, "Une reconciliation insaisissable."

98　Sandra Gwyn, "Papineau, Talbot Mercer," in *Dictionary of Canadian Biography*, vol. 14 (University of Toronto/Université Laval, 2003), http://www.biographi.ca/en/bio/papineau_talbot_mercer_14E.html?print=1.

99　Keelan, "Canada's Cultural Mobilization," 377.

100　*Montreal Daily Mail*, 5 August 1916, 1.

101　*Le Devoir*, 5 August 1916, 4.

102　*Montreal Star*, 25 April 1916 1; 26 April 1916.

103　"Have Huns Been Landing Arms in Ireland…? John Redmond Calls on Followers to Come to the Aid of the Military," *Montreal Standard*, 29 April 1916, 1. The *Gazette* also emphasized Casement's role and stressed that the fighting was confined to Dublin, as did *La Presse* and *La Patrie*.

104　*Le Nationaliste*, 6 August 1916, 1.

105　Deutsch, "War Finance," 540.

106 Wage and price indices report increases in wage rates that kept pace with the cost of living until 1917. Deutsch, "War Finance," 542. Wage rates are only part of the story of family income.

107 Quebec, *Annual Report of the Quebec Department of Labour* (1916), 57.

108 Examples from *La Patrie*, Saturday edition, July–August 1916.

109 *Le Pays*, 4 March 1916, 4; *La Patrie*, 4 March 1916, 14.

110 *Passe temps* is available on the BANQ site. We have not located copies of *Montréal qui chante*.

111 For details on the temperance/prohibition movement in Montreal, see *Montreal Weekly Witness*, 2 January 1917, 4, and each subsequent issue. For the Montreal Brewers Association counteroffensive see *Le Monde Ouvrier/Labour World*, which regularly published articles demanding the exemption of beer, the working man's beverage.

112 *Montreal Standard*, 9 January 1917.

113 *Le Pays*, 26 August 1916, 1.

114 This account is from the *Montreal Standard*, 6 August 1916, 1; *Le Pays*, 19 August 1916, 4; *Le Canard*, 20 August 1916, 8; 24 September 1916, 2. See also *Débats de Assemblé legislative*, 14th Parliament, 1st session, 4 December 1916. See also Dagenais, "Culture urbaine et homosexualité."

115 Nominal Roll, 148th Battalion CEF, LAC.

116 Matthew K. Barrett, "The Currie Advocate, Lieut-Colonel Alan Magee," in "Patriots, Crooks and Safety-Firsters: Colonels of the Canadian Expeditionary Force," https://matthewkbarrett.com/2015/02/16/the-lawyer/.

117 Vennat, *Les "poilus" québécois*, 1.287–8; *La Presse*, 15 June 1915, 1.

118 Gagnon, *Le 22e Battalion*, 162.

119 "150th Battalión Amalgamation," RG 24, vol. 1569, File HQ683-188-3, LAC.

120 Nominal Roll, 178th Battalion CEF, LAC.

121 LAC, *Guide to Sources Relating to Units of the Canadian Expeditionary Force*, 150th Battalion, 490.

122 Letter, Barré to Kemp (minister of overseas services), 14 February 1918, cited in Barrett, "Patriots, Crooks and Safety-Firsters: Colonels of the Canadian Expeditionary Force," https://matthewkbarrett.com/2015/11/09/the-disgruntled/.

123 One draft of 98 men from the 150th was sent to the 87th Battalion. Their war diary notes, "A good looking lot apparently well trained." Duguid, *Canadian Grenadier Guards*, 154.

124 "*Poil-aux-pattes*" was a French Canadian term used to describe men who were bold or daring.

125 Olivar Asselin, "Les proceeds de l'abbé d'Amours," *L'Action*, 9 October 1915, 1. A week later in a column titled "Pour la liberte de parole" Asselin announced publication in pamphlet form of a series of articles, "L'Action Catholique, Les évêques et le guerre." See also Wade, *The French Canadians*, 2.677–8.

126 See Pelletier-Baillargeon, *Olivar Asselin*, 1.657–8.

127 *Montreal Gazette*, 22 January 1916, 4. See also the commentary by A. Labelle on the behaviour and motivation of the students, *Le Pays*, 29 January 1916, 5.

128 The 206th began recruiting in February 1916. In September 103 men transferred to the 163rd in Bermuda. Two drafts of 50 men were sent to other French Canadian battalions. Gagnon, "Canadian Soldiers in Bermuda," 9–36.

129 Pelletier-Baillargeon, *Olivar Asselin*, 2.26–9.

130 Lieut.-Gen. Sir George Bullock's report is quoted in Pelletier-Baillargeon, *Olivar Asselin*, 2.41–3.

131 LAC, *Guide to the Sources Relating to the Units of the Canadian Expeditionary Force*, 163rd Battalion, 518. The 163rd reached England on 6 December 1916.

132 Pelletier-Baillargeon, *Olivar Asselin*, 2.51.

133 The other French-language Quebec battalions recruiting in mid-1916 were the 167th (Quebec City), 171st (Valcartier), and 189th (Fraserville, or modern day Rivière-du-Loup).

134 *Le Canada*, 28 July 1916, 3.

135 LAC, *Guide to Sources Related to Units of the Canadian Expeditionary Force Pioneer Battalions*, 31.

136 Recruiting Poster, 5th Pioneer Battalion, C 233-2-4-0-211, Archives of Ontario.

137 Nominal Roll, 5th Pioneer Battalion, LAC.

138 My thanks to Garison Ma and Mike Kelly for examining the attestation papers of the other ranks who enlisted in the 199th Battalion.

139 See also Burns, "Montreal Irish"; Jolivet, *Le vert et le bleu*, 169–211.

140 *Montreal Gazette*, 31 July 1916, 3.

141 199th Battalion Attestation Papers Database. We have not been able to locate a Nominal Roll, for the 199th.

142 Inspection Report, 199th Battalion, RG II-B-5, vol. 7; Inspections, LAC.

143 Major Knox-Leet was returned to Canada before the 60th Battalion entered battle in France. Personnel file, Edward Knox-Leet, LAC.

144 Borden Papers, Reel C-4323, LAC. Cited in Brendan O'Driscoll, *The 199th Irish Canadian Rangers* (unpublished paper, LCMSDS Archives, 2015).

145 Burns, "Montreal Irish," 75.

146 Drysdale, *Canada to Ireland*, 6.

147 *The Tablet*, 3 February 1917, 26.

148 Drysdale, *Canada to Ireland*, 6.

149 Finnan, *John Redmond*, 199. Sinn Fein won a by-election in May 1917 but it was the East Clare by-election of July 1917 won by Eamon de Valera that marked the end of Redmond's influence.

150 Duguid, *Canadian Grenadier Guards*, 183. O'Donahoe commanded the battalion through the first months of 1917, but when the 199th became the core of a reserve battalion in April he returned to France to lead the 87th. He died of wounds sustained in action during April 1918.

5 Attrition

1 Hynes, *A War Imagined*, xiv.
2 Revisionism began with John Terraine's biography *Douglas Haig: The Educated Soldier*. See also Sheffield, *Forgotten Victory*, for a recent example of the revisionist approach.
3 Fischer, *Germany's Aims*, 98–107.
4 Doughty, *Pyrrhic Victory*, 18.
5 Doughty, *Pyrrhic Victory*, 107.
6 Harris, *Douglas Haig* , 154.
7 Sheffield and Bourne, *Douglas Haig*, 137.
8 Harris, *Douglas Haig*, 176.
9 The Canadians burned sulphur-infused waste to imitate a gas cloud. Nicholson, *Canadian Expeditionary Force*, 121.
10 Nicholson, *Canadian Expeditionary Force*, 97.
11 This account of Aubers Ridge and Festubert is based on Harris, *Douglas Haig*, 132–52.
12 Nominal Roll, 23rd Battalion CEF, LAC.
13 Potter, "Smile and Carry On," 84.
14 Iarocci, *Shoestring Soldiers*, 194.
15 Rawling, *Surviving Trench Warfare*, 43.
16 Iarocci, *Shoestring Soldiers*, 203. For the phrase "between mutiny and obedience" and the most detailed account of agency and proportionality among front-line soldiers, see Smith, *Between Mutiny and Obedience*.
17 Nicholson, *Canadian Expeditionary Force*, 103.
18 Haycock, *Sam Hughes*, 269.
19 Haycock, *Sam Hughes*, 271.
20 Delaney, "Mentoring the Canadian Corps," 931–53.
21 Clements, *Merry Hell*, 65.
22 Campbell, "Divisional Experience in the CEF."
23 Speaight, *Vanier*, 43–6.
24 The 5th Brigade reported 23 men killed in action and 95 wounded during February 1916, a month of trench routine. War diary, 5th Brigade, LAC.
25 Macphail, *Official History: The Medical Services*, 54.
26 "Monthly Strength Infantry 2nd Division," statistics compiled by C.E.F. Registry, Director of Records, Department of National Defence, LCMSDS Archive.
27 War diary, 42nd Battalion, November 1915, LAC.
28 Doughty, *Pyrrhic Victory*, 269–89.
29 Sheffield, *Haig Diary*, 29 March 1916, 183.
30 Haycock, *Sam Hughes*, 268–9. See Hughes to Kitchener, 24 March 1915; *Montreal Witness*, 20 June 1916, 6.

31 Plumer was under pressure from Haig, who was unhappy with Second Army's performance. Stewart, *Embattled General*, 84.

32 Edmonds, *Military Operations, France and Belgium, 1916*, vol. 1, pt. 1, 185.

33 Stewart, *Embattled General*, 87.

34 Tim Cook, *At the Sharp End*, 328. See also Cook, "Blind Leading the Blind," 24–36.

35 Edmonds, *Military Operations, France and Belgium, 1916*, vol. 1, part 1, 191.

36 Fetherstonhaugh, *The 24th Battalion*, 46.

37 The 22nd Battalion lost 7 men with a further 30 wounded holding the line for three days. War diary, 22nd Battalion, 14–17 April 1915, LAC.

38 Stewart, *Embattled General*, 104–11.

39 Haycock, *Sam Hughes*, 297–8.

40 Stewart, *Embattled General*, 104–9.

41 Williams, *Byng of Vimy*. Williams notes that Byng "wrote no memoirs … and had his personal papers destroyed" (10); we therefore know little about Byng's thoughts or planning.

42 Nicholson, *Canadian Expeditionary Force*, 148.

43 Edmonds, *Military Operations, France and Belgium, 1916*, vol. 1, pt. 1, 229–30.

44 Nicholson, *Canadian Expeditionary Force*, 134.

45 Edmonds, *Military Operations, France and Belgium, 1916*, vol. 1, pt. 1, 231.

46 Topp, *The 42nd Battalion RHC*, 56. The war diary of the 42nd Battalion provides more detail.

47 Currie later recalled cautioning Byng against an immediate counterattack but did not comment on Hoare-Nairne's role. Dancocks, *Sir Arthur Currie*, 70.

48 "Counter Attack on Maple Copse and Observatory Ridge Positions Night of June 2/3 1916," war diary, 14th Battalion, June 1916.

49 D Company of the 14th Battalion, originally formed from 65th Regiment volunteers, ceased to be a French-language unit in March 1916 when the surviving members were scattered among all four companies. Radley, *We Lead, Others Follow*, 81–2.

50 Fetherstonhaugh, *The 13th Battalion*, 102.

51 Hooge, once a village on the Menin Road, was on the forward, western slope of the Ypres Ridge and therefore subject to observed artillery fire from British and Canadian artillery.

52 Edmonds, *Military Operations, France and Belgium, 1916*, vol. 1, part 1, 242.

53 Humphries, *A Weary Road*, 113–14.

54 The full text of the letter was published in the *Montreal Gazette* and other newspapers on 14 June 1916, 4.

55 Borden diary, 6 June 1916, Sir Robert Borden Fonds, Manuscript Group 26, vol. 450, LAC.

56 *Montreal Gazette*, 8 June 1916, 4.

57 Fetherstonhaugh, *McGill University at War*, 11.

58 LAC, *Guide to Sources Related to Units of the Canadian Expeditionary Force Infantry Battalions*, 665.

59 On 26 August 1916, as recruiting for the 245th Battalion was to begin, units recruiting in Montreal needed 2,537 additional volunteers. *Montreal Standard*, 26 August 1916, 10.

60 Duguid, *Canadian Grenadier Guards, 1760–1964*, 130.

61 Nominal Roll, 245th Battalion CEF, LAC.

62 The French army provided just eleven divisions to "support" what Joffre saw as a British offensive. Doughty, *Pyrrhic Victory*, 291. On 1 July the British employed fourteen divisions, the French six. Harris, *Douglas Haig*, 229.

63 Edmonds, *Military Operations, France and Belgium, 1916*, vol. 1, pt. 1, 252.

64 Harris, *Douglas Haig*, 216–20.

65 Prior and Wilson, *The Somme*, 41.

66 Censors must have prevented news of the scale of losses from reaching the public. There was no reference to the disaster that overwhelmed the Newfoundland Regiment on 1 July in Montreal.

67 Sheffield, *Haig Diary*, 2 July 1916, 197.

68 Sheffield, *Haig Diary*, 29 July 1916, 213.

69 The full text of the memo is reproduced in Churchill, *World Crisis*, 3.188–94.

70 Sheffield, *Haig Diary*, 2 August 1916, 214.

71 This summary of the Somme is drawn from Copp, *The Somme*.

72 Fetherstonaugh, *13th Battalion*, 130–1.

73 Williams, *Byng of Vimy*, 136.

74 Sheffield, *Haig Diary*, 2 August 1916, 214.

75 Sheffield, *Haig Diary*, 5 September 1916, 227.

76 Harris, *Douglas Haig*, 261.

77 Miles, *Military Operations, France and Belgium 1916*, vol. 1, pt. 1, 302.

78 Nicholson, *Canadian Expeditionary Force*, 170–1.

79 War diary, 5th Brigade, September 1916, appendix 25, LAC. See also Fetherstonaugh, *24th Battalion*, 88–90. For divisional casualties and the reinforcement problem see Stewart, *Embattled General*, 136–7; Campbell, "A Forgotten Victory: Courcelette," 27–48.

80 Clements, *Merry Hell*, 152.

81 See, for example, *Le Devoir*, 23 September 1916. *La Presse* editors provided readers with the most detailed stories about the role played by the 22nd at Courcelette. See Vennat, *Les "polius*," 1.274–83. See also Keelan, "Il a bien merité de la patrie."

82 The phrase became the unofficial motto of the Royal Tank Regiment and the Royal Canadian Armored Corps.

83 Nicholson, *Canadian Expeditionary Force*, 178–9.

84 Adamson, *Letters of Agar Adamson*, 225.

85 Sheffield, *Haig Diary*, 2 October 1916, 236.

86 Hughes to Carson, 14 October 1916, cited in Stewart, *Embattled General*, 152.

87 Sheffield, *Haig Diary*, 2 October 1916, 236.
88 Nicholson, *Canadian Expeditionary Force*, 186.
89 Duguid, *Canadian Grenadier Guards*, 113–14.
90 Sheffield, *Haig Diary*, 12 November 1916, 254.
91 Nicholson, *Canadian Expeditionary Force*, 196–7.
92 Duguid, *Canadian Grenadier Guards*, 125. Overall, 4th Division suffered 4,311 casualties in the last weeks of the Somme Campaign. Godefory, "4th Canadian Division," 214.
93 Hutchison, *73rd Battalion*, 84.
94 Humphries, *A Weary Road*, 157–97.
95 Sheffield, *Haig Diary*, 5 November 1916, 252.
96 Prior and Wilson, *The Somme*, 101–2. See also McRandle and Quirk, "Blood Test Revisited," 667–701.
97 Miles, *Military Operations, France and Belgium 1916*, vol. 2, pt. 2, 457.
98 Harris, *Douglas Haig*, 272–3.
99 The memorandum is reproduced in full in Lloyd George, *War Memoirs*, 2.833–45.
100 Lloyd George, *War Memoirs*, 2.850. See also Dalin, *French and German Public Opinion*, 1933).
101 Lloyd George, *War Memoirs*, 2.862–73.
102 Scott, *Official Statements*, 1–3.
103 See Keelan, "Catholic Neutrality," 108.
104 Brown, *Robert Laird Borden*, 2.70.

6 Conscription

1 Brown, *Robert Laird Borden*, 2.61–3.
2 Holt, *Filling the Ranks*, 177–83. From September 1916 to the end of the war a monthly average of 6,051 infantry other ranks were required to maintain the four divisions at full strength (179).
3 Macphail, *Official History: The Medical Services*, 253.
4 Nicholson, *Canadian Expeditionary Force*, 224.
5 Stewart, "Frustrated Belligerence."
6 Holt, *Filling the Ranks*, 177–83.
7 The quotations are from Brown, *Robert Laird Borden*, 2.67–8.
8 Morton, *Peculiar Kind of Politics*, chap. 6, "Gaining Control."
9 Borden, *Robert Laird Borden*, 1.613; *Montreal Gazette*, 7 December 1916, 3.
10 Brown, *Robert Laid Borden*, 2.64.
11 For an interesting study of the way the war was presented to the public in Quebec and Ontario, see Djebabla, "La confrontation des civils Québecois."
12 René Castonguay, "Chase-Casgrain, Thomas," in *Dictionary of Canadian Biography*, vol. 14 (University of Toronto/Université Laval, 2003), http://www .biographi.ca/en/bio/chase_casgrain_thomas_14E.html.

13 Bélanger, *L'impossible défi*, 232–51.
14 See especially the cartoons in the *Le Nationaliste*, 14 and 21 January 1917.
15 Lloyd George, *War Memoirs*, 4.1731.
16 Brown, *Robert Laird Borden*, 2.72.
17 *Montreal Star*, 3 February 1917, 12.
18 Tulchinsky, *Canada's Jews*, 154. See also Stedman, *Angels of the Workplace*, 95–6.
19 Lyon Cohen (1867–1937) was a successful clothing manufacturer and community leader who co-founded the *Canadian Jewish Times* and the Jewish Immigrant Aid Services. Two of his sons, Nathan Bernard Cohen (father of Leonard Cohen) and Horace Rives Cohen, served in the Canadian Expeditionary Force. Lyon Cohen became the first president of the Canadian Jewish Congress in 1919.
20 Tulchinsky, *Canada's Jews*, 155.
21 Tulchinsky, *Canada's Jews*, 159.
22 Ewen, "International Unions," 83.
23 Copp, *Anatomy of Poverty*, 133.
24 For an overview see Robin, "Registration, Conscription," 101–18; and Heron, "Labourism," 45–76. Both authors make only passing reference to Montreal. Ewen, "Ideas of Gustav Franq," adds a Montreal discussion.
25 On 1 May 1917, two to three thousand marchers set off on a rainy evening with the Red Flag leading the procession. At Place D'armes speeches were made before separate contingents of French, English, Yiddish, German, Italian, and Russian participants. *Montreal Gazette*, 2 May 1917.
26 "100th Anniversary of City's National Hockey Team," *North Bay Nugget*, 28 November 2016, tells the story of the 228th Battalion hockey team.
27 Based on the sports pages of the *Montreal Gazette*, *La Patrie*, and the *Ottawa Citizen*. The Seattle Metropolitans won the Stanley Cup.
28 See especially the *Montreal Standard*, 27 January 1917, and *La Patrie*, "L'automobile un triomphe," 20 January 1917.
29 See the appropriate entries in the *International Encyclopedia of the First World War* and firstworldwar.com.
30 Nicholson, *Canadian Expeditionary Force*, 233–44. See also the casualty lists of the period in *Montreal Gazette*, 3 January–April 1917.
31 *Montreal Star*, 9 April 1917, 19.
32 *Montreal Gazette*, 26 April 1917, 10.
33 Miller, *Our Glory and Our Grief*, 196.
34 Doughty, *Pyrrhic Victory*, 323–36.
35 Cook, "A Proper Slaughter," 7–23.
36 The 73rd suffered 161 casualties in the raid. Morton, *Peculiar Kind of Politics*, 101–2; Hutchinson, *73rd Battalion*, 97.
37 Nicholson, *Canadian Expeditionary Force*, 250–1.
38 Fetherstonhaugh, *Royal Montreal Regiment*, 141.

39 The 13th Battalion (Royal Highlanders of Canada) were in reserve on 9 April. As they waited for their hot meal, "the cookhouse used by three companies was shelled and the cooks killed consequently the soup was lost." War diary, 13th Battalion, 9 April 1917, LAC.

40 Nicholson, *Canadian Expeditionary Force*, 253.

41 Fetherstonaugh, *Royal Montreal Regiment*, 148.

42 Iarocci, "1st Canadian Division,"166.

43 Campbell, "2nd Canadian Division," 171–87.

44 Geoffrey Hayes, "3rd Canadian Division," 206.

45 Duguid, *Canadian Grenadier Guards*, 144.

46 Cook, *Vimy*, 147.

47 *Montreal Witness*, 17 April 1917, 1.

48 *Le Canada*, 14 April 1917, 4.

49 Steven Smith, "'That Day Was Like a Scythe': Montreal and the Casualty Lists of Vimy Ridge," CBC News, 7 April 2017. The story is based on the work of Caitlin Bailey, curator of the Canadian Centre for the Great War in Montreal.

50 Cited in Barrett, "Lt. Col. Blondin," in "Patriots, Crooks and Safety Firsters: Colonels of the Canadian Expeditionary Force," https://matthewkbarrett.com /2017/04/10/lt-col-blondin/.

51 *Montreal Star*, 7 May 1917, 12.

52 *Le Canada*, 7 May 1917, 1.

53 Atherton, *Report of the Proceedings of the Win the War and National Unity Convention* (Montreal, 1917).

54 Brown, *Robert Laid Borden*, 2.83. All of the city newspapers carried the text of Borden's statement on conscription.

55 Brown, *Robert Laid Borden*, 2.83.

56 Nicholson, *Canadian Expeditionary Force*, 220.

57 Brown, *Robert Laid Borden*, 2.84. The text of Borden's speech was published in the major daily newspapers on 19 May 1917. For more detailed discussion of the background to the conscription decision, see Granatstein and Hitsman, *Broken Promises*; Sharpe, "Enlistment"; Brown and Loveridge, "Unrequited Faith"; Morton, "Did the French Canadians."

58 *Le Devoir*, 28–29 May 1917, 1. See also Anctil, *"Do What You Must,"* 118–19.

59 Canada, *Debates of the House of Commons*, 12th Parliament, 7th Session, vol. 2 (18 May 1917), 1547.

60 *Le Canada* 30 May 1917, 4.

61 *Le Canada*, 31 May 1917, 4.

62 Durflinger, "Vimy's Consequences,"161.

63 Durflinger, "Vimy's Consequences," 169.

64 Durflinger, "Vimy's Consequences," 172.

65 Cited in Eberle, "Conscription Policy," 118.

66 *Le Canada*, 26 June 1917, 8.

67 *Montreal Witness*, 5 June 1917, 1.

68 The story is most easily followed in the *Star* and *Standard.* See also the coverage in *Le Devoir* using the term "dynamitards." See also Millman, *Popularity, Patriotism and Dissent*, chap. 5.

69 Durflinger, "Vimy's Consequences," 177.

70 *La Patrie*, 29 August 1917, 1.

71 Durflinger, "Vimy's Consequences," 181. For more on the reaction of military intelligence and the Dominion Police, see Eberle, "Conscription Policy."

72 *Montreal Star*, 28 June 1917, 2. In the course of a three-hour speech at the Monument National, Bourassa announced his support for Laurier's referendum policy, which he insisted was a nationalist proposal.

73 English, *Decline of Politics*, 134–5.

74 *Montreal Star*, 4 July 1917, 3. A more complete account of the meeting was reported in *Le Canada*, 4 July 1917, 8.

75 Versions of the interview differ slightly. This quotation is from the *Montreal Star*, 3 July 1917, 11.

76 English, *Decline of Politics*, 142–5.

77 The debate on second reading began 22 August 1917. For press coverage see, for example, *Le Canada*, 23 August 1917, 1; and 24 August 1917, 4.

78 Graham, *Arthur Meighen*, 1.169.

79 "Overall there were twelve Tory ministers, nine Liberals and one 'Labour' (Gideon Robertson). Most of the senior portfolios … continued to be held by Tories. The Liberals seemed both outnumbered and outranked." English, *Decline of Politics*, 157.

80 Ferraro, "English Canada." Ferraro demonstrates that most Laurier Liberals elected outside Quebec favoured conscription.

81 Brookfield, "Divided by the Ballot Box," 473–501.

82 *Labour World*, 3 November 1917, 4.

83 *Montreal Gazette*, 16 August 1918, 1.

84 Cook, *No Place to Run*, is the best account of gas warfare. See also Cook, "Fire Plan," 125–6; Engen, "Force Preservation," 173–4; Humphries, "Best Laid Plans," 78–101.

85 *Montreal Gazette*, 17 August 1917, 1.

86 Foley, "Other Side," 198.

87 Jackson, "Anything but Lovely." For memorial and memory on Hill 70, see Durflinger, "A Battle Forgotten?"

88 *Montreal Gazette*, 27, 29, 30, August 1917.

89 Stewart, "Frustrated Belligerence," 43.

90 Sheffield, *Douglas Haig*, 335.

91 Nicholson, *Canadian Expeditionary Force*, 312–13.

92 Humphries, *Selected Papers*, 54–6.

93   Humphries, *Selected Papers*, 66.
94   *Montreal Gazette*, 27 October 1917, 1. See also Keshen, *Propaganda and Censorship*.
95   The *Gazette*, *Star*, and *La Presse* printed the official casualty lists as they were made available. The quotations are from the *Gazette*, 17 November 1917, 20.
96   *Montreal Gazette*, 20 November 1917, 1.
97   *Montreal Witness*, 20 November 1917, described the controversy and the reaction of the British and French press but added no comment of its own.
98   Machin, *Report*, 42.
99   English, *Decline of Politics*, 191–2.
100   English, *Decline of Politics*, 192.
101   All newspapers reported on Laurier's declaration. This quotation is from the thoughtful editorial in the *Montreal Witness*, 11 December 1917, 1 which argued that Laurier's position allowed "win the war" advocates to vote Liberal.
102   *Le Devoir*, 9 November 1917, 1; 10 November 1917, 1.
103   Dutil and Mackenzie, *Embattled Nation*, 180–1.
104   Based on a review of the daily press. See J. Castell Hopkins, "General Elections of 1917," *Canadian Annual Review 1917*, 587–643, for a summary of the campaign; and Granatstein and Hitsman, *Broken Promises*, chap. 3.
105   Extensive coverage of the Halifax explosion began on 7 December and continued for several days. See Armstrong, *Halifax Explosion*.
106   The text of the "Lansdowne Letter" is available online. See also Newton, "Lansdowne Peace Letter of 1917," 16–39.
107   *Le Devoir*, 1 December 1917, 1. See also Keelan, "Catholic Neutrality.
108   *Le Pays*, 8 December 1917, 1. See also Lévesque, *Freethinker*.
109   Barlow, "House of the Irish, 165–8.
110   *Canadian Jewish Chronicle*, 4 September 1914, 4; 11 September 1914, 2.
111   Rosenberg, *The Jewish Community*, 2.174.
112   LAC, *Guide to Sources Related to Units of the Canadian Expeditionary Force*, Miscellaneous Infantry Units, Jewish Reinforcing Company.
113   Tulchinsky, *Canada's Jews*, 174–5. See also Kay, "A Note on Canada," 171–7; Keren and Keren, *We Are Coming, Unafraid*.
114   Tulchinsky, *Canada's Jews*, 169–70.
115   *Canadian Jewish Chronicle*, 1 June 1917, 1.
116   *Canadian Jewish Chronicle*, 22 June 1917, 1.
117   *Canadian Jewish Chronicle*, 25 May 1917, 2; 13 July 1917, 2.
118   *Canadian Jewish Chronicle*, 21 December 1917, 1.
119   Skelton, *Life and Letters*, 2.542.
120   As John English has demonstrated, the Unionist caucus was dominated by Presbyterians and Methodists many of whom saw the war as a crusade which would bring regeneration in the form of social and moral reform. *Decline of Politics*, 200.
121   Morton, *Peculiar Kind of Politics*, 148.

7 1918

1 All daily newspapers covered the debate, with particular attention to Gouin's speech. The quotations are from the *Sherbrooke Daily Record*, 25 January 1918, 1. See *Le Canada*, 24 January 1918, 1, for a fuller text.
2 Machin, *Report*, 42, 44.
3 Machin, *Report*, 50.
4 Skelton, *Life and Letters*, 2.544–55.
5 *Le Canada*, 5 February 1918, 8. See also Dennis, *Reluctant Warriors*, 53.
6 *Le Pays*, 19 January 1918, 1. *Le Pays* described the grave situation confronting Quebec if prohibition was adopted.
7 *Le Mond Ouvrier/Labour World* was the voice of both organizations.
8 For the Catholic Church and La ligue antialcoolique, see Gagnon and Hamelin, *Histoire du catholicisme québécois*, 3.197–209. The pages of the *Montreal Witness* provide the best source for English-speaking prohibition. For Mitchell's speech to the legislature, see *Montreal Witness*, 12 February 1918, 3. See also *Canadian Annual Review* 1919, 686–8.
9 *La Patrie*, 2 January 1918, 3; *Le Canada*, 4 January 1918, 2.
10 *Le Devoir*, 20 September 1918, 7.
11 All daily newspapers reported on the tragedy. See especially *La Patrie*, 15 February 1918, 1; *La Presse*, 15 February 1918, 1.
12 *Le Pays*, 9 March 1918, 1. The writer suggested citizens were being asked to "ouvrez vos bourse, fermez vos bouches."
13 *Literary Digest*, 5 January 1918, 22.
14 *Le Canada*, 7 March 1918, 8. The *Herald* also carried a series of front-page stories on infant deaths in the city, noting on 4 March 1918 that 53,000 babies under two years of age had died in Montreal in the past twelve years.
15 Lalonde, "La revanche des berceaux."
16 Montpetit, "La veillée des berceaux". The talk was also reproduced in *Le Devoir*, *Le Canada*, and other newspapers, 7 March 1918. See also Baillargeon, "Entre la revanche."
17 Montreal Board of Health, *Annual Report*, 1918, 14.
18 Baillargeon, *Babies for the Nation*. See also Nathalie Lampron, "Growing Up Healthy in the 20th Century," McCord Museum, http://collections.musee-mccord.qc.ca/en/keys/webtours/VQ_P4_4_EN.
19 *Montreal Gazette*, 9 January 1918, 1.
20 The most recent and balanced account of the Allies' 1918 manpower crisis is Greenhalgh, "David Lloyd George," 397–421.
21 Sam Hughes cited the views of the War Office in an Ottawa speech advocating the six-division plan. *Montreal Herald*, 5 March 1918, 4.
22 Currie's original proposal was to strengthen the infantry battalions and increase the artillery. The additional engineer and machine gun units were later additions. Humphries, *Selected Papers,* 80–2.

23 Herwig, *The First World War*, 382–432.

24 Harris, *Douglas Haig*, 447.

25 Sheffield and Bourne, *Douglas Haig*; diary entries for 10 April 1918, 405; 5 May 1918, 410.

26 Cronin and Adair, *Wearing of the Green*, 96. See also Jolivet, *Le vert et le bleu*, 209; and Barlow, *Griffintown*.

27 Gregory, "You Might as Well Recruit Germans."

28 Rudy, "Do You Have the Time?" 531–54.

29 *Montreal Gazette*, 23 May 1918, 17.

30 *La Bonne Parole*, May 1910, 1. See also Lévesque, *Freethinker*, 266–70.

31 *Le Devoir*, 28 March 1918, 1. For a full account of Bourassa's views see Trofi-menkoff, "Henri Bourassa." See also *Le Monde Ouvrier*, 6 April 1918, for a contemporary critique of Bourassa by Eva Circé Côte.

32 Rodolphe Lemieux's speech on the issue in the House of Commons was typical. Canada, *Debates of the House of Commons*, 13th Parliament, 1st Session, vol. 1 (11 April 1918), 652.

33 The austerity measures implemented by the council led to a strike by police and firemen in December 1918. Dagenais, *Des pouvoirs et des hommes*, 52.

34 All six daily newspapers opposed Martin's urging voters to protect the reputation of French Canadians and the city by voting for Ainey. See, for example, *Le Canada*, 28 March 1918, 4.

35 Henri-Edgar Lavigueur was the Liberal MP for Quebec County as well as mayor of Quebec City from 1916 to 1920.

36 The most recent and detailed study of the riots is Auger, "On the Brink of Civil War," 503–40.

37 Power, *A Party Politician*, 85.

38 Borden diary, 30 March 1918, Sir Robert Borden Fonds, Manuscript Group 26, vol. 450, LAC.

39 Power, *Party Politician*, 85–6; Auger, "On the Brink of Civil War," 517–18.

40 Auger, "On the Brink of Civil War," 517–18.

41 Auger, "On the Brink of Civil War," 519.

42 *Montreal Gazette*, 3 April 1918, 1.

43 Canada, *Debates of the House of Commons*, 13th Parliament, 1st Session, vol. 1 (3 April 1918), 284.

44 Borden, *Memoirs*, 2.789.

45 Borden diary, 9 and 10 April 1918, Sir Robert Borden Fonds, Manuscript Group 26, vol. 450, LAC.

46 *Montreal Star*, 5 June 1918, 6.

47 *Montreal Standard*, 6 April 1918, 1.

48 *Le Pays*, 6 April 1918, 1. See Keelan, *Duty to Dissent*, 186–7.

49 *Montreal Star*, 8 May 1918, 2; 17 June 1918, 1.

50 *Montreal Star*, 27 May 1918, 5.

51 Auger, "On the Brink of Civil War," 553.
52 *Montreal Standard*, 6 April 1918, 1.
53 Borden diary, 10 April 1918, Sir Robert Borden Fonds, Manuscript Group 26, vol. 450, LAC.
54 *Le Canada* 18 April 1918, 4, reprints the *La Patrie* editorial and offers its own view. For *Le Devoir*, see Keelan, *Duty to Dissent*, 188–9; and Keshen, *Propaganda and Censorship*. The order-in-council was issued on the same day that Borden received a "secret telegram" from Lloyd George with details about the situation confronting the Allies. It was a plea for help, and Borden responded by calling a closed session of Parliament to announce the cancellation of exemptions.
55 Canada, *Debates of the House of Commons*, 13th Parliament, 1st Session, vol. 1 (19 April 1918), 937–9.
56 *Montreal Star*, 8 May 1918, 2.
57 Keshen, *Propaganda and Censorship*, 77.
58 *Montreal Star*, 17 June 1918, 1.
59 *Montreal Star*, 27 May 1918, 5.
60 *Montreal Star*, 6 June 1918, 2.
61 Granatstein and Hitsman, *Broken Promises*, 94.
62 *La Presse*, 7 May 1918, 1. Translation available in *Montreal Star*, 8 May 1918, 2.
63 *Montreal Gazette*, 13 July 1918, 3.
64 *Montreal Gazette*, 10 July 1918, 3.
65 Borden diary, 3, 4 April 1918, Sir Robert Borden Fonds, Manuscript Group 26, vol. 450, LAC.
66 *Montreal Star*, 7 May 1918, 2.
67 *La Presse*, 7 May 1918, 2.
68 *Montreal Gazette*, 13 July 1918; 20 July 1918.
69 All newspapers carried the Canadian Press story or the Supreme Court decision, 20 July 1918. For the text of the decision, see *Judgements of the Supreme Court of Canada* Re: Edwin Gray, https://scc-csc.lexum.com/scc-csc/scc-csc/en/item /9496/index.do.
70 Machin, *Report*, 26.
71 Machin, *Report*, 3.
72 *La Patrie*, 9 August 1918, 1.
73 *Montreal Star*, 12 August 1918, 1.
74 Machin, *Report*, 26.
75 My thanks to Mark Humphries for this perspective on Currie's position.
76 Brown, *Robert Laird Borden*, 2.809–12.
77 Brown, *Robert Laird Borden*, 2.827.
78 *Le Canada*, 18 May 1917, 4.
79 Brown, *Robert Laird Borden*, 2.841.
80 See Fischer, *Germany's Aims*, 697–8, for a description of Germany's war aims in July 1918.

81 Herwig, *The First World War*, 417.

82 Harris, *Douglas Haig*, 486–7.

83 Dennis, *Reluctant Warriors*, 55–6. See Holt, *Filling the Ranks*, 205. More than 10,000 men, largely conscripts, arrived in England in the first three months of 1918.

84 Holt, *Filling the Ranks*. Our random sample of names recorded on the Commonwealth War Graves Commission website produced the following estimates of the percentage of conscripts killed in action during selected battles of the Hundred Days.

Amiens, 8–12 August	3%
Arras, 26–8 August	8%
Canal du Nord	19%
1–11 November	26%

In the samples, a large majority of conscripts killed in action were from Ontario and the west.

85 The paragraphs on the events of the "Hundred Days" are from Copp et al., *Canadian Battlefields*, and are based on Nicholson, *Canadian Expeditionary Force*; Harris, *Douglas Haig*; and Humphries, *Sir Arthur Currie*. See also Granatstein, *The Greatest Victory*; Schreiber, *Shock Army*; Dennis, *Reluctant Warriors*; and Cook, *Shock Troops*.

86 War diary, 13th Battalion 8 August 1918.

87 Fetherstonhaugh, *24th Battalion*, 226–7.

88 Fetherstonhaugh, *24th Battalion*, 228.

89 Jacques Castonguay, "Brillant, Jean," in *Dictionary of Canadian Biography*, vol. 14 (University of Toronto/Université Laval, 2003), http://www.biographi.ca /en/bio.php?id=brillant_jean_14F.html.

90 For a detailed account of the action of the 13th and 14th Battalions at Amiens and beyond see Fetherstonhaugh's *13th Battalion* and *14th Battalion*, both of which are available online.

91 Potter, "Smile and Carry On," 268–79.

92 Canadian Press, *Montreal Gazette*, 10 August 1918.

93 Official statement, 12 August 1918. *Montreal Gazette*.

94 Casualties were in fact heavy: 3,868 on 8 August 1918; 11,822 between 8 and 20 August. Nicholson, *Canadian Expeditionary Force*, 419.

95 Nicholson, *Canadian Expeditionary Force*, 426.

96 See, for example, Pepin, "Need to Advance," 37–42.

97 Fetherstonhaugh, *24th Battalion*, 237, 245. The 24th lost 21 officers in the battle and reported total casualties of 666 men in August.

98 The battlefield is little changed today, and it is possible to identify the positions held by each of the three battalions on the slope. I have not found remnants of the barbed wire.

99 Clements, *Merry Hell*, 214–15.

100 Nicholson, *Canadian Expeditionary Force*, 432.

101 Olivar Asselin, who joined the 87th in October, reported that 25 per cent of the battalion was French Canadian by then. Pelletier-Baillargeon, *Olivar Asselin*, 2.221.
102 Duguid, *Canadian Grenadier Guards*, 181; personnel file, John Francis Young, LAC.
103 *Montreal Gazette*, 4 September 1918, 1.
104 Harris, *Amiens to the Armistice*, 153–4.
105 Nicholson, *Canadian Expeditionary Force*, 460.
106 Lloyd George, *War Memoirs*, 6.3259.
107 Herwig, *The First World War*, 426.
108 Lloyd George, *War Memoirs*, 6.3279.
109 Lloyd George, *War Memoirs*, 6.3288–9.
110 Ząbecki, *The Generals' War*, 256.
111 See Sharpe, *The Last Day*.
112 Livesay, *Canada's Hundred Days*.
113 Humphries, "Horror at Home," 235–60.
114 Humphries, *The Last Plague*, 113.
115 Humphries, *The Last Plague*, 113.
116 All newspapers carried news of the regulations on the dates included. See also Humphries, *The Last Plague*, 114–17.
117 Montreal, *Report of the Board of Health 1918* (Montreal, 1919), 19.
118 Zhang et al., "Transmissibility: 27–31; Humphries, *The Last Plague*, 142–7.
119 Humphries, *The Last Plague*, 142–7.
120 This account is drawn from Fong, *J.W. McConnell*, 138–41. There is extensive coverage in the daily newspapers.

Conclusion

1 Sandra Gwyn, "Papineau, Talbot Mercer," in *Dictionary of Canadian Biography*, vol. 14 (University of Toronto/Université Laval, 2003), http://www.biographi.ca/en/bio/papineau_talbot_mercer_14E.html.
2 There is full coverage of the fire in Montreal's daily newspapers.
3 Casement's trial and execution were also "forgotten" until the publication of his Black Diaries. See Inglis, *Roger Casement*. The Carreau affair was also restored to history in the twenty-first century. See Dagenais, "Culture urbaine et homosexualité."
4 *Montreal Gazette*, 5 May 1915.
5 Gregory, *The Last Great War*, 282.
6 Marsh, *Health and Unemployment*, 141.
7 *La Presse* promoted the idea of a French Canadian brigade throughout the war. See Vennat, *Les "poilus" québécois*, vol. 2.
8 Litalien, *Dans la tormente*.

9 Canada, *Debates of the House of Commons*, 13th Parliament, 1st Session, vol. 1 (19 April 1918), 935.

10 A ratio of one in seven deaths among men who served overseas is used to calculate this estimate.

11 Gregory, *The Last Great War*, 252.

12 Vance, *Death So Noble*, 3.

13 *Le Canada*, 19 April 1916; *Montreal Standard*, 22 April 1916.

14 *Montreal Standard*, 21 April 1917, 1.

15 *Le Canada*, 28 April 1918, 4.

16 The quotation is from Smith, "How the Yearning for Peace," 37.

17 The meetings are described in detail in Cook, "Sir Robert Borden," 371–95.

18 Canada, *Debates of the House of Commons*, 13th Parliament, 1st Session, vol. 2 (18 May 1917), 1526–38.

19 *Le Canada*, 19 May 1917, 4.

Bibliography

Adamson, Agar, ed. *Letters of Agar Adamson, 1914 to 1919: Lieutenant Colonel, Princess Patricia's Canadian Light Infantry.* Ottawa: CEF Books, 1997.

Anctil, Pierre, ed. *"Do What You Must": Selected Editorials from* Le Devoir *under Henri Bourassa, 1910–1932.* Toronto: Champlain Society, 2016.

Anctil, Pierre, *Through the Eyes of the Eagle.* Montreal: Véhicule, 2001.

Armstrong, John Griffith. *The Halifax Explosion and the Royal Canadian Navy: Inquiry and Intrigue.* Vancouver: UBC Press, 2002.

Atherton, William H. *Montreal, 1535–1914.* 3 vols. Montreal: S.J. Clarke, 1914.

Atherton, William H. *Montreal under British Rule.* 2 vols. Montreal, 1914.

Atherton, William H. *Report of the Proceedings to Win the War and National Unity Convention.* Montreal: Canadian Unity and Win the War League, 1917.

Auger, Martin. "On the Brink of Civil War: The Canadian Government and the Suppression of the 1918 Quebec Easter Riots." *Canadian Historical Review* 89, no. 4 (2008): 503–40.

Bacchi, Carol Lee. *Liberation Deferred?: The Ideas of the English-Canadian Suffragists.* Toronto: University of Toronto Press, 1983.

Baillargeon, Denyse. *Babies for the Nation: The Medicalization of Motherhood in Quebec, 1910–1970.* Waterloo: Wilfrid Laurier University Press, 2009.

Baillargeon, Denyse. "Entre la revanche et la veillée des berceaux." In *Children's Health Issues in Historical Perspective*, edited by Veronica Strong-Boag and Cheryl Lynn Krasnick Walsh, 101–20. Waterloo: Wilfrid Laurier University Press, 2005.

Barber, Marilyn. "The Ontario Bilingual Schools Issues: Sources of Conflict." *Canadian Historical Review* 47, no. 3 (1966): 227–48.

Barlow, Matthew. *Griffintown: Identity and Memory in an Irish Diaspora Neighborhood.* Vancouver: UBC Press, 2017.

Barlow, Matthew. "The House of the Irish: Irishness, History, and Memory in Griffintown, Montreal 1868–2009." PhD diss., Concordia University, 2009.

Barrière, Michelle. "Montréal, microcosme du theatre lyrique Nord-Américain (1893–1913)." In *Québécois et Américains: La culture québécoise aux XIXe et XXe siècles*, edited by Gerard Bouchard and Yvan Lamonde, 369–85. Montreal: Fides, 1993.

Bélanger, Réal. *Henri Bourassa*. Quebec: Laval University, 2013.

Bélanger, Réal. *L'impossible défi: Albert Sévigny et les conservateurs fédéraux, 1902–1918*. Quebec: Presses de l'Université Laval, 1983.

Berman, Marshal. *All That Is Solid Melts into Air: The Experience of Modernity*. New York: Penguin, 1988.

Boivin, Aurélien, and Kenneth Landry. "Françoise et Madeleine, pionnières du journalisme féminin au Québec." *Voix et Images* 4, no. 2 (1978): 233–43.

Borden, Henry, ed. *Robert Laird Borden: His Memoirs*. 2 vols. New York: Macmillan, 1938.

Bradbury, Bettina. *Working Families: Age, Gender, and Daily Survival in Industrializing Montreal*. Toronto: University of Toronto Press, 2007.

Brisebois, Marilyne. "La Fédération Nationale Saint-Jean-Baptiste et la constitution d'un Réseau Catholique Feminin Transnational 1907–1920." *Histoire Sociale/ Social History* 49, no. 98 (2016): 105–24.

Brookfield, Tarah. "Divided by the Ballot Box: The Montreal Council of Women and the 1917 Election." *Canadian Historical Review* 80, no. 4 (2008): 473–501.

Brown, Michael. *Jew or Juif? Jews, French Canadians, and Anglo-Canadians, 1759–1914*. Philadelphia: Jewish Publication Society, 1986.

Brown, Robert, and Donald Loveridge. "Unrequited Faith: Recruiting the CEF 1914–1918." *Canadian Military History* 24, no. 1 (2015): 61–87.

Brown, Robert Craig. *Robert Laird Borden: A Biography*. 2 vols. Toronto: Macmillan, 1975.

Bryce, John Stephen. "The Making of Westmount, Quebec 1870–1929." MA thesis, McGill University, 1990.

Burns, Robin. "The Montreal Irish and the Great War." *Canadian Catholic Historical Association* 52 (1985): 67–81.

Cameron, Brian. "The Bonne Entente Movement, 1916–1917: From Cooperation to Conscription." *Journal of Canadian Studies* 13, no. 2 (1998): 42–55.

Campbell, David. "The Divisional Experience in the CEF: A Social and Operational History of the 2nd Division 1915–1918." PhD diss., University of Calgary, 2003.

Campbell, David. "A Forgotten Victory: Courcelette 15 September 1916." *Canadian Military History* 16, no. 2 (2007): 27–48.

Campbell, David. "The 2nd Canadian Division." In Hayes, Bechthold, and Iarocci, *Vimy Ridge*, 171–87.

Campbell, Peter. *Rose Henderson: A Women for the People*. Montreal/Kingston: McGill-Queen's University Press, 2010.

Carnegie, David. *The History of Munitions Supply in Canada, 1914–1918*. London: Longmans, Green, 1925.

Carr, Iona K. *A Story of the Canadian Red Cross Information Bureau during the Great War*. Montreal, 1917.

Chickering, Roger. *Imperial Germany and the Great War, 1914–1918*. 2nd ed. Cambridge: Cambridge University Press, 2004.

Choquette, Arthur. *Language and Religion: A History of English-French Conflict in Ontario*. Ottawa: University of Ottawa Press, 1975.

Churchill, Winston. *The World Crisis*. 5 vols. New York: C. Scribner's Sons, 1927.

Clarke, Nic. *Unwanted Warriors: The Rejected Volunteers of the Canadian Expeditionary Force*. Vancouver: UBC Press, 2015.

Clements, Robert N. *Merry Hell: The Story of the 25th Battalion (Nova Scotia Regiment), Canadian Expeditionary Force 1914–1919*. Toronto: University of Toronto Press, 2013.

Collard, Edgar Andrew. *The Irish Way: The History of the Irish Protestant Benevolent Society*. Montreal: Irish Protestant Benevolent Society, 1992.

Cook, Gordon L. "Sir Robert Borden, Lloyd George and British Military Policy 1917–1918." *The Historical Journal* 14, no. 2 (1971): 371–95.

Cook, Ramsay. "Bourassa to Bissonnette: The Evolution of Castor-Rougeism." In *Watching Quebec*, edited by Ramsay Cook, 133–41. Montreal/Kingston: McGill-Queen's University Press, 2005.

Cook, Tim. *At the Sharp End: Canadians Fighting in the First World War, 1914–1916*. Toronto: Viking Canada, 2007.

Cook, Tim. "The Blind Leading the Blind: The Battle of St. Eloi Craters." *Canadian Military History* 5, no. 2 (1996): 25–36.

Cook, Tim. "The Fire Plan: Gas, Guns, Machine Guns, and Mortars." In Delaney and Gardner, *Capturing Hill 70*, 102–36.

Cook, Tim. *No Place to Run: The Canadian Corps and Gas Warfare in the First World War*. Vancouver: UBC Press, 1999.

Cook, Tim. "A Proper Slaughter: The March 1917 Gas Raid at Vimy Ridge." *Canadian Military History* 8, no. 2 (1999): 7–23.

Cook, Tim. *Shock Troops: Canadians Fighting the Great War, 1917–1918*. Toronto: Viking Canada, 2008.

Cook, Tim. *Vimy: The Battle and the Legend*. Toronto: Penguin, 2018.

Copp, John Terry. *The Anatomy of Poverty: The Conditions of the Working Class in Montreal, 1897–1929*. Toronto: McClelland and Stewart, 1974.

Copp, Terry. *The Somme: Newfoundland Regiment and Canada's Sacrifice in the Trenches*. Edited by Eric Harris. Ottawa: Canvet, Legion, 2016.

Copp, Terry, Mark Humphries, Nick Lachance, Caitlin McWilliams, and Matt Symes. *Canadian Battlefields of the First World War: A Visitor's Guide*. Waterloo: LCMSDS, 2015.

Crofton, Morgan. *Massacre of the Innocents: The Crofton Diaries, Ypres 1914–1915*. Edited by Gavin Roynon. Stroud: Sutton, 2004.

Cronin, Mike, and Daryl Adair. *The Wearing of the Green: A History of St. Patrick's Day*. London: Routledge, 2002.

Croteau, Jean-Phillipe. "La financement des Écoles Publiques à Montréal et Toronto (1841–1997): Un baromètre pour mesurer les rapports entre la majorité et la minorité." *Historical Studies in Education* 24, no. 2 (2012): 1–30.

Dagenais, Michèle. "Culture urbaine et homosexualité: Pratiques et identités homosexuelles à Montréal, 1880–1929." PhD diss., Université du Québec a Montréal, 2017.

Dagenais, Michèle. "Culture urbaine et pouvoirs publics locaux à Montréal au début du 20e siècle." *Loisir et Société/Society and Leisure* 18, no. 2 (1995): 273–85.

Dagenais, Michèle. *Des pouvoirs et des hommes: L'administration municipal de Montreal, 1900–1950.* Montreal/Kingston: McGill-Queen's University Press, 2000.

D'Agostino, Peter R. *Rome in America: Transnational Catholic Ideology from the Risorgimento to Fascism.* Chapel Hill: University of North Carolina Press, 2004.

Dales, John H. *Hydroelectricity and Industrial Development: Quebec, 1898–1940.* Cambridge, MA: Harvard University Press, 1957.

Dalin, Ebba Dahlin. *French and German Public Opinion on Declared War Aims, 1914–1918.* New York: AMS, 1933.

Dancocks, Daniel G. *Sir Arthur Currie: A Bibliography.* Toronto: Methuen, 1985.

Danylewycz, Marta. *Taking the Veil: An Alternative to Marriage, Motherhood and Spinsterhood in Quebec, 1840–1920.* Toronto: McClelland and Stewart, 1987.

Davidson, Melissa. "'Private Sorrow Becomes Public Property': Canadian Anglican Sermons and the Second Battle of Ypres, May 1915." *Historical Papers/Canadian Society of Church History* (2011): 171–80.

Delaney, Douglas E. "Mentoring the Canadian Corps: Imperial Officers and the Canadian Expeditionary Force, 1914–1918." *Journal of Military History* 77, no. 3 (2013): 931–53.

Delaney, Douglas E., and Serge Marc Durflinger, eds. *Capturing Hill 70: Canada's Forgotten Battle of the First World War.* Vancouver: UBC Press, 2016.

Dennis, Patrick. *Reluctant Warriors: Canadian Conscripts and the Great War.* Vancouver: UBC Press, 2017.

Deutsch, J. "War Finance and the Canadian Economy, 1914–20." *Canadian Journal of Economics and Political History* 6 (1940): 525–42.

Djebabla, Mourad. "La confrontation des civils Québecois et Ontarien a la Première Guerre mondiale 1914–1918: Le répresentations de la guerre au Québec et en Ontario." PhD diss., Université du Québec a Montréal, 2008.

Domeier, Norman. *The Eulenburg Affair: A Cultural History of Politics in the German Empire.* Translated by Deborah L. Schneider. Rochester: Camden House, 2015.

Dorais, Lucie. *Morrice and Lyman in the Company of Matisse.* Toronto: Firefly Books, 2014.

Doughty, Robert A. *Pyrrhic Victory: French Strategy and Operations in the Great War.* Cambridge, MA: Harvard University Press, 2008.

Drysdale, A.M. *Canada to Ireland: The Visit of the "Duchess of Connaught's Own."* London: T. Fisher Unwin, 1917.

Duguid, A.F. *History of the Canadian Grenadier Guards, 1760–1964.* Montreal: Gazette Printing, 1965.

Duguid, A.F. *Official History of the Canadian Forces in the Great War 1914–1919*. 2 vols. Ottawa: Ministry of National Defence, 1938.

Durflinger, Serge. "A Battle Forgotten? Remembering Hill 70 in Its Time and Ours," in Delaney and Durflinger, *Capturing Hill 70*, 226–51.

Durflinger, Serge Marc. "Vimy's Consequences: The Montreal Anti-Conscription Disturbances May to September 1914." In *Turning Point 1917: The British Empire at War*, edited by Douglas E. Delaney and Nikolas Gardner, 160–87. Vancouver: UBC Press, 2017.

Durocher, René. "Henri Bourassa, les évêques et la guerre de 1914–1918." *Historical Papers* 6, no. 1 (1971): 248–75.

Dutil, Patrice. "'Adieu, demeure chaste et pure': Godfroy Langlois et la virage vers la progressisme Liberal." In *Combats libereaux au tourant du XX siècle*, edited by Yvan Lamonde, 247–75. Montreal: Fides, 1995.

Dutil, Patrice. "Against Isolationism: Napoléon Belcourt, French Canada, and 'La Grande Guerre.'" In *Canada and the First World War: Essays in Honour of Robert Craig Brown*, edited by David Mackenzie, 96–137. Toronto: University of Toronto Press, 2005.

Dutil, Patrice. *Devil's Advocate: Godfroy Langlois and the Politics of Liberal Progressivism in Laurier's Quebec*. Montreal: R. Davies, 1994.

Dutil, Patrice, and David Mackenzie. *Embattled Nation: Canada's Wartime Election of 1917*. Toronto: Dundurn, 2017.

Eberle, Donald Charles. "Conscription Policy, Citizenship and Religious Conscientious Objectors in the United States and Canada during World War One." PhD diss., Bowling Green State University, 2013.

Edmonds, J.E. *Military Operations, France and Belgium, 1915*. London: Macmillan, 1927.

Edmonds, J.E. *Military Operations, France and Belgium, 1916*. 2 vols. London: Macmillan, 1932.

Engen, Robert. "Force Preservation: Medical Services." In Delaney and Durflinger, *Capturing Hill 70*, 162–86.

English, John. *The Decline of Politics: The Conservatives and the Party System, 1901–20*. Toronto: University of Toronto Press, 1977.

Ewen, Geoffrey. "The International Unions and the Worker's Revolt in Quebec 1914–1925." PhD diss., York University, 1998.

Ewen, Geoffrey. "The Ideas of Gustav Franq on Trade Unionism and Social Reform as Expressed in Le Monde Ourvrier/Labour World." M.A. thesis, University of Ottawa, 1981.

Ferraro, Patrick. "English Canada and the Election of 1917." MA thesis, McGill University, 1972.

Fetherstonhaugh, R.C. *McGill University at War, 1914–1918, 1939–1945*. Montreal: McGill University, 1947.

Fetherstonhaugh, R.C., ed. *No. 3 Canada General Hospital (McGill) 1914–1919*. Montreal: Gazette Printing, 1928.

Fetherstonhaugh, R.C. *The Royal Montreal Regiment, 1925–1945*. Westmount: Royal Montreal Regiment, 1927.

Fetherstonhaugh, R.C. *The 13th Battalion Royal Highlanders of Canada, 1914–1919*. Toronto: 13th Battalion, 1925.

Featherstonhaugh, R.C. *The Royal Montreal Regiment, 14th Battalion, CEF, 1914–1925*. Montreal: Gazette Printing, 1927.

Fetherstonhaugh, R.C., ed. *The 24th Battalion, C.E.F., Victoria Rifles of Canada 1914–1919*. Montreal: Gazette Printing, 1930.

Figler, Bernard. *Sam Jacobs, Member of Parliament*. Harpell's, 1970.

Finnan, Joseph. *John Redmond and Irish Unity, 1912–1918*. Syracuse: Syracuse University Press, 2004.

Fischer, Fritz. *Germany's Aims in the First World War*. New York: W.W. Norton, 1967.

Foley, Robert T. "The Other Side of the Hill." In Delaney and Durflinger, *Capturing Hill 70*, 187–204.

Fong, William. *J.W. McConnell*. Montreal/Kingston: McGill-Queen's University Press, 2008.

Fong, William. *Sir William C. Macdonald*. Montreal/Kingston: McGill-Queen's University Press, 2007.

Fournier, Ovila. *Un pionnier de l'économique au Québec: Joseph Versailles (1881–1931), le fondateur de Montréal-Est*. Saint-Étienne de Bolton: Les Éditions de la Libellule, 1974.

Fowler, Michelle. "'Death Is Not the Worst Thing': The Presbyterian Press in Canada, 1913–1919." *War & Society* 25, no. 2 (2006): 23–38.

Gaffield, Chad. *Language, Schooling, and Cultural Conflict: The Origins of the French-Language Controversy in Ontario*. Montreal/Kingston: McGill-Queen's University Press, 1987.

Gagnon, J.P. "Canadian Soldiers in Bermuda in World War One." *Histoire Sociale/Social History* 23, no. 45 (1990): 9–36.

Gagnon, J.P. *Le 22e Battalion (Canadian-Français) 1914–1918*. Ottawa: Laval University Press/Department of National Defence, 1986.

Gagnon, Nicole, and Jean Hamelin. *Histoire du catholicisme québécois, le XX Siecle 1898–1940*. Vol. 3. Montreal: Boréal Express, 1984.

Gagnon, Robert. *Histoire de la Commission des Écoles Catholiques de Montréal*. Montreal: Boréal Express, 1996.

Gauvin, Michel. "The Municipal Reform Movement in Montreal, 1886–1914." MA thesis, University of Ottawa, 1972.

Germain, Lacasse, Massé Johanne, and Poirier Bethsabée. *Le diable en ville: Alexandre Silvio et l'émergence de La Modernité Populaire au Québec*. Montreal: Presses de l'Université de Montréal, 2012.

Gervais, Reginald. *The Silent Sixtieth 100 Years On: The Story of the 60th Canadian Overseas Battalion, Canadian Expeditionary Force in the Great War*. Victoria: Friesen, 2014.

Gilland, Jason. "Redimensioning Montreal: Circulation and Urban Form, 1846–1918." PhD diss., McGill University, 2001.

Glassford, Sarah Carlene. "Marching as to War: The Canadian Red Cross Society, 1885–1939." PhD diss., York University, 2007.

Godefory, Andrew. "The 4th Canadian Division." In Hayes, Bechthold, and Iarocci, *Vimy Ridge*, 211–24.

Gopnik, Adam. "How Montreal Perfected Hockey." *McGill News,* 12 August 2011.

Graham, Roger. *Arthur Meighen*. Vol. 1. Toronto: Clarke & Irwin Limited, 1960–5.

Granatstein, J.L. *The Greatest Victory: Canada's One Hundred Days, 1918*. Don Mills: Oxford University Press, 2014.

Granatstein, J.L., and J.M. Hitsman. *Broken Promises: A History of Conscription in Canada*. Toronto: Oxford University Press, 1977.

Greenhalgh, Elizabeth. "David Lloyd George, Georges Clemenceau, and the 1918 Manpower Crisis." *Historical Journal* 50, no. 2 (2007): 397–421.

Gregory, Adrian. *The Last Great War: British Society and the First World War*. Cambridge: Cambridge University Press, 2008.

Gregory, Adrian. "'You Might as Well Recruit Germans': British Public Opinion and the Decision to Conscript the Irish in 1918." In *Ireland and the Great War*, edited by Adrian Gregory and Senia Pašeta, 113–32. Manchester: Manchester University Press, 2002.

Haas, K.B. "The Purple Cross for Wounded and Sick Army Horses." *Veterinary History* 20, no. 2 (1997): 37–9.

Hanaway, Joseph, Richard L. Cruess, and James Darragh. *McGill Medicine,* vol. 2: *1885–1936*. Montreal/Kingston: McGill-Queen's University Press, 2006.

Harris, J.P. *Amiens to the Armistice: The BEF in the Hundred Days' Campaign, 8 August–11 November 1918*. London: Brassey's, 1998.

Harris, J.P. *Douglas Haig and the First World War*. Cambridge: Cambridge University Press, 2008.

Hawthorn, Ramon. "Sarah Bernhardt and the Bishops of Montreal and Quebec." *Canadian Catholic Historical Association* 53 (1986): 97–120.

Haycock, Ronald. *Sam Hughes: The Public Career of a Controversial Canadian, 1885–1916*. Waterloo: Wilfrid Laurier University Press, 1986.

Hayes, Geoffrey. "3rd Canadian Division." In Hayes, Bechthold, and Iarocci, *Vimy Ridge*, 193–210.

Hayes, Geoffrey, Michael Bechthold, and Andrew Iarocci, eds. *Vimy Ridge: A Canadian Reassessment*. Waterloo: Wilfrid Laurier University Press, 2007.

Heron, Craig. "Labourism and the Canadian Working Class." *Labour/Le Travail* 13 (1984): 45–76.

Herwig, Holger H. *The First World War: Germany and Austria-Hungary, 1914–1918*. London: St. Martin's Press, 1997.

Holt, Richard. *Filling the Ranks: Manpower in the Canadian Expeditionary Force, 1914–1918*. Montreal/Kingston: McGill-Queen's University Press, 2017.

Horne, John, and Alan Kramer. *German Atrocities: A History of Denial*. New Haven: Yale University Press, 2001.

Howie, David, and Josephine Howie. "Irish Recruiting and the Home Rule Crisis of August-September 1914." In *Strategy and Intelligence: British Policy during the First World War*, edited by M.L. Dockrill and David French, 1–22. London: Hambledon, 1996.

Humphries, Mark. "The Best Laid Plans: Sir Arthur Currie's First Operations as Corps Commander." In Delaney and Durflinger, *Capturing Hill 70*, 78–101.

Humphries, Mark Osborne. "The First Use of Poison Gas at Ypres." *Canadian Military History* 16, no. 3 (2007): 57–74.

Humphries, Mark Osborne. "The Horror at Home: The Canadian Military and the Great Influenza Epidemic of 1918." *Journal of the Canadian Historical Association* 16, no. 1 (2005): 235–60.

Humphries, Mark Osborne. *The Last Plague: Spanish Influenza and the Politics of Public Health in Canada*. Toronto: University of Toronto Press, 2013.

Humphries, Mark Osborne, ed. *The Selected Papers of Sir Arthur Currie: Diaries, Letters, and Report to the Ministry, 1917–1933*. Waterloo: LCMSDS, 2008.

Humphries, Mark Osborne. *A Weary Road: Shell Shock in the Canadian Expeditionary Force, 1914–1918*. Toronto: University of Toronto Press, 2018.

Huston, Lorne. "The 1913 Spring Exhibition on the Art Association of Montreal: Anatomy of a Public Debate." *Journal of Canadian Art History* 34, no. 1 (2013): 13–55.

Hutchison, Paul P. *The 73rd Battalion Royal Highlanders of Canada, 1915–1917*. Montreal: Royal Highlanders of Canada, 2011.

Hynes, Samuel. *A War Imagined: The First World War and English Culture*. London: Bodley Head, 1990.

Iarocci, Andrew. "The 1st Canadian Division: An Operational Mosaic." In Hayes, Bechthold, and Iarocci, *Vimy Ridge*, 155–70.

Iarocci, Andrew. *Shoestring Soldiers: The 1st Canadian Division at War, 1914–1915*. Toronto: University of Toronto Press, 2008.

Inglis, Brian. *Roger Casement*. London: Hodder and Stoughton, 1973.

Jackson, Geoff. "Anything but Lovely: The Canadian Corps at Lens in the Summer of 1917." *Canadian Military History* 17, no. 1 (2008): 5–16.

Jaramowycz, R. "Montreal and the Battle of Ypres 1915: One Hundred Years." *Canadian Military History* 25, no. 1 (2015): 343–59.

Johal, R.P. "Responses to Change: Labour, Capital and the State – A Study of the Montreal Working Class through an Examination of Strikes and Lockouts 1901–1914." MA thesis, Queen's University, 1999.

Johnston, Hugh. *The Voyage of the Komagata Maru: The Sikh Challenge to Canada's Colour Bar*. Vancouver: UBC Press, 1989.

Jolivet, Simon. *Le vert et le bleu*. Montreal: Presses de l'Université de Montréal, 2011.

Kay, Zachariah. "A Note on Canada and the Formation of the Jewish Legion." *Jewish Social Studies* 29 (1967): 171–7.

Keelan, Geoffrey. "Canada's Cultural Mobilization during the First World War and a Case for Canadian War Culture." *Canadian Historical Review* 97, no. 3 (2016): 377.

Keelan, Geoffrey. "Catholic Neutrality: The Peace of Henri Bourassa." *Journal of the Canadian Historical Association* 22, no. 1 (2011): 99–132.

Keelan, Geoff. *Duty to Dissent: Henri Bourassa and the First World War.* Vancouver: UBC Press, 2019.

Keelan, Geoffrey. "'Il a bien merité de la patrie': The 22nd Battalion and the Memory of Courcelette." *Canadian Military History* 19, no. 3 (2014): 29–40.

Kerby, Martin. *Sir Philip Gibbs and English Journalism in War and Peace.* London: Palgrave Macmillan, 2016.

Keren, Michael, and Shlomit Keren. *We Are Coming, Unafraid: The Jewish Legions and the Promised Land in the First World War.* Lanham: Rowman and Littlefield, 2010.

Keshen, Jeffrey. *Propaganda and Censorship during Canada's Great War.* Edmonton: University of Alberta Press, 1996.

Kilbourn, William. *The Elements Combined: A History of the Steel Company of Canada.* Toronto: Clarke Irwin, 1960.

Kirkland, Elizabeth. "Mothering Citizens: Elite Women in Montreal, 1890–1914." PhD diss., McGill University, 2011.

Kloot, William van der. "April 1915: Five Future Nobel Prize Winners Inaugurate Weapons of Mass Destruction and the Academic-Military-Industrial Complex." *Notes and Records of the Royal Society of London* 58, no. 2 (2004): 149–60.

Kramer, Alan. *Dynamic of Destruction: Culture and Mass Killing in the First World War.* Oxford: Oxford University Press, 2007.

Lachiver, Alban. "Le soutien humanitaire Canadien-Français à La France en 1914–1918." *Guerres Mondiales et Conflicts Contemporains*, no. 179 (1995): 147–73.

Lacombe, Danyèle. "Marie Gerin-Lajoie's Hidden Crucifixes: Social Catholicism, Feminism and Québec Modernity 1910–1930." MA thesis, University of Alberta, 1998.

Lalonde, Louis. "La revanche des berceaux." *L'Action Française* 263 (1918).

Lamonde, Yvan, and Raymond Montpetit. *Le Parc Sohmer de Montréal, 1889–1919: Un lieu populaire de culture urbaine.* Quebec: Institut Québécois de Recherche sur la Culture, 1986.

Langlois, Godfroy, *Still Paddling after All These Years.* Montreal, 1913.

Laperrière, Guy. "Le Congrès eucharistique de Montréal en 1910: Une affirmation du Catholicisme Montréalais." *Études d'histoire Religieuse* 77 (2011): 21–39.

Legault, Rejean. "Architecture et Forme Urbaine: L'example du Triplex à Montreal de 1870–1914." *Urban History Review* 18, no. 1 (1989): 1–10.

Le Moine, Roger. "Deux loges Montréalaises du Grand Orient de France." *Montréal Laboratoire d'urbanité* 34, no. 3 (1993): 526–7.

Le Naour, Jean-Yves. "Les narraines de guerre: L'autre famille des soldats." *Les Chemins de la memoire*, no. 181 (March 2008): 7–10.

Lévesque, Andrée. "Éteindre le Red Light: Les réformateurs et la prostitution à Montréal entre 1865 et 1925." *Urban History Review* 17, no. 3 (1989): 191–201.

Lévesque, Andrée. *Freethinker: The Life and Works of Éva Circé-Coté.* Translated by Lazer Lederhendler. Toronto: Between the Lines, 2017. Originally published as *Éva Circé-Coté, Libre-Penseuse 1871–1949.* Montreal: Les Éditions de la Libellule, 2011.

Lévesque, Andrée. *Making and Breaking the Rules: Women in Quebec, 1919–1929.* Toronto: University of Toronto Press, 1994.

Lew, Byron, and Bruce Cater. "Canadian Emigration to the U.S., 1900–1930: Characterizing Movers and Stayers, and the Differential Impact of Immigration Policy on the Mobility of French and English Canadians." Paper presented at meeting of the Canadian Network for Economic History, Banff, Alberta, 26–28 October.

Lew, Byron, and Marvin McInnis, "Guns and Butter: World War I and the Canadian Economy." 2021. https://www.researchgate.net/publication/228434035_Guns _and_Butter_World_War_I_and_the_Canadian_Economy.

Lewis, Robert. *Manufacturing Montreal: The Making of an Industrial Landscape, 1850 to 1930.* Baltimore: Johns Hopkins University Press, 2000.

Linteau, Paul-André. "Factors in the Development of Montreal." In *Montreal Metropolis, 1880–1930,* edited by Isabelle Gournay and Franc Vanlaethem, 25–33. Toronto: Canadian Centre for Architecture/Stoddart, 1998.

Linteau, Paul-André. *Histoire de Montréal depuis la Confederation.* Montreal: Boréal, 1992.

Linteau, Paul-André. *The Promoters' City: Building the Industrial Town of Maisonneuve, 1883–1918.* Toronto: J. Lorimer, 1985.

Litalien, Michel. *Dans la tourmente: Deux hôpitaux militaires canadiens-français dans la France en guerre, 1915–1919.* Outremont: Athena, 2003.

Litalien, Michel. "Un projet trop ambitieux? L'Hôpital La Presse ou l'échec d'une aide à la France, 1914–1915." *Bulletin d'histoire Politique* 17, no. 2 (2009): 75–87.

Livesay, J.F.B. *Canada's Hundred Days: With the Canadian Corps from Amiens to Mons, Aug. 8–Nov. 11, 1914.* Toronto: T. Allen, 1919.

Lloyd George, David. *War Memoirs.* 6 vols. London: Nicholson and Watson, 1933.

Lowe, C.J. "Britain and Italian Intervention, 1914–1915." *Historical Journal* 12, no. 3 (1969): 533–48.

MacDonald, Heidi. "Who Counts?: Nuns, Work, and the Census of Canada." *Histoire Sociale/Social History* 43, no. 86 (2010): 369–91.

MacFadyen, Joshua D. "'Nip the Noxious Growth in the Bud': Ortenberg v. Plamondon and the Roots of Canadian Anti-Hate Activism." *Canadian Jewish Studies* 12 (2004): 73–96.

Machin, H.A.C. *Report of the Director of the Military Service Branch to the Honourable the Minister of Justice on the Operation of the Military Service Act, 1917.* Ottawa: Department of Justice, 1919.

MacKenzie, Scott. *Screening Québec: Québécois Moving Images, National Identity, and the Public Sphere*. Manchester: Manchester University Press, 2004.

MacLeod, Roderick, and Mary Anne Poutanen. "Little Fists for Social Justice: Anti-Semitism, Community, and Montreal's Aberdeen School Strike, 1913." *Labour/Le Travail* 70 (2012): 61–99.

MacLeod, Roderick, and Mary Anne Poutanen. *A Meeting of the People: School Boards and Protestant Communities in Quebec, 1801–1998*. Montreal/Kingston: McGill-Queen's University Press, 2004.

MacMillan, Margaret. *The War That Ended Peace: The Road to 1914*. New York: Random House, 2013.

Macphail, Andrew. *Official History of the Canadian Forces in the Great War 1914–19: The Medical Services*. Ottawa: F.A. Acland, 1925.

Marsh, Leonard C. *Health and Unemployment: Some Studies of Their Relationships*. Montreal: Oxford University Press, 1938.

Marshall, David B. *Secularizing the Faith: Canadian Protestant Clergy and the Crisis of Belief, 1850–1940*. Toronto: University of Toronto Press, 1992.

Marti, Steve. "For Kin and Country: Scale, Identity and English-Canadian Voluntary Societies, 1914–1918." *Histoire Sociale/Social History* 47, no. 94 (2014): 333–51.

McCalla, Douglas. "The Economic Impact of the Great War." In *Canada and the First World War: Essays in Honour of Robert Craig Brown*, edited by David Mackenzie, 138–53. Toronto: University of Toronto Press, 2005.

McKeagan, David. "The First Fifty Years of the École Des Haut Etudes Commerciales de Montréal." *Historical Studies in Education* 26, no. 1 (2014): 1–25.

McRandle, James, and James Quirk. "The Blood Test Revisited: A New Look at German Casualty Counts in World War I." *Journal of Military History* 70, no. 3 (2006): 667–701.

Melnycky, Peter. "Badly Treated in Every Way: The Internment of Ukrainians." In *The Ukrainian Experience in Quebec*, edited by M. Diakowsky and A. Biega, n.p. Toronto: Basilian, 1994.

Metcalfe, Alan. *Canada Learns to Play: The Emergence of Organized Sport, 1807–1914*. Toronto: McClelland and Stewart, 1987.

Miles, Wilfrid. *Military Operations France and Belgium 1916, 2nd July to the End of the Battle of the Somme*. 2 vols. London: Macmillan, 1938.

Miller, Deborah L. "The Big Ladies Hotel: Gender, Residence and Middle Class Montreal: A Contextual Analysis of Royal Victoria College 1899–1931." MA thesis, McGill University, 1998.

Miller, Ian. *Our Glory and Our Grief: Torontonians and the Great War*. Toronto: University of Toronto Press, 2002.

Montpetit, Edouard. "La veillée des berceaux." *L'Action Française* (1919).

Morris, Philip H. *The Canadian Patriotic Fund: A Record of Its Activities from 1914 to 1919*. 1920.

Morton, Desmond. "Did the French Canadians Cause the Conscription Crisis of 1917?" *Canadian Military History* 24, no. 1 (2015): 89–99.

Morton, Desmond. "Entente cordiale? La section montréalaise du Fonds patriotique canadien, 1914–1923, le bénévolat de guerre à Montréal." *Revue d'histoire de l'Amérique Française* 53, no. 2 (1999): 207–46.

Morton, Desmond. *Fight or Pay: Soldiers' Families in the Great War*. Vancouver: UBC Press, 2004.

Morton, Desmond. "French Canada and the Canadian Militia, 1868–1914." *Histoire Sociale/Social History* 2, no. 3 (1969): 32–50.

Morton, Desmond. *A Peculiar Kind of Politics: Canada's Overseas Ministry in the First World War*. Toronto: University of Toronto Press, 1982.

Morton, Desmond. "The Short Unhappy Life of the 41st Battalion CEF." *Queen's Quarterly* 81, no. 1 (1974): 70–9.

Newton, Douglas. "The Lansdowne Peace Letter of 1917 and the Prospects of Peace by Negotiation with Germany." *Australian Journal of Politics and History* 48, no. 1 (2002): 16–39.

Nicholson, G.W.L. *Canadian Expeditionary Force 1914–1919: Official History of the Canadian Army in the First World War*. Montreal/Kingston: McGill-Queen's University Press, 2015.

Nuhuet, Robert. "Une experience canadiene la Taylorism, les usines Angus du Canadien pacifique." MA thesis, Université du Québec à Montréal, 1984.

O'Keefe, Kevin. *A Thousand Deadlines: The New York City Press and American Neutrality, 1914–17*. The Hague: Nijhoff, 1972.

Otter, W.D. *Internment Operations, 1914–1919*. Montreal, 1921.

Pearson, Robert Harry. "The Decline of Professional Baseball in Montreal: A Case Study of the Montreal Royals and the Montreal City League 1910–1917." BA thesis, Concordia University, 1996.

Pearson, Robert Harry. "Montreal's Delorimier Downs Baseball Stadium as Business and Centre of Mass Culture." MA thesis, Queen's University, 1998.

Pelletier-Baillargeon, Hélène. *Olivar Asselin et son temps*. 2 vols. St. Laurent: Fides, 1996.

Pepin, Carl. "The Need to Advance: The Battle of Chérisy and the Massacre of Québeçois Troops (August 1918)." *Canadian Military Journal* 15, no. 3 (2015): 37–42.

Philpott, William James. "Britain, France and the Belgian Army." In *Look to Your Front: Studies in the First World War*, edited by Brian Bond, 121–36. Staplehurst: Spellmont, 1999.

Pickles, Katie. *Transnational Outrage: The Death and Commemoration of Edith Cavell*. Basingstoke: Palgrave Macmillan, 2007.

Pineault, Virginie. "Les clubs de 'Manches de Ligne' et du Dr. Geoffrion: Sociabilités gaies, discours, publiques et repression dans la region du Montréal 1860–1910." MA thesis, University of Montreal, 2012.

Piovesana, Roy H. "Laurier and the Liberal Party." MA thesis, Lakehead University, 1969.

Pollard, John F. *The Unknown Pope: Benedict XV (1914–1922) and the Pursuit of Peace.* London: Geoffrey Chapman, 1999.

Potter, Stephanie E. "'Smile and Carry On': Canadian Cavalry on the Western Front, 1914–1918." PhD diss., University of Western Ontario, 2013.

Power, Charles Gavan. *A Party Politician: The Memoirs of Chubby Power.* Edited by Norman Ward. Toronto: Macmillan, 1966.

Price, Enid M. *Industrial Occupations of Women.* Montreal: Canadian Reconstruction Association, 1919.

Primeau, Francis. "Le libéralisme dans la pensée de Mgr Bruchesi." *Mens: Revue D'Histoire Intellectuelle de l'Amerique Francoise* 7, no. 2 (2007): 241–77.

Prince, Lorenzo. *Montreal Old and New.* Montreal: International Press Syndicate, 1915.

Prior, Robin, and Trevor Wilson. *The Somme.* New Haven: Yale University Press, 2005.

Quiney, Linda J. "'Bravely and Loyally They Answered the Call': St. John Ambulance, the Red Cross, and the Patriotic Service of Canadian Women during the Great War." *History of Intellectual Culture* 5, no. 1 (2005): 1–19.

Radley, Kenneth. *We Lead, Others Follow: First Canadian Division, 1914–1918.* St. Catherines: Vanwell, 2006.

Rawling, Bill. *Surviving Trench Warfare: Technology and the Canadian Corps, 1914–1918.* Toronto: University of Toronto Press, 1992.

Roby, Yves. *Les Franco-Americains de la Nouvelle-Angleterre.* Sillery: Septentrion, 1990.

Rome, David. *Early Anti-Semitism: The Imprint of Drumont.* Montreal: Canadian Jewish Congress, 1985.

Rosenberg, Stuart E. *The Jewish Community in Canada.* Vol. 2. Toronto: McClelland and Stewart, 1971.

Rudy, Jarrett. "Do You Have the Time? Modernity, Democracy, and the Beginnings of Daylight Saving Time in Montreal, 1907–1928." *Canadian Historical Review* 93, no. 4 (2012): 531–54.

Rumilly, Robert. *Henri Bourassa: La vie publique d'un Grand Canadien.* Montreal: Editions Chantecler, 1953.

Ryan, William. *The Clergy and Economic Growth in Quebec (1896–1914).* Quebec: Presses de l'Universite Laval, 1966.

Salvatore, Filippo. *Ancient Memories, Modern Identities: Italian Roots in Contemporary Canadian Authors.* Translated by Domenico Cusmano. Toronto: Guernica Editions, 1999.

Sandwell, B.K. *The Call to Arms: Montreal's Roll of Honour, European War, 1914.* Montreal: Southam, 1914.

Schreiber, Shane. *Shock Army of the British Empire: The Canadian Corps in the Last 100 Days of the Great War.* London: Praeger, 1997.

Scott, James Brown. *Official Statements of War Aims and Peace Proposals, December 1916 to November 1918*. Washington, DC: Carnegie Endowment for International Peace, Division of International Law, 1921.

Senecal, N.H. "The No. 5 Terminal Grain Elevator in the Port of Montreal." MA thesis, Concordia University, 2001.

Sharpe, Chrise. "Enlistment in the Canadian Expeditionary Force 1914–1918." *Canadian Military History* 24, no. 1 (2015): 17–60.

Sharpe, Robert J. *The Last Day, the Last Hour: The Currie Libel Trial*. Toronto: Carswell, 1988.

Sheffield, Gary. *Forgotten Victory: The First World War Myths and Realities*. London: Review, 2002.

Sheffield, Gary, and John Bourne, eds. *Douglas Haig: War Diaries and Letters, 1914–1918*. London: Weidenfield and Nicolson, 2005.

Skelton, Oscar D. *Life and Letters of Sir Wilfrid Laurier*. Vol. 2. London: Oxford University Press, 1922.

Smith, Jamie. "How the Yearning for Peace after a Trench War's Horror Gave Way to Vapid 'Vimyism.'" *CITC Canadian Issues* (Fall 2015): 36–9.

Smith, Leonard V. *Between Mutiny and Obedience: The Case of the French Fifth Infantry Division during World War I*. Princeton: Princeton University Press, 1994.

Speaight, Robert. *Vanier: Soldier, Diplomat and Governor General: A Biography*. London: Collin and Harvill, 1970.

Stagni, Pellegrino. *The View from Rome: Archbishop Stagni's 1915 Reports on the Ontario Bilingual Schools Question*. Translated by John Zucchi. Montreal /Kingston: McGill-Queen's University Press, 2002.

Stedman, Mercedes. *Angels of the Workplace: Women and the Construction of Gender Relations in the Canadian Clothing Industry, 1890–1940*. Toronto: Oxford University Press, 1997.

Stewart, William. *The Embattled General: Sir Richard Turner and the First World War*. Montreal/Kingston: McGill-Queen's University Press, 2015.

Stewart, William. "Frustrated Belligerence: The Unhappy History of the 5th Canadian Division in the First World War." *Canadian Military History* 22, no. 2 (2015): 31–47.

Talbot, Robert. "Une reconciliation insaisissable: Le movement de la Bonne Entente, 1916–1930." *Mens: Revue d'histoire Intelectuelle et Cultuvelle* 3, no. 2 (2003): 31–47.

Taschereau, Henri. *The Social Evil: Toleration Condemned*. Montreal: City of Montreal, 1905.

Terraine, John. *Douglas Haig: The Educated Soldier*. London: Hutchinson, 1963.

Trofimenkoff, Susan Mann. "Henri Bourassa and 'the Woman Question.'" *Journal of Canadian Studies* 10, no. 4 (1975): 3–11.

Topp, C. Beresford. *The 42nd Battalion C.E.F. Royal Highlanders of Canada*. Montreal: Gazette Printing, 1931.

Tulchinsky, Gerald. *Canada's Jews: A People's Journey*. Toronto: University of Toronto Press, 2008.

Vance, Jonathan. *Death So Noble: Memory, Meaning and the First World War.* Vancouver: UBC Press, 1997.

Van Nus, Walter. "A Community of Communities." In *Montreal Metropolis, 1880–1930*, edited by Isabelle Gournay and Franc Vanlaethem, 59–67. Toronto: Canadian Centre for Architecture/Stoddart, 1998.

Vaughan, Walter. *The Life and Work of Sir William Van Horne*. New York: Century, 1920.

Vennat, Pierre. *Les "poilus" québécois de 1914–1918: Histoire des militaires canadiens-français de la Première Guerre mondiale*. 2 vols. Montreal: Du Méridien, 1999.

Ventresco, T.B. "Italian Reservists in North America during World War I." *Italian Americana* 4, no. 1 (1998): 92–122.

Vigneault, Michel. "The Cultural Diffusion of Hockey in Montreal, 1890–1910." MA thesis, University of Windsor, 1985.

Vigneault, Michel. "La naissance d'un sport organisé au Canada: Le hockey à Montréal 1875–1917." PhD diss., Laval University, 2001.

Wade, Mason. *The French Canadians, 1760–1967*. Vol. 2. Toronto: Macmillan, 1968.

Walker, Franklin A. *Catholic Education and Politics in Upper Canada*. Vol. 2. Toronto: Federation of Catholic Education Association of Ontario, 1976.

Williams, Jeffrey. *Byng of Vimy: General and Governor General*. London: Leo Cooper, 1983.

Williams, Jeffrey. *First in the Field: Gault of the Patricias*. St. Catherines: Vanwell, 1995.

Wilson, Keith M., ed. *Decisions for War, 1914*. New York: St. Martin's Press, 1995.

Ząbecki, David T. *The Generals' War: Operational Level Command on the Western Front in 1918*. Bloomington: Indiana University Press, 2018.

Zhang, Shenghai, Ping Yan, Brian Winchester, and Jun Wang. "Transmissibility of the 1918 Pandemic Influenza in Montreal and Winnipeg of Canada." *Influenza and Other Respiratory Viruses* 4, no. 1 (2010): 27–31.

Index

Printed and bound by CPI Group (UK) Ltd, Croydon, CR0 4YY

13/04/2025

14656519-0003